MYTH AND MASCULINITY IN THE JAPANESE CINEMA

MYTH AND MASCULINITY IN THE JAPANESE CINEMA

Towards a Political Reading of the 'Tragic Hero'

Isolde Standish

CURZON

First Published in 2000
by Curzon Press
Richmond, Surrey
http://www.curzonpress.co.uk

© 2000 Isolde Standish

Typeset in Garamond by LaserScript Ltd, Mitcham, Surrey
Printed and bound in Great Britain by
Biddles Ltd, Guildford and King's Lynn

All rights reserved. No part of this book may be reprinted or reproduced or utilised in any form or by any electronic, mechanical, or other means, now known or hereafter invented, including photocopying and recording, or in any information storage or retrieval system, without permission in writing from the publishers.

British Library Cataloguing in Publication Data
A catalogue record of this book is available from the British Library

Library of Congress Cataloguing in Publication Data
A catalogue record for this book has been requested

ISBN 0-7007-1291-7

The Publishers gratefully acknowledge the generous contribution of the Japan Foundation in support of the publication of this book.

Contents

List of Illustrations	vii
Acknowledgements	ix
Notes on Janapese Names and the Romanisation of Japanese Words	xi

Introduction — 1
- Discursive Traditions — 7
- Theoretical Framework — 11
- *Chūshingura*, Myth or History? — 15

Chapter 1 – Backgrounds — 24
- The Invention of the *Kokutai* and Early Cinema — 24
- The Quest for the Pure Self and the 'Samurai-isation' of the Lower Classes — 34
- The Death of Romance — 51

Chapter 2 – The *Kamikaze* Film and the Politics of the Collective — 68
- Fallen Blossoms — 78

Chapter 3 – Uniformed Politicians: The Enemy Within — 119
- The Post-war Rebirth of Romance — 121
- The Individual Versus an Anthropocosmic World-View — 128
- The Individual and the Multifarious Relations of Power — 132
- *I Want to be Reborn a Shellfish* and the War Crimes Trials — 141

Chapter 4 – Facts, Fictions and Fantasy 158
   The *Nagare-mono*: Takakura Ken, Metaphorical
      Representation of *Iji* 159
   The *Nagare-mono* and the Symbolic Meaning of Violence 165
   'Reflexive Masochism' and the Aesthetics of Violence 171
   Jingi naki tatakai and the Crisis of the Patriarchy 181

Conclusions 193
   Historicity and the Sensual Imperative of Imaged
      Masculinity 193

Notes 202
Bibliography 222
Index 234

Illustrations

1-2 *Ningen gyorai kaiten* 1955	86
3-4 *Kumo nagaruru hateni* 1953	88
5-8 *Kumo nagaruru hateni* 1953	91
9-10 *Kumo nagaruru hateni* 1953	92
11-12 *Kumo nagaruru hateni* 1953	93
13-14 *Gonin no sekkōhei* 1938	94
15 *Nikudan* 1968	101
16 *Nikudan* 1968	106
17-20 *Nikudan* 1968	112
21-22 *Nikudan* 1968	113
23-24 *Nikudan* 1968	114
25 *Ningen no jōken* 1959-1961	124
26 *Ningen no jōken* 1959-1961	136
27-28 *Ningen no jōken* 1959-1961	140
29-30 *Abashiri bangaichi: Arano no taiketsu* 1966	178
31-33 *Abashiri bangaichi: Arano no taiketsu* 1966	180
34-35 *Abashiri bangaichi* 1965	182
36-38 *Abashiri bangaichi: Aku e no chōsen* 1967	183
39 *Jingi naki tatakai* 1970	185
40 *Jingi naki tatakai* series - Hiroshima Dome 1970	186
41-42 *Jingi naki tatakai* 1970	200

Acknowledgements

I am indebted to many people for their help and support in the production of this work, in particular I would like to thank my supervisors at the University of London, School of Oriental and African Studies, Professor Drew Gerstle and Dr Lola Martinez, as well as my two PhD examiners Dr Mark Morris and Dr Brian Powell for their many helpful suggestions. I would also like to thank the Ouseley Memorial Scholarship for the three years of financial support and the Japan Foundation for the Fellowship I received enabling me to study under the film historian, Professor Iwamoto Kenji, at Waseda University in Tokyo. Finally, I would also like to thank the Nagasawa family for their friendship and support.

All the illustrations included in this work were taken by the author from video prints produced by the following companies. Nikkatsu (*Gonin no sekkôhei*), Nihon ATG (*Nikudan*), Shin Tôhô (*Ningen gyorai kaiten*), Shôchiku (*Ningen no jôken*), Tôei (*Abashiri bangaichi*) and (*Jingi naki tatakai*). The illustrations for *Kumo nagaruru hateni* were taken from a video of an NHK screening of the film. Without access to these and the many other Japanese films available for private viewing in Japan on video, this study would not have been possible.

Notes on Japanese Names and the Romanisation of Japanese Words

Japanese Names appear in traditional Japanese manner of surname followed by given name. Regarding the romanisation of Japanese words in the text, macrons indicate long vowels, but are not used in words and place names commonly referred to in English.

All translations from the original Japanese are my own unless otherwise stated.

Introduction

What men think about the world is one thing; the terms in which they think about it, another. (Hobsbawm 1992a:266)

I therefore claim to show, not how men think in myths, but how myths operate in men's minds without their being aware of the fact. (Lévi-Strauss 1990:12)

Ancient or not, mythology can only have an historical foundation, for myth is a type of speech chosen by history: it cannot possibly evolve from the 'nature' of things. (Barthes 1981:110)

The mythology of a nation is the intelligible mask of that enigma called the 'national character'. Through myths the psychology and world view of our cultural ancestors are transmitted to modern descendants, in such a way and with such power that our perception of contemporary reality and our ability to function in the world are directly, often tragically affected. (Slotkin 1973:3)

This study evolves around two central questions in relation to post-war Japanese popular films and historical consciousness: What is the relationship between history, myth and memory? And, how are individual subjectivities defined in relation to the past? In attempting to shed light on these questions, this study accepts the proposition that 'all histories are in some sense [non-objective] interpretations' (White 1985:51). As Carr elaborates, the historian selects certain 'facts' from a potentially infinite number of incidents which took place in the past, giving predominance to some while rejecting others.

> When we [the historians] attempt to answer the question 'What is history?' our answer, consciously or unconsciously, reflects our own position in time, and forms part of our answer to the broader question what view we take of the society in which we live. (Carr 1990:8)

This applies no less to filmmakers who take an historical incident or period as their mise-en-scène. It can be argued that an analysis of the processes of selection and reconstruction carried out by the historian/filmmakers can tell us more about the historian/filmmakers and the period in which the history was written or the film was made, than about the incident described.

There are many problems involved in writing about film, as it is impossible to convey in words the experience of viewing a film. It is even more difficult for the film theorist/historian to convey this emotional and intellectual experience to a reader who is unlikely to have seen the films in question. Therefore, this study does not attempt to convey the aesthetic experience of viewing these films, but explores through a political analysis how masculine subjectivity interacts with the past in the light of the present, in relation to the 'tragic hero' narrative structure dominant in Japanese films.

From his structuralist study of western literature, Frye (1957) concluded that there are 'four narrative pregeneric elements of literature' which he calls '*mythoi* or generic plots', they are tragedy, comedy, romance and satire. Obviously these classifications are based on an analysis of western narratives, but the underlying principle that 'pregeneric' structures or '*mythoi*' govern creative works is in general agreement with Lévi-Strauss and his theory of myth. Hayden White elaborating on Frye's theory argues that:

> historical interpretation, like a poetic fiction, can be said to appeal to its readers as a plausible representation of the world by virtue of its implicit appeal to those 'pregeneric plot-structures' or archetypal story-forms that define the modalities of a given culture ... Historians, no less than poets, can be said to gain an 'explanatory affect' – over and above whatever formal explanations they may offer of specific historical events – by building into their narratives patterns of meaning similar to those more explicitly provided by the literary art of the cultures to which they belong. (White 1985:58)

INTRODUCTION

This study is an examination of one of Japan's most prolific narrative structures upon which *Chūshingura* (the story of the forty-seven loyal retainers) is based. I shall argue that this narrative forms a 'pregeneric' plot-structure which in its cinematic form, particularly in the post-war period, has crossed genre boundaries forming an interpretive structure upon which war-retro and yakuza films are based. This study will demonstrate how this 'tragic hero' mythic structure in its cinematic form grew to prominence after the Second World War and was instrumental in providing a figurative structure around which the Japanese people could interpret the events of the war, offering the spectators avenues of exculpation from a foreign-imposed sense of guilt that followed the War Crimes Trials. As Onuma (1993) has explained, early post-war Japanese discourse on the war was framed by American foreign policy concerns and the trials within a totalitarian/democratic dichotomy. As such, the reaction of Japanese people was to distance themselves from former rightist ideologies and responsibility for government policy during the war period. This manifested in popular reactions as (a) I was against the war from the start; (b) I was a victim of the war; and (c) I resisted the wartime military institutions. War-retro films can similarly be divided into three broad if at times overlapping categories according to thematic concerns which elaborate on the above listed reactions. For example, *Ningen no jōken (The Human Condition)* corresponds to both (a) and (b), as do certain films based on the *kamikaze* (Special Attack Forces); *Genbaku no ko (Children of the Atomic Bomb)* and the subsequent films made about the bomb all correspond to (b) as do films based on the War Crimes Trials, such as *Watashi wa kai ni naritai (I Want to be Reborn as a Shell-fish)* and the Okinawa films, such as *Himeyuri no tō (Memorial to the Lilies)*. Imai Tadashi's (1912–) 1991 film *Sensō to seishun (War and Youth)* is an example of (c).

Apart from films such as *Kaigun (Navy)* (1943) and a series of B grade films made just after the Shanghai Incident of 1932,[1] the 'tragic hero' structure had been limited to its original home in *jidai geki* (period) films and in particular *Chūshingura*. However, in the light of the judgements following the War Crimes Trials, the 'tragic hero' mythic form took on new life as emblematic of (a) Japan's purity of spirit – expressed through a willingness to die for a cause; and (b) through the allegoric meaning of death which increasingly became encoded as victimisation and not, as previously, sacrifice.

The earlier meaning of sacrifice reappeared in the 1960s in yakuza films and films based on the 26 February Incident of 1936. As the subsequent analysis will demonstrate, in both these genres, the 'tragic hero' mythic structure took on a radical anti-establishment inflection based on the construction of ideal masculine types such as the star persona of Takakura Ken (1931–).

This study is primarily concerned with cinema as a mediative mechanism and its contribution to social and historical discourse in post-war Japan. Here I am indebted to Foucault's concept of 'discourse' as applied in his *History of Sexuality*. However, granted that 'discourse' in this sense has been used as an organising concept to explore the relationship between linguistic codes and consciousness, in this study I have expanded the concept by incorporating a discussion of how visual structures form syntagmatic elements which function at an empathetic or emotional level reinforcing and occasionally challenging dominant discourses. For example, it is through these visual codes that the concept of *ishin denshin* defined as 'the immediate communication (of truth) from one mind to another' (*Kenkyūsha* 1985) is conveyed to the film spectator. *Ishin denshin* as a concept of non-verbal communication is central to the 'tragic hero' mythic narrative and is the governing principle of communication between allies, comrades and lovers in popular Japanese films.

Another useful concept upon which this study draws is that of the 'diegetic process'. As Burch explains, 'it combines a mental process (the development of the spectator's "absorption"), and a process of "writing": the implementation on the screen of the "codes" which catalyse that absorption' (Burch 1979:19). As such, it goes beyond narrative as an analytic concept in its acknowledgement of the spectator. However, it must be remembered that in the reception of film, the meaning a spectator constructs from the chain of cinematic signifiers, both verbal and visual, is dependent on not only the construction of the film's narrative and mise-en-scène, but also the socio-political context of the spectator's own viewing perspective.

The internalised techniques employed by a spectator in the construction of meaning in a film are based on two interrelated cultural processes. First, for a person to fully comprehend the intended meaning of a film, he/she must be conversant with the cultural codes, conventions, and practices employed. This knowledge is acquired while living within a given culture. The second aspect is that the act of successfully constructing meaning from a chain of signifiers in a film is in itself pleasurable as it reaffirms the spectator's position within the hegemonic culture. As Zavarzadeh argues, this act of constructing meaning is political, as the spectator pieces together 'the ideological syntax of the culture', he/she is able to comprehend 'the diverse codes of culture, such as gender, sexuality, class, parenting, and to establish a relation among them' (Zavarzadeh 1991:11). Obviously, there are openings for aberrant readings and this in itself can be pleasurable, as much of the recent work on 'gay' and minority audiences has shown. However, on the whole, the syntax of commercial films directs the spectator to a preferred or dominant reading from which we gain pleasure and with which this study is primarily concerned. This is not to say that the diegetic process is determined by a single dominant ideology, but rather that the contextual environment (i.e. the socio-historical period) in which films are produced and received also plays a significant role in determining the extent of ideological contestation in any given film. For example, from 1939, Japanese officials had to implement a series of harsh film laws to contain a diverse industry and the 'proletarian film movement' of the 1930s (Shimizu 1994:66-69). Contrary to popular belief, restrictions on freedom of expression in films made during the early war period (from 1931) seem not to be as great as has been made out. In fact, it would appear from a study of wartime productions, that the extreme formulaic nature of Japanese popular films is largely a post-war phenomenon and can be attributed to (a) the post-war American Occupation's support for the rationalisation of the industry and (b) the increasing cost of production related to technical innovations which contributed to a reduction in the number of independent companies. Both of these phenomena would seem to have been more effective in containing the thematic concerns of Japanese films from the mid-1950s on than the outright coercive implementation of the 1939 film law. Social realist filmmakers such as Uchida Tomu (1908-1972) were still able to make films like *Tsuchi* (*Earth*) as late as 1939, long after the 1932 initial crackdown on socialist filmmakers. In the post-war era similar filmmakers were marginalised and forced to find funding through small independent Japanese film companies or abroad, as for example Ōshima Nagisa who left Shōchiku after the withdrawal of his film *Nihon no yoru to kiri* (*Night and Fog in Japan*) in 1960 after only a four-day run. He then went on to make films such as *Kōshikei* (*Death by Hanging*) 1968, *Shinjuku dorobō nikki* (*Diary of a Shinjuku Thief*) 1968 and *Shōnen* (*Boy*) 1969 through an independent Japanese film company, ATG. In the 1970s he received international acclaim making the following films with foreign backing, *Ai no kōrida* (*In the Realm of the Senses*) 1976, *Ai no bōrei* (*Empire of Passion*) 1978 for Anatole Dauman's Argos Films and *Merry Christmas, Mr Lawrence* 1983 for the British producer Jeremy Thomas and *Max, Mon Amour* 1986 for Serge Silverman. This line of enquiry raises questions of why post-war critics sought to paint such a bleak picture of the wartime industry. The answer must lie in the first instance in the politics of defeat and the War Crimes Trials.

Films made in Japan during the immediate post-war period also provide explicit examples of films as the site of contestation of a multiplicity of competing ideologies, as they reflect the political confusion characteristic of Japanese society in that period. Therefore, they are excellent examples of open, polysemic texts whose spectators, whether American censors or the Japanese public, were able to construct independent and distinct readings from the same text by employing their respective culturally specific codes and practices.

Kurosawa's 1948 *Yoidore tenshi* (*Drunken Angel*) is a case in point. The dialogue of Dr Sanada on the rights of women[2] while no doubt appealing to the Civil Information and Education Section (CIE) censorship board, is simultaneously juxtaposed with images of the 'new woman' (Nanae, Matsunaga's mistress) who contradicts visually the spoken word. Quite apart from the fact that Japanese, at least mythically, equate action above dialogue in evaluating sincerity, in purely filmic terms, images are often more powerful than dialogue in eliciting empathetic responses[3]. Hence the American censors, working mainly from translations of the screenplay, could feel content that women's rights were being championed, while Japanese audiences, I would argue, could construct an alternative reading which followed the dominant pre-war (ideo)logic that the traditional female role was more desirable than the counter-hegemonic view the Americans sought to impose.

INTRODUCTION

Discursive Traditions

> ... since anthropologists dealing with Japan have rarely been interested in film, and since film critics are rarely interested in Japanese social organisation, the paradox between an ideology based on harmony and a popular culture which ... makes much of unharmonious activities has rarely been addressed. (Moeran 1989:161)

Generally speaking, texts currently available in English on Japanese cinema can be divided into two broad categories, according to the academic backgrounds of their authors. First, there are film theorists with an interest in Japanese cinema. Mellen (1976) was one of the earliest, followed by Burch (1979), Bordwell (1988) and Desser (1988). Then there are those with a Japanese academic background and an interest in film; Anderson and Richie (1959), Richie (1975, 1982) and Keiko McDonald (1983) are good examples of this group. Obviously, there are difficulties inherent in both approaches. Burch and Bordwell both seem to have overcome potential problems, particularly the language barrier; Burch by confining his analysis to the pre-war silent era of film and Bordwell by employing four Japanese translators. They have also both studied Japanese history and society extensively.

Perkins, in his first chapter, 'The Sins of the Pioneers', in *Film as Film* (1974), discusses the critical positions of early western film commentators and journalists who, in an over-zealous attempt to elevate cinema to the level of high culture, established a film critique based on an 'aesthetics of taste'. This 'aesthetics of taste' became an orthodox view founded on a social class position and had the effect of limiting critical discourse to an (educated) individual's response to a particular work. This 'dogma', Perkins goes on to explain 'not only [failed] to provide a coherent basis for discussion of particular films but actively [obstructed] understanding of cinema' (Perkins 1974:11). Early western critics and historians of Japanese cinema similarly established an orthodox theory of Japanese film. Here I am using 'orthodox' in the classical Greek sense of the word: *orthos* (right) and *doxa* (opinion). In their attempts to link Japanese cinema to Zen Buddhism and such ephemeral concepts as *mono no aware* (the pathos of things), they have established an *ortha doxa* view of

Japanese cinema as a unique aesthetic form, which however inadvertently, has only added fuel to the myths surrounding *nihonjinron* (theories of Japaneseness). Their concern with prestige (high culture) is evident in the very directors selected for critical discussion, that is, directors whose films have featured prominently in the *Kinema Junpō* awards and at international festivals such as the Venice Film Festival, in particular Ozu, Kurosawa, Mizoguchi and more recently, from the 1960s avant-garde Ōshima and Teshigahara among others, none of whom is truly representative of Japanese popular cinema and none of whom has produced consistent box office hits. This is not to argue that it is not important to study these 'auteurs', but merely to point out that they form a clique of 'art' or 'high culture' filmmakers around whom a critical *ortha doxa* has formed. This tendency of western critics to focus on the oeuvre of a few 'art' directors raises questions of the western critics' approach to Japanese cinema as 'other'. Has 'difference' been equated with originality and therefore art, and has this search for the artist led to predominantly auteur-based studies?

Bordwell (1988), while staying within the auteur tradition in his study of Ozu, applies a theoretical framework based on an 'historical poetics' which challenges the aesthetics of taste established by earlier film critics and historians. His analysis demonstrates the fact that Ozu's oeuvre grew out of the age in which Ozu lived and that his films were influenced by the popular culture of the Meiji, Taishō and early Shōwa periods and, perhaps even more importantly, Hollywood narrative structures. Bordwell even quotes Ozu as saying, 'They [foreign critics] don't understand, that's why they say it is Zen or something like that' (Bordwell 1988:27).

Burch (1979), in contrast, examines the early works of Ozu and Mizoguchi among others from a structuralist perspective, taking up and expanding many of the points raised by Roland Barthes in his essay, *Empire of the Signs* (1982). Burch's basic premise is that the cinematic modes of spatio-temporal relations evident in the early silent films (1912–1930) remained faithful to the representational systems evident in the traditional arts. As such, the early films of Ozu and Mizoguchi, for example, have been neglected by western analysts due to the relative incompatibility of these films with the ideology of representation and signification informing the dominant cinema of the west. The Japanese cinema of the early period developed its own system of representations and narrative structures which were by and large not influenced by western (Hollywood) cinematic modes until the advent of sound. From a socio-historical perspective, Burch, in *To the Distant Observer*, traces the development of these traditional modes of representation from the Heian period (794–1185), when he states they were first formulated, through to the Tokugawa period (1615–1867) and the development of *kabuki* and *bunraku*, and on up to their incorporation in the pre-1930s cinema.

From this historical survey of traditional Japanese art forms, Burch concludes that there are four basic contentions. First, intertextuality; 'tradition inclines the Japanese to read any given text ... in relation to a body of texts'; secondly, 'the sacrosanct value placed on originality, the taboo placed on "borrowing" and on "copying", in the west is as utterly foreign to Japan as are Western "individualism" and the primacy of the person or subject'; thirdly, 'the linear approach to representation is not a privileged one'; finally, 'the precedence given to "content" over "form", or rather the hypostasis of meaning to the detriment of its *production*, is a specifically Western attitude' (Burch 1979:53).

These four contentions form the basis of his subsequent analysis of the works of various Japanese directors and are important points to be considered in the post-war development of the Japanese studio system which has consistently favoured generic continuity and the use of the film series to an extent unprecedented in western cinema. Also, his point about originality helps to explain why Japanese directors often remake the same film over and over again. The ninety-one films of *Chūshingura* made between 1908 and 1994 and the fourteen films based on the 26 February Incident 1936 made between 1951 and 1988 are cases in point.

Alternatively, Japanese film scholarship generally centres on the historical and conforms to traditional pedagogical structures of the dissemination and acquisition of knowledge. This is not generally speaking based on the European Enlightenment tradition of theoretical paradigms underpinning an analytical approach, but rather a process of 'the getting of wisdom'. Traditionally, it is a forward-flowing imparting and acquisition of knowledge from master to apprentice, father to son and from the person's anecdotal recounting of his experiences to the student. Hence the great importance attached to the *sensei/seito* (teacher/pupil), *senpai/kōhai* (senior/junior) and *oyabun/kobun* (father-figure/son) relationships.

Modern history, when understood from within this tradition, relies on the linear recounting of experience. A vast majority of the books written on World War II fall into this experiential generic tradition (Iguchi and Nakajima 1984; Gomikawa 1990; Morimoto 1992; Shimizu 1994; and Nakasone 1995). This is not only a 'popular' form of historical narration but, as the above citations indicate, informs scholastic writings which can generally be divided into two categories or genres: (a) experiential writings and (b) the recounting of 'facts', i.e. dates, places and names (Nakamura 1994), and the reprinting of source materials (Kōno 1993; Itō and Kita 1995). Within these discursive traditions, interpretation in terms of theoretical paradigms is kept to a minimum. This does not mean that these modes of historical discourse are any the less ideological in the historical world-view which they inform, but it does mean that they encourage a view which denies its own reflexive nature by linking it closer to 'reality'. Recounted experience, when framed within this academic paradigm, is easily connoted as 'past reality' and not subjective interpretation or experience. As this study will demonstrate, in Japanese historical films there is a conflation of these two discursive traditions through the incorporation of actual news(*real*) footage and authoritative voice-over into the subjective experiential representations of the protagonists' story.

Japanese film scholarship similarly conforms to these two historical discursive traditions, (a) experiential writings evident in the vast quantity of material published by directors under such titles as *Taiken-teki sengo eizō-ron (A Personal Account of Post-War Image Theory)*, (Itami 1973; Ōshima 1978, 1993; Suzuki 1991; Ishii, T. & K. Fukuma 1992; Ozu 1993; Ichikawa, K. & Y. Mori 1994); and (b) factual writings (Iwamoto, K. & T. Saiki 1988, 1991; Yamamoto 1990; Sakuramoto 1993; Shimizu 1994; Satō 1995, 1996). Works falling into this latter category provide copious information on the film industry: who directed and starred in what, when and where interspersed with detailed plot summaries. Sakuramoto (1993) and Shimizu (1994) both attempt to contextualise films produced during the war period from a political perspective. Satō similarly in *Nihon no eiga to Nihon no bunka (Japanese Film and Japanese Culture)* 1989 attempts to place various post-war films in their socio-historical perspectives. However, these accounts often include anecdotal evidence in support of their arguments. To summarise, Japanese film scholarship has tended to centre on the historical and in so doing has stayed within pre-established discursive traditions that privilege the factual over and above the analytical. Only recently in some avant-garde journals such as *Imago* have attempts been made to incorporate western film (psychoanalytic) theory into Japanese scholarship.

Theoretical Framework

At this point, it is important to set out some notes leading to a working definition of two crucial terms: ideology and myth.

I intend to adopt the classical concept of 'ideology' developed by Louis Althusser in his paper 'Ideology and the Ideological State Apparatus' (1971). Althusser makes a distinction between what he terms 'theoretical ideologies' (his example is the work of bourgeois political economists), that is, the formal conscious beliefs of a class or other social group; and 'ideology in its practical state', by which he means the way 'ruling imperatives' are actually transmitted into forms of routine behaviour, becoming the characteristic world-view or general perspective ('common sense' in Gramsci's terms) of class or other social group. It is this latter meaning Althusser explicates in his paper and which I am concerned with here. In short, Althusser recognised the fact that the 'reproduction of existing social relations' is not only dependent on the reproduction of material conditions of life, e.g. food, clothing and shelter, but is also dependent on the reproduction of a system of shared beliefs and values. This system constitutes a dominant ideology which in the modern world is diffused throughout society by means of the institutions of the 'Ideological State Apparatus'[4]. Under this general heading, Althusser lists social institutions such as the family, education, religion and the media. Therefore, Althusser defines ideology in a broad sense, relating it to the material processes of the production of ideas, beliefs and values of social life. In other words, ideology alludes to our actual relation with the world through beliefs, often both unconscious and reflexive, masking existing (power) relations and the 'reality of lived' experience as natural and commonsensical. In Althusser's own words: *'Ideology is a "Representation" of the Imaginary Relationship of the Individuals to their Real Conditions of Existence'* (Althusser 1971:162). This definition accepts the principle that ideologies are frequently obscurantist rather than false, as their discourses of the 'real' and 'accepted practice' are often grounded in empirical fact. However, this raises a further question: is it possible to say whether a particular 'world-view' is either true or false? Surely not, since a 'world-view' held by a particular social group or interest is predicated on a certain mode of perception. It is constructed in accordance with a specific 'grammar' – 'a system of rules for organising its various elements, which cannot be spoken of in [simple] terms of truth and falsehood'. It is also predicated on the 'material base' specific to given societies of those beliefs, as Althusser explains:

> the existence of the ideas of [an individual's] belief is material in that *his ideas are his material actions inserted into material practices governed by material rituals which are themselves defined by the material ideological apparatus from which derive the ideas of that subject.* (Althusser 1971:169)

Therefore, as this study is concerned to locate in war-retro and yakuza films a Japanese masculine perception of 'reality' and the position of the male 'self' in that historical reality, I propose the following definition. Starting from Althusser's initial premise that ideology is a system of 'lived' relations to society promoting a set of beliefs or world-view supportive of sectorial interests (Althusser 1990:233), it follows that, if we invert the perspective to that of the subject, ideology can be understood as a representational structure in which the individual conceives or imagines his or her 'world-view' and his or her place within that 'reality'.

Myth and ideology are closely related concepts which have tended to become conflated in recent sociological and historical studies (for example, Gluck 1985, *Japan's Modern Myths: Ideology in the Late Meiji Period*). However, even if there are strong parallels, in that myth and ideology are conceptions of symbolic meanings with social functions and effects, there are also points of significant divergence, as argued by Ben Halpern in his article on 'Myth and Ideology in Modern Usage' (1961). Halpern attempts to define myth and ideology as distinct cultural processes in history. He makes the following two distinctions by extrapolating common usages from contemporary studies:

1. The study of myth is a study of the origin of beliefs out of historic experience. The study of ideology is a study of the moulding of beliefs by social situations. 2. The social function

of myth is to bind together social groups as wholes or, in other words, to establish a social consensus. The social function of ideology is to segregate and serve special interests within societies in the competition of debate. (Halpern 1961:137)

From these divergences, it becomes obvious that myth is the more capacious concept, concerned with metaphysical questions; whereas ideologies are generally more specific and pragmatic and, while often encompassing similar issues as myth, they bring them to bear more directly on questions of power. It is this relationship with power which is crucial to a theoretical understanding of myth's ideological function as the cement binding a social group together. As Eagleton states, 'myth is thus a particular register of ideology, which elevates certain meanings to numinous status' (Eagleton 1991:189).

This point is supported by Lévi-Strauss when he demonstrates through his structural analysis of myths that their primary function is to 'insure the permanency of the group' (Lévi-Strauss 1968:309). This is achieved through their ameliorating social function – the providing of (imaginary) resolutions to real contradictions. It is in this, their political capacity to reconcile real social contradictions, that they resemble ideology. As this study is concerned with the interrelationship between myth and ideology in Japanese cinema, it is important to make the distinction between aspects of ideologies which are mythical and those which are not.

Barthes' (1981) now famous deconstruction of the *Paris Match* photograph of the young black soldier saluting provides an excellent example of the ideological function of myth. Here, the 'narrative syntax' of the photograph forms a mythical structure providing a resolution to the contradictions inherent in French imperialistic policy. The 'Negro', a symbol of a colonial subject, is seen in French military uniform, eyes uplifted, saluting what is presumed to be the tricolour. He is presented as sharing the same values and beliefs as the indigenous French themselves and is therefore seen to be a fully integrated member of the French Empire and thereby, in Lévi-Strauss' words, 'insur[ing] the permanency of the group' (Lévi-Strauss 1968:309). In this photograph, the black soldier's representational meaning has been inflected with a mythical meaning embedded in French imperialistic ideologies. The Japanese in China, Taiwan (Formosa) and Korea during the occupation period attempted to construct similar mythic narratives in films like *Soshū no yoru* (*Suchow Nights*) 1942 and *Sayon no kane* (*Sayon's Bell*) 1943 which depict colonial Chinese happily integrating into Japanese society.

Myths, as part of an hegemonic process, are never static, but are themselves constantly being altered and inflected with new meanings and interpretations, as an analysis of the publicity photograph for *Rikugun* (*Army*) 1944 will illustrate. The photograph is a medium close-up of the mother, acted by Tanaka Kinuyo (1909-1977). This is a still from the final scene of the film that was the subject of some controversy at the time of the first release. In this scene, the mother anxiously watches as her son marches off to war and, according to the Japanese censors, she was somewhat too anxious. The film was later banned by the American censors, but, due to the wartime controversy surrounding the scene, this photograph has become symbolic of those 'humanistic directors' who, as many Japanese and western film critics have argued, consciously opposed government interference in film productions during the war[5]. This interpretation supports post-war myths first propagated by Japan's ruling elite led by Yoshida Shigeru (Prime Minister for most of the occupation) at the time of the purges which blamed 'uniformed politicians' (Yoshida's term) for Japan's involvement in the war. In the post-war era, this photograph has taken on a cluster of meanings which are connected to Yoshida's 'reverse course' policy of the late 1940s and early 1950s. Amongst other things, this policy included the reinstatement of previously classified war criminals. The post-war meanings attached to the photograph bear no relationship to those it had when first published in 1944. It therefore provides a good example of the mythic process.

As the above examples have illustrated, myths form part of the hegemonic process of cultural discourse through their ameliorating social function by providing resolutions to real social contradictions. This comes about, as the examples have demonstrated, through an historical, cultural process – a chain of signifiers forms a meaning around an 'object' which 'impoverishes' the purely representational meaning of the 'object'. In short, myths help to make ideological concepts intelligible. They encourage the development of an 'inter-subjectivity' in which individual subjective responses are shared to a certain extent by most of the members of a social group. They therefore function as the cement binding individuals to a social group through a set of shared meanings, values and beliefs.

Finally, in film studies, there is often a temptation to select the films to fit the theory. In order to avoid this pitfall, the principal criterion I applied when selecting films for analysis was their popularity not only at the time of initial release, but also with regard to their general availability to contemporary audiences. By this criterion, all the films analysed in this study are classics of Japanese popular culture, being readily available for rent and sale in most suburban video outlets.

Although much of this study is an exploration of Japanese discourses in relation to the Second World War, it is in no way concerned with 'moral' questions of right and wrong in relation to the war, but rather with an exposition of Japanese strategies for constituting 'reality'. Also, with regard to methodology and the current debates raging around traditional disciplinary paradigms, I have attempted to follow Hayden White's advice in that:

> when it is a matter of speaking about human consciousness, we have no absolute theory to guide us; everything is under contention. It therefore becomes a matter of choice as to which model we should use to mark out, and constitute entries into, the problem of consciousness in general. Such choices should be self-conscious rather than unconscious ones, and they should be made with a full understanding of the kind of human nature to the constitution of which they will contribute if they are taken as valid. (White 1985:22-23)

Chūshingura, Myth or History?

> The past is intelligible to us only in the light of the present; and we can fully understand the present only in the light of the past. (Carr 1990:55)

> Just as there can be no explanation in history without a story, so too there can be no story without a plot by which to make of it a story of a particular kind. (White 1985:62)

[*Chūshingura*] was an incident that at once reflected and affected cultural metamorphosis: it not only indicated the ways in which the honor culture of the samurai was changing; it inspired the future course of that culture. (Ikegami 1995:223)

For the purposes of this study, I have chosen *Chūshingura* as a point of entry for the following reasons; first, its great popularity in puppet theatre, *kabuki*, and in cinema; secondly, the rise in popularity of its cinematic form was congruent with the first major phase of Japanese industrialisation, the second phase of industrialisation being the immediate post-war period which saw the development of the archetypal 'tragic hero' in the war-retro film. This same period also saw the birth of the yakuza genre which I shall demonstrate is based upon the same mythic patterns. Therefore, this study will argue that *Chūshingura* in particular and the 'tragic hero' in his other various manifestations have achieved mythic status in contemporary Japan.

Lévi-Strauss (1981) argues that myths exist independently of any particular author as autonomous cultural objects. Therefore, it is the process of re-narration that distinguishes individually created works from myths. He goes on to explain that all works of art are potential myths; it is only when they are 'adopted by the collectivity' that they achieve mythic status and become part of a collective tradition. When this occurs, only the structural level of the original narrative will remain intact as successive narrators transmogrify the basic structure and adjust it to the requirements of the historical period and the variabilities of their personalities. Lévi-Strauss (1990) demonstrated that the basic pattern of a myth is inherent in all its manifestations and so to search for the origins of a particular myth is superfluous. Ivan Morris (1980) in his study of the 'tragic hero' in Japanese culture provides examples from the fourth century on. The important point for the present study is not so much when this form of mythic narrative first developed, but its dominance and immense popularity. In one sense, the point of entry into a study of this kind is purely arbitrary. As Lévi-Strauss has stated: 'this code ... has neither been invented nor brought in from without. It is inherent in mythology itself, where we simply discover its presence' (Lévi-Strauss 1990:12).

The few known historical facts upon which the ninety-one film versions of *Chūshingura* made between 1908 and 1994 are ostensibly based are as follows. The incident took place in Edo between 1701 and 1703. On the fourteenth day of the third month of the year *Genroku* 14 (1701),[6] Asano Takumi-no-kami, Lord of Akō *han* (estate) in Harima in the eastern section of the Inland Sea,[7] attacked and wounded Kira Kōzuke-no-suke in the Shōgun's castle. In the subsequent investigation, when questioned, Lord Asano reported it had been a private grievance, and when Kira was similarly questioned, he replied he did not know what had provoked the attack. After the results of this investigation were made known to the Shōgun, Lord Asano was ordered to commit ritual suicide (*seppuku*); his lands were confiscated, his family disinherited, and his retainers dismissed. On the fifteenth day of the twelfth month of *Genroku* 15 (1702), Ōishi Kuranosuke and forty-six of Asano's former retainers attacked Kira's home in Edo, beheading him before surrendering to the *bakufu* (the *shōgunate*). On the fourth day of the second month in *Genroku* 16 (1703), the forty-six retainers also committed *seppuku*.

Satō (1976) makes the point that the attack of the forty-seven on Kira's house could be construed in one of two ways: (a) it could be taken as an act of extreme loyalty to their dead Lord Asano, or (b) it could be taken as an act of rebellion against the *bakufu*. As Satō explains, Ōishi Kuranosuke and the forty-six retainers and indeed the *bakufu*, all had a vested interest in promoting the first option. Satō suggests that Ōishi and the forty-six were concerned with their honour. Therefore, if it had been construed that their actions were rebellious, they would have been executed as traitors, and their families would have suffered for generations to come. To avoid this outcome, Horibe Yahei and the other forty-six wrote a proclamation to the Shōgun stating that they accepted the fact that their Lord Asano was at fault in striking Kira within the castle precincts. They went on to say that, had Asano not been restrained at the time, he would surely have killed Kira. Thus, in order to placate the spirit of their dead Lord, they felt it was their duty out of loyalty to him to complete the deed. To bring moral backing to their argument, they altered the Confucian precept upon which revenge killings were permitted by law during the Edo period (1615-1867)[8] - 'one should not live under heaven with the enemy of one's father' (*chichi no teki totomo ni ten o itadakazu*). This they changed to - 'one should not live under heaven with the enemy of one's lord' (*kunpu no teki totomo ni ten o itadakazu*). As Satō (1976) explains, it was commonly accepted that a child or younger brother could seek vengeance against a person who had killed their father or elder brother, however, there were no recorded cases of retainers taking vengeance for their lord.[9] Until the attack of the forty-seven on Kira's house, Japanese Confucianism laid emphasis on the *kō* of filial piety and not the *chū* of loyalty. Therefore, Satō concludes that it was from this period on that absolute loyalty to one's lord became the central concept of *bushidō* (the way of the warrior). Prior to the events of the *Chūshingura* Incident, bravery (*buyō*) and honour (*meiyo*) were central to the *bushi* tradition. To reinforce this line of argument, he points to the many examples of *bushi* who changed their allegiance to lords to advance their own positions during the Sengoku period (1482-1558).

> To the *bushi* the honour and respect of their house was more important than loyalty, but after *Chūshingura*, this ideology descended to the level where honour and respect were equated with loyalty. (Satō 1976:31)

Satō argues that the motivating force behind the attack of the forty-seven was probably resentment at losing their lands and stipends through no fault of their own. Loyalty became an issue of expediency in their attempt to protect their honour and their families from the consequences of their act. However, by accepting their own deaths as a necessary requisite of their deed, they caught the public's imagination. This, Satō states, was in part due to the fact that so many retainers were involved. If it had just been one or two, he suggests, they would have been dismissed as eccentrics. The strong public support the forty-seven enjoyed after the attack on Kira's house, Satō argues, was a decisive factor in the *bakufu's* handling of the incident. If it was construed that Kira had provoked Asano, it could be argued that the *bakufu's* judgement on Asano to commit *seppuku* and lose his lands was unjust under the *kenka ryōseibai* system, which stipulated that before the law both parties in a disagreement were equally to blame and should both be punished. In order not to provoke public opinion further, the *bakufu* distanced itself from Kira's household and accepted the forty-seven *rōnins'* (masterless samurai) statement that 'this act of vengeance was in no way an attempt to attain justice, but was simply a private expression of devotion' (Satō 1976:17). As such, they were permitted to commit *seppuku* rather than be executed as traitors.

Satō further raises the issue that at the time of the incident, loyalty was not a particularly popular theme of story-tellers (*kōdanshi*) or theatrical plays. He points out that the populace favoured stories that praised the strong, as for example, the Soga Brothers.[10] However, this began to change at about the time when the first *Kanadehon Chūshingura* was performed in 1748. At this time, the lives of historical figures such as Sugawara Michizane (845-903)[11] and Kusunoki Masashige (1294-1336)[12] were being introduced into schools as exemplary examples of loyalty. The *Kanadehon Chūshingura* further helped to institutionalise absolute loyalty as the dominant concept of *bushidō* Here Satō is intimating that the emerging emphasis afforded Sugawara Michizane, Kusunoki Masashige and *Chūshingura* at this time laid the foundations in popular consciousness for the Meiji Restoration (1868) and the *tennōsei* (absolute loyalty to the Emperor) ideology of the war period.

In answer to the question why did *Chūshingura* capture the people's imagination at this time, Satō believes that it appealed to both the ruled and the ruling class. The ruled enjoyed the subversive element of the rebellion theme, likening it to other popular plays of the period based on some of the many peasant uprisings occurring during the Edo (Tokugawa) period, such as *Sakura Sōgorō*,[13] while the ruling class enjoyed the theme of absolute loyalty. This is certainly a valid observation, but it provides only a partial answer to the question why the 'tragic hero' narrative and *Chūshingura* in particular grew to such prominence as a narrative form in Japanese popular consciousness. This study will suggest that the answer lay in the ability of the narrative to work out and resolve contradictions that arose in the nature of human relations accompanying the transition from a feudal to a market industrial economy. As Ikegami (1995) has argued, due to the centralisation of power, samurai were increasingly being excluded from the 'land as a source of economic independence' and being incorporated into the 'bureaucratic hierarchy' of the Tokugawa hegemony.

When reduced to their simplest elements, the structures of relationships in fictional accounts of *Chūshingura* since 1748 provide a figurative framework in which the transition from filiative to affiliative social relations are worked out through the narrative.

If a filial relationship was held together by natural bonds and natural forms of authority – involving obedience, fear, love, respect, and instinctual conflict – the new affiliative relationship changes these bonds into what seem to be trans-personal forms – such as guild consciousness, consensus, collegiality, professional respect, class, and the hegemony of a dominant culture. (Said 1991a: 20)

By placing the events of the incident within a filiative/affiliative binary opposition, fictional accounts of *Chūshingura* changed the ideological foundation of relations within the collective (i.e. those relationships between Asano and his vassals, and between the vassals themselves), converting them into a filiative, i.e. natural relationship, through the altered meaning of loyalty. As Ikegami states:

Although it was the organizational "system" of the Japanese state that empowered the samurai class, the system's optimal operation depended upon the ideology of vassalage, which always presupposed a "personal" relationship between master and followers. (Ikegami 1995:237)

Thus the narrative posits two potential and distinct forms of social relations; the first between Asano and the forty-seven, portrayed as pseudo-filiative, that is the 'ideology of vassalage', and the second between Kira and Asano, representative of the affiliative.

The fact that no reason for the attack was ever recorded allowed story-tellers, playwrights and filmmakers the freedom to cast the historical characters as they pleased. Kira is almost universally cast as the villain, Asano, the wronged if imprudent country lord and Ōishi, his loyal retainer, is cast as the ultimate hero of the piece. Within these scenarios, Ōishi and to a certain extent Asano are symbolic of all the positive aspects of nature and life, while Kira, the aging, sophisticated court official, is symbolic of all the negative aspects of culture and society. In film versions, the character of Kira is almost always constructed as a bad-tempered (*ijiwarui*) old man who, as a result of being dissatisfied with the gift he receives from Asano, proceeds to misadvise him on court procedure,[14] therefore humiliating Asano and provoking the attack. Within this scenario, a nature/culture divide is similarly established. Asano's status as a country *daimyō* is emphasised in many productions when Kira disparagingly refers to him as 'a country lord' (*inaka daimyō*) or refers to his retainers as 'country samurai' (*inaka zamurai*). The fact that Asano makes the mistake in the type of gift required in the first instance shows that he lacks the social knowledge and graces of court life. Within these fictional reconstructions of the events, two forms of social relations are portrayed and contrasted. On the one hand, there is the pseudo-filial relationship of absolute loyalty between Asano and his retainers; and on the other, there are the various bureaucratic relationships between Kira and his associates clearly based on financial dealings (often the giving and receiving of bribes) and self-interest. In these scenarios, the Kira/Asano relationship is cast in the mould of the *senpai/kōhai* (senior/junior) relationship dominant in all spheres of Japanese social, political and economic life. The sense of frustration and humiliation Asano feels is, according to Satō, inherent in this system which encourages the humiliation (both mental and physical) of underlings in the guise of strengthening the spirit (*kurō wa ningen o kitaeru* – suffering forges the man). This point would in part explain the enormous popularity of the film versions appearing between 1908 and the early 1940s – a period of great social and economic upheaval characterised by mass migration from the country to the cities.

Following Lévi-Strauss' definition of myth, this study argues that through constant repetition, *Chūshingura* has become part of the Japanese collective tradition. Moreover, film versions have come to rely on the 'iconic memory' of their viewing audience in the creation of meaning. Jackie Stacey defines 'iconic memory' as memories of a 'frozen moment; a moment removed from its temporal context and captured as pure image' (Stacey 1994:318). Many film versions reject the linear narrative style of cause and effect, stringing together a series of iconic moments as motifs carrying far greater meanings than their purely representational form suggests.

Kira's character in early versions, for example, Mizoguchi Kenji's 1941–1942 *Genroku Chūshingura*, is developed through the depiction of the *bakufu's* investigation of the attack. However, in many post-war productions, his character as an ill-tempered old man is reduced to close-up shots of his contorted face. In the 1994 *Chūshinguragaiden Yotsuyakaidan*, which entwines a traditional ghost story around the *Chūshingura* narrative, Kira is virtually absent from the screen. An aging retainer of Kira's house who plays a significant role in the ghost story sub-narrative is constructed to carry iconic meanings associated with more traditional representations of Kira. In contrast Asano, in his *seppuku* scene, is constantly shrouded in falling cherry blossoms. This *sakura*/death motif may seem clichéd to western audiences, but is still most evocative for Japanese spectators. The falling *sakura* of the *seppuku* scene is contrasted with the falling snow of the final scene – the revenge attack on Kira's house. While loyalty (*chūgi*), which this study will demonstrate is an ideological metaphor for a homosocial love upon which the Japanese male collectivity is founded, is expressed through a close-up shot of a tear-stained cheek which invariably forms part of a sequence of direct eye-line match reverse-cut shots. These sequences provide some of the best examples of the non-verbal communication (*ishin denshin*), central to the ideal masculine image constructed in these films. In Mizoguchi Kenji's *Genroku Chūshingura*, this motif is conveyed through the soundtrack as the impersonal shooting style of 'one scene, one shot', generally characteristic of Mizoguchi's films, does not permit the use of close-ups. Perhaps one of the best examples of the dramatic intensity of these sequences is found in the 1938 Makino Masahirō/Ikeda Tomiyasu collaboration *Chūshingura/Ten no maki/Chi no maki* (*Chūshingura/The Heavenly Scroll/The Earthly Scroll*). In this version, Kataoka Chiezō (1903–) plays both the Asano and Tachibana roles. In standard film versions of *Chūshingura*, Ōishi and Asano do not meet. However, in this version, Kataoka Chiezō's star persona transcends the two characters he portrays. So it is possible to read the Ōishi/Tachibana scene as a scene between Ōishi and Asano. The moving interchange of reverse-cut shots is therefore ambiguous and can be viewed as an expression of affection between Ōishi and Asano. Alternatively, due to the star personas of both Kataoka Chiezō and Bandō Tsumasaburō (1901–1953) (Ōishi), it is possible to read the scene as a moment of bonding between the two stars. These key motifs rely on the spectator's 'iconic memory' for their meaning. The narratives or genres into which they are inserted are continually changing, but as this study will demonstrate, the iconic core meanings inscribed into these motifs have remained constant.

Satō (1976), in his interpretation of the development of *Chūshingura* as a popular narrative, attempts to ground the two dominant themes of loyalty and rebellion in the few historically known facts relating to the incident. However, as with all similar attempts, in the final analysis, it is based on supposition. This in no way detracts from Satō's account, which provides one of the best

INTRODUCTION

outlines of the incident as a topic of popular discourse (as opposed to academic accounts). The important point for this study is not whether this interpretation is accurate, but rather that it is generally accepted as accurate. Therefore, it provides an analytic key as to why filmmakers used *Chūshingura* or more specifically the 'tragic hero' narrative as an organising figurative structure to explain the traumatic events of the war and defeat, a discussion of which will be developed in the analysis of war-retro films in chapters two and three. Chapter four will be concerned with the yakuza genre. These films are primarily based on the rebellion theme and through an analysis of the allegoric meanings of death, it will become clear how they are at one and the same time liberating and constraining.

In popular modern histories of Japan both visual (i.e. film and television accounts) and written, there has been a tendency to classify events within discreet historical time frames. This periodisation of history has helped perpetuate a view which sees the end of the Second World War as an historical closure and that what developed after, in the post-war period, as somehow different and unrelated to the past. In contrast, this study approaches the development of Japanese cinema from the perspective of continuity through a socio-historical analysis of the 'tragic hero' pregeneric narrative form. This narrative form in its two dominant themes of loyalty and rebellion has been, and is instrumental as a figurative structure by which (a) the traumatic events of the war are worked out, and (b) the contradictions between filiative and affiliative social relations are similarly resolved, therefore forming an integral part of the popular post-war discourse *nihonjinron*. However, before launching into an analysis of war-retro films, it is important to explore the socio-political background out of which nationalist ideologies of the *kokutai* based on pseudo-filial social relations developed and how they were manifested in early Japanese cinema.

CHAPTER 1

Backgrounds

The Invention of the *Kokutai* and Early Cinema

Nationalism – the principle of homogenous cultural units as the foundation of political life, and the obligatory cultural unity of rulers and ruled – is indeed inscribed neither in the nature of things, nor in the hearts of men, nor in the pre-conditions of social life in general, and the contention that it is so inscribed is a falsehood which nationalist doctrine has succeeded in presenting as self evident. (Gellner 1990:125)

In Japan, the connection between a person and his ... *ie*, [household] is at the same time the link between the individual and the nation. Today, if we but probe a little, we realise that the faithful subjects and loyal retainers of history are our ancestors, and we are aware, not just vaguely but in a concrete way, of the intentions of our ancestors. The awareness that our ancestors have lived and served under the imperial family for thousands of generations forms the surest basis for the feelings of loyalty and patriotism (*chūkun aikokushin*). If the *ie* were to disappear, it might even be difficult for us to explain to ourselves why we should be Japanese. As our individualism flourished, we would come to view our history no differently from the way we view that of foreign countries. (from a speech made by Yanagita Kunio to the Greater Japan Agricultural Association in 1906, quoted in Irokawa 1985:288)

Lévi-Strauss, through the deconstruction of the mythology of the Indians of South America, concluded that a binary opposition of nature/culture underlined these myths. Thus he saw them as offering a solution to 'the philosophical problems arising from the introduction of an agricultural mode of life' (1990:186). This study suggests that a similar binary opposition based on nature/culture is inherent in *Chūshingura*; nature as defined in nativist ideologies of the *kokutai* (national polity)[1] and family state (*kazoku kokka*) is contrasted with the 'corrupting' influences associated with the introduction of western culture.[2] Furthermore, I shall argue that the adoption of *Chūshingura* into the collective tradition of modern Japanese mythology in the form of the 'tragic hero' was precisely because it offered a solution to some of the philosophical problems arising from the development of a market economy in the latter half of the Tokugawa period (1615-1867) and the subsequent introduction of western technology in the Meiji period (1868-1912). Beasley stated that in eighteenth-century Japan 'feudalism was facing a crisis in that its political forms had outlived its economic base' (Beasley 1973:72). This crisis[3] is evident in the historical events upon which the narratives of *Chūshingura* are ostensibly based. The Confucian scholar Ogyū Sorai's (1666-1724) assessment and solution to the problem posed by the actions of Ōishi Kuranosuke and his followers was an attempt to reach a compromise between the old ideologies of political legitimacy and the new rule of law emerging as Japan was entering the period of transition from a feudal to a market economy. Ogyū Sorai posed the question, 'If a private principle predominates over a public principle, how can the law of the world stand?' (quoted in Ikegami 1995:233). As Beasley points out 'by 1700 Japan's merchants were already highly specialized' (Beasley 1973:43). Their economic advance not only threatened the samurai class financially, but also challenged the Confucian-based status divisions upon which the society was founded. The *sankin kōtai*[4] (alternative attendance) system was in part responsible for the advanced state of the economy in the major towns at this time. The *daimyō* (feudal lords) and samurai who were forced into maintaining expensive homes in the capital stimulated market activities that contributed to the moneterisation of the economy.

To understand the ideological roots of the nature/culture binary discourse inherent in the 'tragic hero' myth, it is necessary to turn to a discussion of the Meiji period and the emergence of the *kokutai* as a concept comprised of several unifying ideologies which ultimately developed at the time of the Russo-Japanese war of 1904-1905 into popular nationalism.

Yoshino (1995) in his study *Cultural Nationalism in Contemporary Japan* argues that the reason for the emergence of cultural nationalism as manifested in concepts of the *kokutai* and the *nihonjinron* was a need to 'regenerate the national community' by creating and/or strengthening a people's cultural identity when it is threatened. Hobsbawm raises a central question which must be addressed if one is to come to terms with the role and function of myths and ideologies of nationalism in social life.

> Why and how could a concept so remote from the real experience of most human beings as 'national patriotism' become such a powerful political force so quickly? It is plainly not enough to appeal to the universal experience of human beings who belong to groups recognizing one another as members of collectivities or communities, and therefore recognizing others as strangers. (Hobsbawm 1992c:46)

Gellner (1990) in part answers this question by tracing in theoretical terms the birth of nationalism from the agrarian (or feudal) stage of development to the industrial phase. His hypothesis is that, contrary to popular thought, a sense of nationalism is the precursor of the birth of the nation and not the other way round. He argues that the conditions for the growth of nationalism are inherent in the social relations required by industrialisation. These are mobility and universal education. Agro-literate societies tended to be sedentary and 'inward-turned' communities dominated by an elite who through the legitimate use of violence maintained order and who were purveyors of the 'official wisdom of the society'. At this stage of social development, Gellner states, 'both for the ruling stratum as a whole, and for the various sub-strata within it, there is a great stress on cultural differentiation rather than on homogeneity' (1990:10). In the Tokugawa period, this ideological differentiation was codified in the four Confucian social divisions of samurai, peasant, artisan and merchant. This system of social ordering was dependent on the maintenance of these social groups as static. However, the growth of the economy ultimately led to an increase in wealthy merchants and, combined with peasant unrest, facilitated the eventual disintegration of the Confucian social order. Ikegami tells us that the factors encouraging economic growth were the reclamation of arable land which led to an accumulation of an economic surplus in many villages; the *sankin kōtai* system;

improvements in agricultural technology; and 'the most important factor stimulating a market economy', the taxation system, whereby tax revenue was paid in rice which was sold for cash in the market place. As Ikegami explains,

> The establishment of a decentralized yet highly integrated political system encouraged economic growth and facilitated the development of a market economy on a national scale. The subsequent social developments stimulated by these gradual economic changes encouraged population and commodity mobility. This new fluidity in turn generated serious problems in many areas for the *bakuhan* system of domination. (Ikegami 1995:172)

The effects of the economic changes were an increasingly mobile population, urbanisation and labour migration. By the mid-eighteenth century, five to seven percent of the population lived in one of the three major cities of Edo, Osaka or Kyoto (Ikegami 1995:173) and between 1897 and 1916 the population of Osaka doubled to 1.5 million and in 1911 only forty percent of Tokyo's population had in fact been born there (Gluck 1985: 33). Relatively stable agricultural communities of the early Tokugawa period, characterised by social differentiation of vertical status divisions and geographically isolated from historical links, were replaced over a period of several hundred years by new urban societies in a state of constant change and flux.

The reproduction of agrarian society was rooted in an educational system that was both localised and intimate. Families passed skills down from one generation to the next. In contrast, industrial labour relations are dependent on a generic core of education transmitted to all potential workers. Skill flexibility is concomitant with mobility, therefore, even though at one level, industrial society is highly specialised 'its educational system is unquestionably the *least* specialized, the most universally standardized, that has ever existed' (Gellner 1990:27). It is the state, in industrial society, which has the monopoly of legitimate education. Gellner explains that as the economy industrialises, it is the education monopoly which becomes more important than the monopoly on violence[5] for the maintenance of social order.[6] To sum up, industrial society requires its workers to be both mobile and flexible and to have a generic training which allows for communication through standard idioms between individuals who do not necessarily know each other. Therefore, in Japan it was in the industrialising phase of development that the Confucian social divisions were eroded (the *bakumatsu* period), and cultural homogeneity, perpetuated through the advent of universal education introduced during the Meiji period, became the dominant theme as nationalist sentiments came to the fore.

Anderson made a similar point when he stated that 'nationalism has to be understood by aligning it, not with self-consciously held political ideologies, but with the large cultural systems that preceded it, out of which - as well as against which - it came into being' (Anderson 1993:12). Therefore Gellner speaks of a cultural hegemony as being the most pervasive form of social control in modern societies; that is, a common culture disseminated through a centralised education system, and I would add, increasingly through centralised mass media.

Therefore an answer to the question of how concepts of the nation-state, which differed in size and scale from the agrarian communities with which individuals had identified, are inculcated in people's minds as real concepts, must lie in the dissemination of the dominant culture. In the early phase of Japanese industrialisation the introduction of universal education in 1872 and conscription in 1873, combined with the standardisation of the language, facilitated the dissemination of the dominant culture to the lower levels of society. The state mobilisation of the population through these institutions, combined with the needs of industry for a mobile and flexible labour force, led to a degree of cultural homogenisation and even social equality. This equality was, theoretically, institutionalised in the Five Articles of the Imperial Charter Oath (*Go-kajō no Seimon*) of April 1868 which, among other things, stipulated that 'high and low would be of one heart in carrying out national policy', that 'merchants and peasants would achieve their ambitions' and that 'uncivilized customs of the past would be abandoned' (Lehmann 1982:185). The Charter Oath encouraged the subsequent use of phrases such as *shimin byōdō* (the equality of all citizens) and *ikkun banmin* (one ruler, many subjects). Both phrases emphasised the abolition of the Confucian class structure and promoted the equality of all subjects within the *kokutai*. This is still reflected today in the Japanese almost universal belief that they are middle-class.[7] As Gellner explains:

> Men can tolerate terrible inequalities, if they are stable and hallowed by custom. But in a hectically mobile society, custom has no time to hallow anything ... Stratification and inequality do exist, and sometimes in extreme form; nevertheless they have a muted and discreet quality, attenuated by a kind of gradualness of the distinctions of wealth and standing, a lack of social distance and a convergence of life-styles, a kind of statistical or probabilistic quality of the differences (as opposed to the rigid, absolutized, chasm-like differences typical of agrarian society), and by the illusion or reality of social mobility. (Gellner 1990:25)

The latter half of the Tokugawa period saw the beginnings of the homogenisation of the traditional social class divisions which continued into the Meiji period with the abolition of the samurai class and the inception of universal conscription in 1873. This included the dissemination of what had been an exclusive dominant culture to the lower echelons of Japanese society. Lehmann (1982) refers to this process as the 'samurai-isation' of the lower classes. The ideals and values of the samurai class were disseminated throughout the entire population by means of, for example, the Imperial Rescript to Soldiers and Sailors of 1882 (*Gunjin Chokuyu*) and the Imperial Rescript on Education of 1890. Lehmann explains:

> For reasons of internal development and defence against perceived external pressures the government required docile and well-disciplined peasants, workers, soldiers and sailors: to achieve that end, it was best not to instill in the hearts and minds of the populace liberal bourgeois values, but rather those samurai virtues of loyalty and obedience. (Lehmann 1982:159)

The 'samurai-isation' of the lower echelons of Japanese society was carried out through a process of deliberate ideological engineering through such mechanisms as the two rescripts which sought to establish the individual's 'personal' relationship with the Emperor. This was part of a policy which Gluck (1985) calls the 'denaturing of politics'. Simultaneously, the Civil Codes of 1898 and 1912 legally established the family as the basic unit of the nation-state and not the individual as in western judicial law. The effect of these combined processes was to situate the individual in a clearly defined, non-abstract position vis-à-vis authority and, by extension, the national *kokutai*.[8]

The process of delineating between the corrupting influences of politics and westernisation and the inherently superior qualities of a traditional Japanese ethos rooted in 'nature' goes back to the Meiji period. This delineation can now be seen as a clear-cut divide in films made during the Second World War and in various other forms in the post-war cinema. Gluck has demonstrated that the oligarchs viewed party politics as inherently divisive, therefore, in an effort simultaneously to secure their own power base and encourage unity vis-à-vis the foreign threat, they suppressed popular participation in politics.[9] The call of Itō Hirobumi (1841-1909) and Kuroda Kiyotaka (1840-1900) for 'transcendental cabinets' reinforced the view that party politics were associated with western bourgeois rationalism and therefore partisan. His Majesty the Emperor's government should be, they argued, comprised of an elite who theoretically represented a non-partisan neutrality. The suppression of politics as a legitimate area of public interest combined with the negative image of political candidates in the popular press had the effect of debasing notions of popular participation which were ultimately subsumed in national sentiments and patriotism.

The Civil Code of 1898 legally codified the customs and traditions of the samurai family as the legal philosophy of the society, applying to all equally. The Code safeguarded filial piety, primogeniture and the subservience of wives to husbands. The revised Civil Code of 1912 further secured the family as the central unit of Japanese society. The power of the male head of the *ie* (house) was now absolute. The family came to represent the 'microcosm' of the Japanese state. 'The power of the *ie*-head was a reflection of the power that the *tennō* [Emperor] should exercise over his children, namely the subjects of the Japanese Empire' (Lehmann 1982:258). The Diet had rejected an earlier draft code compiled by Gustave Émile Boissonade de Fontarbie (1825-1910), which had been based on the Napoleonic Code, as this was seen to be overtly concerned with the rights of the individual and therefore, not compatible with Japanese traditions. The Constitution of 1889 had guaranteed some basic rights to Japanese citizens; however, these 'were granted only within the framework of the law' (Lehmann 1982:259). Therefore, these rights were but privileges that the government could rescind through legislation.

> It is clear ... that in matters of jurisprudence the state appropriated to itself the role of an absolute central authority. It is also clear that by insisting on the autocratic and hierarchic nature of the family according to the provisions of the civil code, the government intended that this basic social unit should serve as the cornerstone for the *kokutai*.
> (Lehmann 1982:259)

The government was clearly engaged in deliberate ideological engineering through both the Imperial Rescripts and the Civil Code, but, as Hobsbawm points out when examining aspects of a national consciousness, it 'would be a mistake to see these exercises as pure manipulation from above' (Hobsbawm1992c:92). The Meiji oligarchy was most successful when they could build on pre-existing national sentiments. To this end the connection between the family, village community and the state was officially promoted (*kazoku kokka*), as the epigraph taken from a speech made by Yanagita (at the beginning of this section) so clearly demonstrates. The link between the *ie* and ancestor worship was extended to include the ancestors of the Imperial family. The Emperor, as symbolic father of the people, ensured that each individual Japanese had a direct link to the Imperial ancestors, the Gods of Japan. This was consolidated through a rationalisation of *Shintō* shrines (between 1906 and 1910, the number of shrines was reduced from 190,000-100,000 nationally), and through the creation of public holidays to celebrate important dates in the *Shintō* calendar.

The reinvention of the Imperial institution was also intended to have a similar unifying effect. The Meiji Emperor's regional tours (*gyōkō*) - he made 102 during his forty-five year reign - and the popular images of him 'bestowing the Constitution, writing poems, reviewing the troops and even drawing his bath' meant that, by the time of his death in 1912, his image had become 'quite human and personal' (Gluck 1985:100). As Gluck continues, 'it appears that by the end of the Meiji period virtually all Japanese were conscious of the emperor's existence for the first time in Japanese history' (Gluck 1985:100).

Fear of western imperialism was another such area that easily stimulated xenophobic sentiments. Nothing binds people together as much as fear of the 'other'. As Lehmann points out, racism as an 'important element in modern Japanese history cannot be underestimated' (Lehmann 1982:172). The late nineteenth and early twentieth centuries were the age of social Darwinism that attempted to give racism some basis in scientific fact. He goes on to explain that:

> As Japan was increasingly opened to the West, as contacts between Japanese and Europeans, both in Japan and Europe, as Japanese officials, the press, and hence the populace, came to a greater appreciation of the nature and motivations and underlying tenets of Western policy, the Japanese became not only aware, but indeed acutely conscious of European racism. (Lehmann 1982:172)

This view was reinforced by such incidents as the Triple Intervention (1895) after the Sino-Japanese war of 1894-1895 and at the League of Nations in 1919. It is important to emphasise the point that, while the Japanese were aware of European racism, they did not appear in this early phase to develop a counter-racist attitude towards westerners. There was rather a reactive element to their anti-western sentiment. This can be seen in films made during the war period (1931-1945) which rarely depict foreigners at all. When they do appear (played by Japanese actors), they are never subjected to the blatant racism which characterised American films of the same period and which is still evident in the Vietnam war genre (e.g. *The Deer Hunter* 1978). In fact, a wartime star, Fujiwara Yoshie (1898-1976), was the son of the Norwegian Consul and a geisha. As Dower's study of racism and the Pacific war confirms, 'whereas racism in the West was markedly characterised by denigration of others, the Japanese were preoccupied far more exclusively with elevating themselves' (Dower 1986:204-205). The Japanese did not attack westerners as racially inferior, but challenged the underlying philosophical principles upon which western society is based. The Japanese films of the war years were concerned with mobilisation of the home front and not the denigration of the enemy.[10]

A further cultural mechanism was the promotion of modern myths with their origins in the historical past, and which in modern times became unifying narratives based on human micro-experiences ultimately becoming metaphors for the national collective, the *kokutai*. These were just some of the mechanisms employed by the oligarchy building upon pre-existing national sentiments for the purpose of creating a national unity to ensure both political stability at home and autonomy in an increasingly imperialistic international setting.

Irokawa, quoting Itō Tasaburō, defines the concept of the Japanese *kokutai* as it was conceived until 1945 as:

> 'the eternal and immutable national polity (*kokutai*)' unlike the easily changeable political system (*seitai*), was nothing less than 'the concept of national morality grounded in the rational consciousness and religious psychology of the people'. It was the 'spiritual force behind the activities of the state' and 'the principle of national unity' ... More concretely, it was derived from 'the harmonious unity of the ruler and the people, the whole nation as one family under the rule of the emperor, his line unbroken for ages eternal.' (Irokawa 1985:247)

In answer to the question why individuals felt the need to become part of the 'imagined community' like the *kokutai*, Hobsbawm suggests that the 'imagined community' fills an 'emotional void' left by the disintegration of 'real human communities and networks' caused by the economic and social shift from collective agricultural practices to industrial structures of social relations. The group model, characteristic of Japanese society, became in the Meiji period the ideological substitute for the co-operative collective model of the 'agro-literate' society of the early Tokugawa period. The competitive individualising ethos inherent in capitalist industrial societies was subsumed beneath the group ethos as a variant feeling 'of collective belonging which already existed and could operate ... on the macro-political scale which could fit in with modern ... nations' (Hobsbawm 1992c:46). The *kokutai* as a nationalist sentiment appealed to a common bond of ethnicity, which, it was argued, had been rooted in the Japanese since the first Emperor Jimmu (circa 660 BC: Sansom 1983:28). The ideological basis for the 'family state' rested on organic theories of filial relationships. These, it was argued, were established in the procreative bonds between parents and children when in fact the village community in the 'agro-literate' period was bound together by affiliative economic ties such as the control of irrigation and common lands. Thus, by the time of the outbreak of hostilities in China in 1931 (the Manchurian Incident) there was in the collective national consciousness a clear division between nature (as represented in the social relations upon which the *kokutai* was founded) and culture (carrying with it negative images of western individualism and self-interest).

The Quest for the Pure Self and the 'Samurai-isation' of the Lower Classes

> The special feature of Japanese films produced during the war to promote a fighting spirit was that they were more concerned with the question of how to portray death heroically than how to promote a hatred of the enemy. (Satō 1986:246)

> Tasaka Tomotaka's *Kaigun* and Kinoshita Keisuke's *Rikugun* are typical examples of films concerned with the process of disregarding the ego and the development of the spirit. (Satō 1986:250)

> *Danjite okonaeba kishin mo kore o oku.* (A resolute will chases even demons away). (*Kaigun* – Makoto's motto)

The above quotations from Satō imply that the Japanese authorities were concerned to promote the spiritual development of the home front (*kokumin seishin no kan'yō*). The directions to screen writers by the Ministry of Internal Affairs (*Naimu-shō*) Censorship Office (*Kenetsu-kyoku*) in July 1938 clearly demonstrate this.

> The permeation of individualism evident in western films is to be removed from Japanese productions; the Japanese spirit, family system and beautiful customs are to be extolled; the Japanese public are to be re-educated through film; frivolous activities are to be eradicated from the screen; and respect for senior members of the family should be emphasised. (Hamada 1995:102)[11]

The concept of the pure self is central to the ideological position of nature inherent in the nativist Confucian tradition. The 1943 film, *Muhō Matsu no isshō,* directed by Inagaki Hiroshi (1905–1980),[12] provides one of the finest examples of a war film that, while not a war film in the western sense, sought to promote an idealised (ideological) view of masculinity. The plot evolves around the relationship of Matsugorō, a rickshaw man, (the lowest position in Meiji society), with a young boy and his mother. The character Matsugorō, acted by Bandō Tsumasaburō, is constructed to illustrate the ideal of pure manhood. His simplicity and innocence (*sobokuna utsukushisa*) are represented by his lack of education and low social position. (At one point in the film, he unashamedly asks the boy's mother to read a notice for him.) As the title suggests and as he reminds his various adversaries when challenged, he is *muhō Matsu*. *Muhō* in the title of the film was translated by Barrett (1989) as 'untamed' and certainly it contains this element. However, *hō* in Japanese carries strong meanings of law, making up the second part of the word *kenpō* (constitution) and is the first character in the word *hōritsu* (legal-law), to give just two examples. *Mu*, in *muhō*, is a character of negation. Hence, *muhō* is often translated as 'unlawful'. However, in the light of the preceding discussion, *muhō* in this instance takes on a different complexion. If we link *hō* to culture within the historical negative context discussed above, the title of the film becomes something like *The Life of Matsu the Pure*, as untamed and unlawful usually carry negative connotations in English.

Matsugorō's relationship with the young boy Toshio is based on a shared innocence. He becomes a heroic figure in Toshio's eyes at the sports meeting when Matsugorō breaks down Toshio's shyness and reserve (feminine qualities). During the various sports events, Toshio had lacked the abandon of the other boys to cheer on his side. The diegesis of the film implies that this was due to his life without a father. (His father dies early in the film leaving the position vacant for Matsugorō to become the surrogate father.) When Matsugorō enters the race, he tells Toshio that he can win if Toshio roots for him. During the actual running of the race, the camera created a dual site of tension through rapid inter-cutting between Toshio, as excitement overtakes inhibition, and Matsugorō as he runs, culminating in the last few seconds of the sequence when Toshio loses his inhibitions and starts cheering Matsugorō on with abandon. At this point, Matsugorō overtakes the leaders and goes on to win the race. At home that evening Toshio and his mother have the following conversation:

Toshio: Mother, uncle is a great man (*erai*) isn't he? He was so fast, when he won it was so exciting, I couldn't bear it.
Mother: But uncle is not a great man just because he can run fast.

Toshio: Mm.
Mother: When Matsugorō-san was born, fate was against him so he became a rickshaw man. Toshio, you are a boy, no matter what you want to do, have courage to do it without reservation like Matsugorō. Do you understand?

Long before the race scene, the film is structured to establish Matsugorō's credentials in the spectator's mind through such incidents as his refusal to accept money from Toshio's mother for bringing the boy home in his rickshaw after an accident on his stilts. Through his talks with the young Toshio whom he affectionately calls Bonbon, his own difficult childhood is revealed in flashback. These scenes are brought into sharp contrast with Toshio's experiences, as he is from an upper middle-class family, his father having been an officer in the army. The diegesis raises Matsugorō's relationship with Toshio's mother far above sexual desire despite her widowed status. The spectator knows from his concern for the mother and son that he loves her, but in the best *Hagakure*[13] tradition, it remains an unrevealed and unconsummated love. It is only after his death that the depth of his feelings becomes apparent when it is revealed that over the years he had made financial provision for her in the form of a savings account amounting to five hundred *yen*, no small sum in the Meiji period. His unmarried status further confirms the purity of his love. However, he does get into fights, usually with authoritative figures often comically dressed in western attire, as for example, Wakamatsu, the police inspector who hits Matsugorō for refusing to take him in his rickshaw. His relations with his clients are often contentious, as he is an independent man and can choose when to work and whom to take. Hence, his character is portrayed as upright and honest; he has no need to bow and scrape to his social superiors. In one scene he is described as being like a piece of split bamboo – a straightforward fellow – (*take o wattayōna otoko*). Nevertheless, in his relations with the adolescent Toshio and his mother, he is again portrayed as instinctively accepting his lower social position.

The episodes of his life are interspersed with close-up shots of the wheels of his rickshaw turning. As the film progresses, these punctuating shots increase as does the speed with which the wheels rotate, representing the cycle of Matsugorō's life. The poetic structure of the film is, at first glance, simple and flowing, thus concealing the often complex juxta-positioning of shots which intensify scenes such as the race, drawing the spectator into Toshio's subjective position as the excitement builds. This is also true in one of the final scenes when Matsugorō plays the *taiko* drum at the *matsuri* (festival). The camera, at an increasingly fast pace and in time with the drum, pans from Matsugorō to the crowd below and back to Matsugorō. He plays the drum by instinct as if it were an extension of his body. The people in the crowd and the growing excitement attest to his superior ability. By contrast, Toshio, now grown up and attending university in Tokyo, has lost his innocence and in a sense has become contaminated by his education – through his contact with culture. The *matsuri* scene builds to a climax and then fades into the rotating rickshaw wheels followed by a close-up of flowers in a field and children dancing. Balloons floating up into the sky are superimposed over this scene followed by fleeting flashbacks of Matsugorō's life interspersed with falling blossoms and the rickshaw wheels which finally come to a halt. The portrayal of his death in abstract shots of balloons, blossom and the rickshaw wheels leaves the spectator with an image of Matsugorō in his prime beating the *taiko*. We do not see his body polluted by age, disease or death, as in the post-war 1958 remake (starring Mifune Toshirō 1920–1997 as Matsugorō) where Matsugorō dies alone in the snow after first drinking himself to death, or the 1956 film about a rickshaw man *Wa ga machi (Our Town)*, directed by Kawashima Yūzō (1918–1963). In the final scenes of this later film, the rickshaw man is ridiculed and assaulted by a group of louts in the street who push his rickshaw into the river, shortly after which he dies alone in his dilapidated room, so that the death of the rickshaw man is symbolic of the death of the past, whereas this wartime version of *Muhō Matsu* is a film in praise of a past tradition of manhood.

In short, Matsugorō is the embodiment of *makoto* (purity). The fact that, unlike Ōishi Kuranosuke, the principal hero in *Chūshingura*, he is a mere rickshaw man intensifies the potential for spectator identification and opens up the possibility for the lower orders of Japanese society to become part of an elite cultural tradition. As such, he has remained popular right through the post-war period, occasionally being screened on television and included in special screenings on the NHK satellite channels. The film is also still being listed by Japanese critics in the best top ten Japanese war films (*Dai Anke-to ni yoru Nihon Eiga Besuto 150*, 1992).

In contrast the 1942 film *Chichi ariki (There was a Father)* directed by Ozu Yasujirō (1903-1963), is concerned not with a natural spontaneous masculinity as *Muhō Matsu*, but with patriarchal authority and responsibility. Like *Muhō Matsu*, the narrative revolves around the relationship between a man and, in this case, his natural son. This relationship between father and son represents in microcosm the symbolic relationship between the individual and authority within the *kokutai*. The film received a Bureau of Information award as an outstanding 'national policy film' (Bordwell 1988: 292).

The father, Horikawa, played by Ryū Chishū (1904-1996), is a widowed schoolteacher living in Kanazawa with his only son, Ryōhei, played as an adult by Sano Shūji (1912-1978). While on a school sightseeing excursion to Tokyo including visits to the Meiji and Yasakuni Shrines, the great Buddha at Kamakura, and Hakone from which Mt. Fuji could be seen, one of his students drowns in a boating accident. Horikawa feels he must accept responsibility for the accident and, placing Ryōhei in a dormitory, resigns from his teaching post and goes to work in a Tokyo textile factory. Thus begins the long years of separation the two must endure - a poignant theme during the war which separated fathers and sons from families.

It is not until the second half of the film when Ryōhei has grown up and is himself a teacher that the aging Horikawa puts into words the philosophy that has guided his reactions to the chain of events which make up the plot of the film. The two meet at Shinabara Onsen (a hot spring), where after bathing they have lunch. Ryōhei suggests he should give up his teaching job in Akita and come to live in Tokyo with his father, as he says, 'I can't bear any more this living apart from you'. His father interrupts him telling his son that his job is a vocation (*tenshoku*) and that he must devote his life to it. Ryōhei silently bows his head in assent, swallowing back his disappointment. After lunch, the two go fishing together, thereby duplicating a scene from earlier in the film when Ryōhei was still a child, during which Horikawa told the young Ryōhei he would have to live in a dormitory. Up until that moment, the movement of the two fishing lines in a continuous sweep of casting had been perfectly synchronised. Momentarily, the young Ryōhei falters. However, after accepting his father's decision, his line again falls into sync. In the latter scene, the mature Ryōhei has accepted his father's decision and is again depicted casting his line in unison

BACKGROUNDS

with his father's, emphasising the total harmony between them. Ozu often incorporates shots of people acting in unison to visually emphasise the rapport between characters.

The following morning, as they are preparing to leave the *ryokan* (hotel), they have the following conversation putting into words the emotions evident in the preceding fishing scene:

Ryōhei: It's a shame. If we had a little more time, we could have done some more fishing
Horikawa: Mm.
Ryōhei: I enjoyed fishing yesterday evening.
Horikawa: Yes, how the time has flown.
Ryōhei: Yes, I had been looking forward to this trip for a long time.
Horikawa: Well, it was really pleasant to spend an evening with you and to be able to talk leisurely ... Are you all right for your train?
Ryōhei: Yes, fine.
Horikawa: The next time we'll meet will be when you have your medical for the army.
Ryōhei: Yes, that's right.
Horikawa: That won't be long. I shall look forward to it.
Ryōhei: Yes.
Horikawa: Look after yourself and don't transfer to Tokyo. Don't get ill or anything.
Ryōhei: No.
Horikawa: At this time there is nothing useful for you to do. You must accept things as they are.
Ryōhei: Yes, all right.
Horikawa: Take care of yourself.
Ryōhei: Father ...
Horikawa: Mm.
Ryōhei: This is just a little spending money (*kozukai*) for you.
Horikawa: Well, *kozukai*, for me?
Ryōhei: Yes, it's only very little, but please accept it ... I hoped you would accept it, it's a little extra, but it's very small ... Please.
Horikawa: Well, shall I accept?
Ryōhei: Yes.
Horikawa: Thank you. I will take it and offer it at the *butsudan* (family Buddhist altar) to show your mother.

Ryōhei: Mm.
Horikawa: Thank you.
Ryōhei: I am sorry about last night.
Horikawa: That's all right.
Ryōhei: I have become so selfish (*wagamama*).
Horikawa: No, I was a little severe, but I am pleased that you understand. Well, do your best in this day and age, we must not waste time. I'll keep on trying. We will both keep on trying, yes.
Ryōhei: Yes, let's.

In this scene, it is apparent that Ryōhei has accepted his father's wishes and will place his duty as a teacher above his personal feelings, thus reconciling Ryōhei's potential dilemma. In these scenes, Ryōhei was faced with two potentially conflicting areas of obligation (*giri*) - his duty to his work and his filial duty to his father - both of which in Confucian terms are important areas of obligation. However, the narrative, by turning filial piety into the simple acceptance of patriarchal authority and conflating Ryōhei's obligation to care for his aging father with personal selfish feelings and desires, the film alters the traditional meanings of Confucian filial piety into an autocratic structure of power in keeping with the ideologies of the *kazoku kokka* (family state). This freed sons from family obligations and reconciled two poignant areas of potential personal conflict and ideological contestation in wartime Japanese society. According to the film's interpretation of filial piety, fathers could no longer admonish their sons on these grounds for placing their 'duty' to the *kokutai* above their duty to their parents.

The giving and receiving of *kozuka*i is a further example of the deflection of the traditional obligations associated with filial piety onto the symbolic exchange of money. In an earlier scene paralleling the above-quoted scene, Horikawa gives the young Ryōhei *kozukai* when he is leaving him at the dormitory. In this scene too, Horikawa is confronted by a similar dilemma between his duty to the *kokuta*i in terms of work and his duty to his son. The latter is again deflected on to personal (selfish) emotions and therefore to be resisted. In both these scenes, a compromise is reached between two potentially conflicting areas of obligation. Public duty, as represented here through work, is given priority over filial obligations that are reduced to mere selfishness (*wagamama*) in the case of Ryōhei, and a parent's obligation to his son in the case of Horikawa. The fulfillment of family obligations is, on the part of Ryōhei, represented in the unquestioning acceptance of patriarchal authority; and in Horikawa's case, it was to ensure that Ryōhei received a good education. Furthermore, in both scenes, it is symbolised by the giving and receiving of *kozukai*.[14]

In *Chichi ariki*, as in his post-war films, Ozu's subject matter is the family group, therefore his films are structured both from the narrative point of view and technically to emphasise the family as a group rather than individuals. This is in marked contrast to films such as *Muhō Matsu* in which the plot revolves around one individual character. As the following discussion will demonstrate, Ozu broke with the traditional narrative structure by introducing a multiplicity of leading characters and interacting sub-plots. This became more complex in some of his post-war films such as *Tōkyō monogatari (Tokyo Story)*, *Ohayō (Good Morning)* and *Samma no aji* (released in the west as *An Autumn Afternoon*), but it is evident in his earlier film *Chichi ariki* and the 1941 film *Todake no kyōdai, (Brothers and Sisters of the Toda Family)* where the classical narrative structure is replaced by a more loosely motivated story line. *Muhō Matsu*, on the other hand, is representative of a linear narrative structure through which the character develops. *Chichi ariki* is comprised of a series of often loosely fitting elements, hence the lack of dramatic accumulation so evident in *Muhō Matsu* as, for example, in the race scene and the *taiko* scene. In Ozu's films, the agents of causality are often external to the characters – the death of Horikawa's student in the boating accident has tremendous implications for both Horikawa's and Ryōhei's lives. Ozu's characters tend to react to a given set of circumstances rather than to instigate them. This is in direct contrast to films based on a more traditional western narrative structure revolving around individual characters as the agents of causality such as *Muhō Matsu*. In Ozu's films continuity is created through character types, many of whom continue from one film to the next bearing the same names and often played by the same actors, e.g. the two young sons in *Tōkyō monogatari*, Isamu and Minoru, reappear in *Ohayō*.

The effect of this form of narrative structure in Ozu's films is to distance the spectator from the characters as individuals and to encourage us to view the situations making up the plot more dispassionately. This is reinforced visually through Ozu's self-imposed restrictions on camera movement, camera placement and a rigidly controlled editing technique. Bordwell rejects the earlier position adopted by some critics that Ozu's low camera placement represents the viewpoint of some unseen observer on the following grounds:

> [Ozu's camera is] almost never at the literal height of a seated observer; ... what sort of observing entity is almost always lower than anything it sees, even in streets, train aisles, and office corridors? ... if the frame represented an invisible squatting witness, it should remain constant. It does not ... [and finally, there are instances when] Ozu changes the camera's height even when filming the same object. (Bordwell 1988:77)

He goes on to interpret its significance:

> Exactly because the camera cannot be representing the viewpoint of an intelligent agent, either a character or a person-like invisible witness, it can serve as the basis of an *impersonal* narrational style. (Bordwell 1988:79)

that is, a narrational style which weakens spectator identification and supports the loosely motivated plot line. This is in marked contrast to the filmic techniques used by Inagaki in *Muhō Matsu* which attempt to draw the spectator into an empathetic response to Matsugorō. This is evident in his use of flashbacks to describe Matsugorō's under-privileged childhood. In one scene, when the young Matsugorō is searching for his father, the camera takes his point of view as he runs through a wood where the trees take on ghostly forms. At other times, the camera takes Toshio's point of view as he looks up at the powerful figure of Matsugorō. Ozu's camera position, on the other hand, is always impersonal and his refusal to use close-up reaction shots combined with his insistence on actor restraint and impassiveness in the expression of emotions are further examples of techniques that limit the spectator's emotional responses to the characters. As Bordwell concludes, 'Ozu's directing thus ruled out empathetic interpretation: the actor became a repository of pictorial behaviors. "You are not supposed to feel, you are supposed to do" (Bordwell 1988:85). Furthermore, the eye-line of medium close-up shots of characters is rarely if ever directed at the spectator, even in the most emotional scenes such as the *onsen* scene quoted above. Due to the low position of the camera, the glances of the characters pass over the top of the camera or, alternatively, the eye-line is directed slightly to the right or left of the camera's lens. Ozu's technique of editing each scene according to time further lessens the emotional build up of his films. 'For the spectator, such repetitive meter creates a subliminal norm. There will be no sudden accelerations, no flurry of rapid shots; the calm pace of cutting will match the unfolding syuzhet events' (Bordwell 1988:75).

By limiting the potential for spectator identification with one particular character through the narrative structure, camera position and editing techniques, Ozu, on the one hand, forces his spectator into a more analytic mode of response and, on the other hand, to view the family group as a whole, unlike Inagaki in *Muhō Matsu* who sought through fades, flashbacks, low-angle shots of Matsugorō and rapidly inter-cut sequences to draw the spectator into the film and into an empathetic mode of response. Both films, though technically diametrically opposed, were successful in promoting an idealised image of masculinity compatible with the dominant ideology of the period. However, while Muhō Matsu is representative of a natural and spontaneous purity, Horikawa and Ryōhei achieve a similar state through self-denial and the acceptance of responsibility, while simultaneously reinforcing a group ethos which is built into the very structure of the film. As Horikawa states, '*Otagai ni kokki no seishin de ganbarō*' (Together we will persist in the spirit of self-denial).

The 1943 film released on the second anniversary of Pearl Harbour in honour of the Special Attack Forces, *Kaigun (Navy)*,[15] directed by Tasaka Tomotaka (1902-1974), combines both the idealised qualities of masculinity evident in *Muhō Matsu* and *Chichi ariki* in the character of Tani Makoto, played by Yamanouchi Akira (1920-). *Kaigun* is arguably one of the first films produced, of what was to become in the post-war period a distinct sub-genre of the war-retro film – the *kamikaze* film. It is also a representative example of the 'tragic hero's' first significant move from his traditional home in the *jidai geki* (period drama) into the *gendai geki* (contemporary drama). As the previous discussion made clear, there was a conscious attempt on the part of the authorities to incorporate the lower classes into the former elite samurai traditions. In films, this was reflected in the appearance of working class heroes, e.g. Matsugorō, the lowly rickshaw man, and Horikawa, at first a provincial teacher and then a factory worker. *Kaigun* took the 'samurai-isation' of the lower classes one step further by allowing a boy from a Kagoshima merchant family (the lowest social position in the Confucian hierarchy) the honour of becoming a 'tragic hero'. The film follows the experiences of the young Makoto from his decision to enter the Naval Academy to his death at Pearl Harbour as a member of the Special Attack Force of submarines (*Sensuikan no Tokkōtai*). Unfortunately, the American Occupation Forces destroyed the final reel of the film, which depicted the actual attack.

The hero's name, Makoto, is a phonetical play on the word for purity; the actual characters which comprise his name are *ma* meaning truth and *koto* meaning person. He is the embodiment of youthful purity and truth. This is reflected in the film through his attitude to his family, his teachers, and in his limited relationships with women. Again Makoto, like Ryōhei, is faced with a dilemma in regard to the potential conflict between his obligations to the family – in this case the family business – and his desire to join the navy. His school friend, Takao, intends to join the navy training school and encourages Makoto to join with him. However, in the early stages of the film, Makoto points out that, as he comes from a merchant family, he would have to go into the family business, at the very least he would do what his mother told him to do (*Haha no iu tōri suru tsumori ja*). It is only after his elder brother has offered to stay in the family business and his mother agrees, that he sits the entrance examinations for the Naval Academy. Again, a compromise is reached whereby parental authority is seen to be upheld and the son is simultaneously released to fulfil his duty to the *kokutai*.

As the film is promoting a meritocratic ethos, Takao acts as a foil to measure Makoto's ability and talent. Takao comes from an affluent family and so it is only natural that he should aspire to a military career. However, in reality Takao is physically weak and short sighted and therefore fails the medical test, leaving the way open for Makoto to rise above his humble merchant background to take centre stage in the making of history. Makoto's purity and singleness of purpose are reinforced in his relationship with Takao's younger sister who is infatuated with him. At each encounter, he spurns her advances. Within the true *kamikaze* tradition, his mother, played by Takihana Hisako (1906-1985), is the only female allowed a place in his heart. Thus, while on leave before his departure for Pearl Harbour, he serves the rice for his mother at their final meal together. Later, he tells his elder brother to look after her. At this stage, the family does not know he will fail to return, therefore increasing the dramatic effect of the scene. Male purity associated with sexual abstinence was similarly evident in Matsugorō's relationship with Toshio's mother and, in *Chichi ariki*, where it is only in the final scenes that a woman appears at all. She is Fumiko, the daughter of Horikawa's friend who, it has been decided, will marry Ryōhei. Up until this point, Horikawa's and Ryōhei's contact with women was symbolised by the *butsudan* in which a tablet of Ryōhei's dead mother is enshrined. In both *Muhō Matsu* and *Chichi ariki*, the father figures become almost iconical virgin symbols (as in a reversal of the Christian virgin birth) of an ideal patriarchal male purity. Makoto, in acknowledging only the affection between mother and son, similarly retains in his relationships with other male characters, and through his numerous visits to *Shintō* shrines, his symbolic relationship with the Emperor, the purity essential to the *Hagakure* tradition.

Makoto's family connections with Kagoshima are also highly significant, as Kagoshima is the capital of Satsuma, the home of one of the two great clans instrumental in the events of the Meiji Restoration. Also, the British bombarded Kagoshima in 1863 in a revenge attack after the murder of Charles Richardson, a British subject, by extremist samurai. Furthermore, it was on Shiro-yama that Saigō Takamori (1827-1877) made his last stand and finally committed *seppuku*. Hence, the many punctuating shots of both Shiro-yama and the smouldering Mt. Sakurajima, and Saigō's statue throughout the film. These all function to harness history to the events of Pearl Harbour and to help the individual to conceive of his sacrifice in terms of a divine mission within an established historical tradition.

In *Kaigun*, through Makoto's reverence to Shintō shrines and his many trips to the grave of Tōgō Heihachirō (1847-1934), a famous son of Kagoshima who was commander of the fleet during the Russo-Japanese war, the individual's relationship to authority is institutionalised. The establishment of a direct link from the individual to authority that in the modern age had become increasingly abstract and alienating facilitated the effective 'samurai-isation' of the lower classes. The Emperor, as symbol of the *kokutai*, provided just such a link. The many shots of Tōgō's grave and photograph in *Kaigun* are similar icons personifying authority, while the 'tragic hero' in this example, Makoto, provides a vicarious personification enabling the individual spectator to conceive of this link in personal terms. Thus, during the war period, it can be seen that these films provided a reconciliation between the rule of law and a nativist Confucian ethic. In both *Chichi ariki* and *Kaigun*, this reconciliation is achieved in the narrative through the conflation of the concept of filial piety and the contractual relationship between the individual and the state to which purity (*makoto*) was added as an essential prerequisite. In *Chichi ariki*, this was achieved subtly in the depiction of patriarchal authority within the family. In *Kaigun*, a direct link is established between authoritative figures such as the Emperor, Saigō Takamori, Tōgō Heihachirō, and Makoto. The absence of Makoto's natural father (he died as a soldier) in *Kaigun* is essential, as it leaves the position vacant for the iconographic figures of the Emperor, Saigō Takamori and Tōgō Heihachirō.

In *Kaigun*, the primary personalised narrative of Makoto, the 'tragic hero', is placed within a secondary historical narrative through the use of actual footage of the Naval Academy, the Japanese fleet and the insertion of newspaper headlines providing a chronology of events leading up to the attack on Pearl Harbour, thus effectively homogenising historical fact and the foreground actions of fictional characters. This docu-drama structure not only institutionalises the relationship between the individual and authority through the foreground narrative, as discussed above, but through the secondary historical setting, explains a complex international situation to a disorientated populace suffering the privations of war. Also and more importantly it harnesses history as a legitimating factor for current political and military policy.

The historical setting which encompasses the actions of Makoto in *Kaigun* is provided in the early part of the film by his teacher, played by Tōno Eijirō (1907-), and military instructor, played by Ryū Chishū. For example, in one scene, after passing the entrance examination for the Naval Academy, Makoto and two other students are invited to their teacher's home for a celebratory supper. Before eating, the teacher gives them a lengthy lecture on foreign policy and the various international conferences Japan had participated in since the end of World War One. He begins with a reference to Japan's withdrawal from the League of Nations in 1933, making the point that, since the establishment of the League in 1919, both the

United States and Britain had sought to restrict Japan's growth as an international power. It must be borne in mind that any reference to the League of Nations carries with it strong connotations of the Japanese delegation's failure to get a declaration on the principle of racial equality inserted into the covenant. As further evidence of the United States' and Britain's negative foreign policy attitudes towards Japan in the build up to World War Two, the teacher makes reference to the Washington Conference of 1921 and the London Naval Disarmament Conference of 1930, both of which sought to restrict the amount of naval tonnage at a ratio of 5:5:3 for Britain, the United States and Japan respectively. The Washington Conference was also significant for ending the Anglo-Japanese Alliance. Therefore, the teacher concludes his talk by calling this 'the period of no treaties' (*mu jōyaku jidai*). During this scene, the camera is in a position behind the three students, thereby identifying with their point of view. This is strengthened as the camera maintains a direct eye-line match with the teacher, further equating the audience with the students and reinforcing the socially authoritative position afforded to teachers in Japanese society. Throughout the film, the camera position and angle places the spectator in Makoto's subjective position in such scenes. Furthermore, after Makoto has graduated from the Naval Academy as an officer, newspaper headlines and actual newsreel footage of the celebrations to mark the 2,600 year founding of Japan (*kigen*) in 1940 are inter-cut with shots of Makoto's family reading a letter describing his participation in these events. In the latter part of the film, as the audience has increasingly become aware that Makoto is going to volunteer for the Special Attack Forces, newspaper headlines are more and more interspersed with the action of the drama. First, the headlines are announcing the ratification of the Triple Alliance and finally, as Makoto and his friends are preparing for the attack, such headlines as 'The American Government Hardens its Attitude' and 'The Negotiations have Reached a Critical Phase' are inter-cut between scenes of Makoto's final leave at home in Kagoshima.

The 1944 film *Rikugun (Army)*, directed by Kinoshita Keisuke (1912–1998), adapts a similar docu-drama format to the primary narrative following the lives of three generations of a Chōshū merchant family (Chōshū was the other clan instrumental in the events of the Meiji Restoration and therefore carries connotations of loyalty to the Emperor) from the battle of Kokura in 1866 and the bombardment of Shimonoseki, through to the grandson's departure for the front in China in the 1930s. Again, in *Rikugun,* a definite attempt is made to incorporate the lower classes into the military samurai tradition, while simultaneously placing the origins of Japan's involvement in World War Two within an historical trajectory extending back to the *bakumatsu* period.

The opening sequence of title shots instantly informs the spectator this is not a film about famous military officers, but is about the ordinary foot soldiers who made up the overwhelming majority of the army. The first shot is a close-up at a low-angle of a young soldier standing to attention. At the command to present arms, the camera cuts to a high-angle shot of the parade ground as the title *Rikugun* is superimposed on the screen. In this sequence, while acknowledging the army as a massive body of men, the images also draw attention to the individual, quickly establishing the subject matter of the film. Events from the lives of each generation of the Takagi family are depicted against a backdrop of historical military events, such as the public protests against the Triple Intervention of 1895, the Russo-Japanese war and finally, the war with China. The 'reality' of these latter events is verified through the inclusion of newspaper headlines from the *Asahi Shinbun* and actual newsreel footage of the Japanese bombardment of Shanghai. The docu-drama editing structure of the film blurs the boundaries between reconstruction and actual footage, merging fact and fiction to produce an institutionalised view of history, the main effect of which is the harnessing of history to legitimate present actions. The personalised narratives of the grandfather, played by Mitsuda Ken (1902-), Tomohiko, played as an adult by Ryū Chishū, and his son Shintarō, played by Hoshino Yasumasa, conflate personal ambition with official government policy. Just as in *Chichi ariki* and *Kaigun*, filial piety is equated with duty to the *kokutai.* For example, the grandfather, on a trip to Tokyo to protest against the Triple Intervention, becomes ill and the young Tomohiko travels to Tokyo to see him. The grandfather, on what is soon to become his death-bed, explains the frustration he feels over the foreign situation and goes on to say that they must be patient until the time when Japan will defeat Russia, thereby effectively predicting the outcome of the Russo-Japanese war. The young Tomohiko is very moved by this speech and when his father asks what he will become, he immediately replies that he wants to become a soldier. True to his father's prediction, he does become a soldier in the Russian campaign. Thus, according to the film's interpretation of the events of the narrative, the son's future is determined by his father's wishes and not by government policy. Similarly, when Shintarō is still a baby, his mother, played by Tanaka Kinuyo, implies that it is the child who will fulfil the father's ambition, i.e. the state policy. In this way, filial piety is presented as symbolic of the individual's relationship to the state.

Muhō Matsu, *Chichi ariki* and *Kaigun*[16] are all films that depict the relationships between males. Women, in these films, are either dead or included as a foil to demonstrate male purity. None of the characters is allowed a fulfilling relationship with a woman. In contrast, *Rikugun* does introduce a positive image of a woman into the narrative, Shintarō's mother, thereby providing an alternative primarily visual sub-narrative which ultimately challenges the hegemonic masculine narrative discussed above and which caused Kinoshita some problems with the censorship office.

In the final scenes before Shintarō leaves for the front, the attitude of the father, who had earlier upbraided his son for not having been sent to the front sooner, is contrasted with the attitude of his mother. True to patriarchal social discourse, the father's position is articulated through dialogue, while the mother's position is presented more subtly through the juxta-positioning of images and Tanaka Kinuyo's acting technique, encouraging the spectator to empathetically respond to the events depicted in the images. Stylistically, this final sequence is very different from the rest of the film as, up to this moment, the secondary historical narrative depicted through newspaper headlines, titles and the dialogue of the two father figures has directed the spectator towards a particular interpretation of the events. Hence, the controversy that surrounds the interpretation of this final sequence, not only amongst wartime censors, but also amongst post-war Japanese critics.

In the final sequence, the subject of the narrative shifts from the three male characters to Shintarō's mother. She is alone in the empty dark shop. She tells a passing neighbour that she did not go with her husband to see Shintarō off because she was afraid she might cry. The camera holds a long medium close-up shot of her as she sits motionless and dazed. Then, in the distance, the faint sound of a bugle signalling the imminent departure of the troops is just audible. Coming out of her dazed state, she goes out into the street to follow the sound of the bugle, leaving the shop unattended. Here the editing pace begins to gradually increase and as she starts to run, the camera cuts from a shot of her feet running to a medium close-up shot of her face as she strains to identify from which direction the sound of the bugle is coming. Other people have come out on to the street and are also running towards the bugle. At one point, the camera quickly tracks back along the street, eventually losing Shintarō's mother in the crowd, heightening the sense of anxiety as to whether she will get there on time to see her son. The camera then cuts to shots of the cheering crowd and the women from the *fujin-kai* (married women's association) waving their flags. The bugle music grows louder as the parade approaches. There is a low-angle shot of the first line of buglers followed by a rooftop high-angle shot of columns upon columns of marching men. Shintarō's mother eventually pushes her way through the throng, and framed by cheering children, watches the men go marching by. The camera continually cuts between medium close-up shots of her anxious face as she searches for her son and the lines upon lines of the marching soldiers until the camera finally identifies Shintarō. At this point, a martial air starts on the soundtrack and Shintarō's mother begins to run again, buffeted by the crowd beside the column of marching soldiers. The camera continues to inter-cut shots of Shintarō from behind with reaction shots of the mother as she struggles through the crowd to catch up with her son. The music gradually crescendos in time with the marching men. Finally, she reaches him and shots of her weeping face are contrasted with his smiling face. After jogging beside him for a while, she is forced back by the crowd and ultimately knocked down. As she gets to her feet, the cheering crowd surges forward and there is a medium close-up of her tear-stained face as she raises her hands and bows her head in prayer. The music reaches a climax and the character for the 'end' is superimposed on the screen.

Shintarō's mother usurps control of the narrative in this final sequence; the pace of the editing and the juxta-positioning of shots all support her point of view, thus foreshadowing a female-centred humanism evident in some early post-war war-retro films such as *Ningen no jōken (The Human Condition)*, *Mata au hi made (Until the Day We Meet Again)* and *Kimi no na wa (What is Your Name?)*. There is virtually no dialogue, just the sounds of the bugle and later the martial music intensifying the emotional effect of the images of a mother's desperate search for one last glimpse of her son. Her plight is heightened by the contrasts inherent in the images; the cheering women from the *fujin-kai*, the stirring martial music and the smiling son are all contrasted with the small vulnerable figure of the weeping mother. This sequence rivals Eisenstein's famed sequence on the steps of Odessa in *Battleship Potemkin* (1925) for the tension and emotion it elicits in the spectator. The opening shots of the film singled out the individual from the massive body of men which comprises the army; these final shots merge him back into the army as he marches off to war.

The Death of Romance

The underlying text inherent in the images of masculinity dominating Japanese films of the late 1930s and early 1940s was a discourse of sexual repression. This manifested in two interrelated forms. First, a denial of romantic love; and secondly, the male usurpation of the nurturing role in the family. In *Muhō Matsu* and *Chichi ariki*, women were virtually excluded from the narrative and, therefore, from their traditional role as nurturers. Virgin fathers became both role models as masculine ideals to which sons should aspire and nurturing figures. *Chichi ariki* opens with shots of Horikawa helping the young Ryōhei get dressed and ready for school. In *Muhō Matsu* Toshio's mother, although present, functions in the film's narrative as the object of Matsugorō's sublimated love. Whenever Toshio is in trouble, as for example when he falls off his stilts, it is Matsugorō who is there to care for him and not his mother. The fact that Matsugorō himself as a small child ran away from a cruel stepmother to be with his father further excludes women from a traditional nurturing role in the film.

Itami Mansaku, recounting his thoughts while engaged in writing the screenplay for *Muhō Matsu* in 1941, stated that the novel *Tomijima Matsugorō den* was an 'odd romance'. He went on to explain:

> There is no doubt that the word 'love' (*ren'ai*) is there, and that the feeling Matsugorō has for Mrs Yoshioka is a true self-sacrificing love. There is no doubt that anyone reading the novel would not want to *sully Matsugorō's pure sentiments by using this commonplace word love. It is for this reason that in our unconscious there is a tendency not to think of this novel as a love story* ... However, if we consider this dispassionately, Matsugorō's sentiment is a form of repressed

love. His self-sacrificing affection for Toshio cannot be explained simply in terms of a paternal instinct, but can only be explained in terms of his sublimated love for Toshio's mother. (Itami 1973 vol 2:251) (emphasis mine.)

In Itami's reminiscences it is evident that the direct expression of love (*ren'a*i) for a woman is incompatible with the heroic masculinity of Muhō Matsu. Hence, the 'unconscious tendency' Itami attributes to readers of the book, to deny this aspect of the novel.

The aim of this section is twofold; first, briefly to trace the dominant narrative trends leading to the rejection of romance and the establishment of a homosocial code of brotherhood, which became evident in the late 1930s and dominant in early 1940s Japanese cinema. (This theme will be taken up at greater length in subsequent chapters.) The second aim is to elucidate how this narrative trend reinforced the interests of masculinity at a time when the on-rush of 'modernism' challenged the traditional foundations of the family.

In the transition from feudal to capitalist economic and social relations that pre-empted the Meiji Restoration and modernisation, the autocratic role (described colloquially as *bōkun* or tyrant) of the father in the traditional family was undermined. Although legally until 1945, the father, as head of the household, had supreme authority over its members, in reality as women and adult children began to gain a degree of economic independence separate from the family enterprise, the father's autocratic role was undermined. Satō (1995 vol 1) links this change from feudal to capitalist social relations with a change in the depiction of fathers in the films of the pre-war and wartime periods. During these periods, the depiction of fathers' roles within the family changed from that of autocrat to that of nurturer. This trend is particularly evident in the *gendai geki* films analysed in the previous section and, Satō asserts, became important from the 1930s on. The affection between father and son, or surrogate father and son was also an important motif in *jidai geki* films such as the 1928 silent film *Hōrō zanmai (The Wandering Yakuza)*, the 1935 *Tange Sazen yowa hyaku-man ryō no tsubo (Tange Sazen and the Secret Story of the Million-ryō Vase)* and even in the swashbuckling series of films that ran from 1927 until the 1960s *Kurama Tengu (The Kurama Devil-The Black-Masked Reformer)*. Yamamoto (1990) and Satō (1995 vol 1) both state that this shift in the patriarchal image from autocrat to caring father was in part a result of western cinematic influences.

Concomitant with the shift to a nurturing role in the depiction of masculine relations within the cinematic family was a more open depiction of romance. When speaking about the trend in the late 1920s of yakuza in *jidai geki* films, and gangsters (in Ozu's silent films) to be in love with their girlfriends, Satō (1995 vol 1) states that this was a direct influence of Hollywood westerns which were imported in large numbers in the 1910s and l920s. The most popular theme being the *gudo baddo* man (the good, bad man) scenario in which the miscreant hero is redeemed by the love of a 'good' woman. An example of this taken from the *jidai geki* would be the 1931 *matatabimono* (wandering yakuza film) *Banba no Chūtarō mabuta no haha* (*Banba Chūtarō's Memories of His Mother*). However, as Iwamoto (1991) points out, the advent of 'modernism' in Japan of the 1920s and 1930s precipitated a change in 'public morals'; this was particularly evident in the cities. This, he argues, was largely due to the fact that women broke out of their traditional space as *okusan* (wives within the home) and entered society for the first time in significant numbers. As such, their image within popular films of the period is often ambiguous, reflecting masculine insecurity and the destabilising effect this trend had on the traditional family. In cinematic narratives, the social response to the new femininity was often to contain it within a 'masculine point of view' or masculine voice.[17] Jeffords defines the 'masculine point of view' as that

> which represents the disembodied voice of masculinity, that which no individual man or woman can realise yet which influences each individually. In this way, it is possible to identify the voice through which dominance is enacted in a narrative representation, though it may not consistently be spoken by any one character. (Jeffords 1989:xiii)

In the films of the early 1940s, discussed in the previous section, this process of containment reached a peak where women were marginalised if not deleted from the narrative completely, thereby reaffirming masculinity and traditional relations of dominance, particularly in relationships between fathers and sons. In earlier films, such as the 1928 *jidai geki* directed by Inagaki Hiroshi, *Hōrō zanmai*, and Ozu's gangster and student films of the silent era, expression of love for wives and lovers was permissible, but only if contained within a masculine voice.

In *Hōrō zanmai*, the love of the hero, played by Kataoka Chiezō (1903-), for his wife is intensified and simultaneously contained within the narrative through a universal masculine point of view by filmic devices such as flash-forwards into the hero's imagination. The hero, returning from Edo as part of the *sankin kōtai* policy, imagines in a series of flash-forwards what will happen when he first greets his wife and son and in his mind's eye he also elaborates on all the preparations she has made for his long- awaited return. The expectations these scenes build up in the spectator who, unlike the hero, is partially aware of the disaster to follow, heightens the impact of the climactic scene. In this scene, he returns home to find his wife, having committed suicide, drawing her last breath in front of the *butsudan* (the Buddhist family altar). The extreme melodrama of this death scene allows the hero to express his love for his wife in a physical embrace as he cradles her in his arms. His wife had been the victim of the implied sexual advances of a senior official of the clan and had accordingly committed suicide, so proving herself worthy of the hero's love within *bushidō* (the way of the warrior) traditions of loyalty and purity. In this way, his masculine status as a samurai who, in the latter half of the film, becomes a *rōnin* (masterless samurai) is not compromised. In the first half of the film the discourses of love, through the mechanisms of flash-forwards and the suicide of the wife, are enunciated solely from within the masculine voice of the hero and the *bushidō* tradition. The character of the wife is thus constructed from the idealised image of her held in her husband's imagination.[18] Unlike the mother in *Rikugun* or Chikako in *Tōkyō no onna (Women of Tokyo)*, she is never given a feminine voice of her own. In this way the hero's love remains 'pure' as Matsugorō's love in *Muhō Matsu*, as in the second half of the film, it is displaced on to the love for his son expressed through his nurturing parent role.

It was only with the rise in popularity of female stars such as Tanaka Kinuyo in the 1930s that a female voice, although muted, was occasionally heard. The scandal following the release of *Rikugun* in 1944 and the Information Office's condemnation of Kinoshita as an 'effeminate director' (*memeshii kantoku*) for having projected a female voice in the final sequences of the film provides a good example. A further example can be found in the 1933 silent film, directed by Ozu Yasujirō, *Tōkyō no onna*. This film also permits the rare inclusion of a female voice, projected through the character Chikako (Okada Yoshiko 1902-), in the final scenes to criticise her brother's inability to come to terms with and survive in a modern industrial society. In this highly sophisticated melodrama, Chikako shares rooms with her brother, the university student, Ryōichi (Egawa Ureo 1902-1970). The early shots of this film establish Chikako in the dual roles of mother figure and provider for Ryōichi. In an early scene, Chikako gives Ryōichi *kozukai* (pocket money) to take his girlfriend Harue (Tanaka Kinuyo) to the cinema. During the course of the film, it is made known to Ryōichi that his sister has been supplementing their income through prostitution, thereby transgressing a clear division in the imaging of women in Japanese popular culture between, on the one hand, mothers and sisters, and on the other hand, women who operate outside the home and who until recently were traditionally sexualised.

The narrative in the film is structured into two distinct segments. The first is an investigation of Chikako. This is initially carried out by a police officer, the legitimate social representative of authority. The camera and dialogue reinforce the inferences drawn from the fact that she is being investigated. By underlining her ability as a typist, through an extreme close-up of her hands typing, the camera and the dialogue make the spectator aware of the fact that she works part-time of an evening helping a university professor with translations. This information is contrasted with her role as surrogate mother figure to Ryōichi. Within popular discourses of the opposition of purity/contamination, and nature/culture, it is easy to discern a similar binary opposition between the pure mother figure and the (over-)educated woman, a defining thematic of the film as the title indicates, Tokyo women/country women. The prejudice inherent in this division is soon confirmed when it is revealed through the police investigation that Chikako is not relying on her education, but on her body as an object of exchange in order to finance Ryōichi's education. The narrative therefore subordinates her threatening competence in the workplace to an investigation of her sexuality. Thus in the first half of the film, the narrative projects a 'universal' masculine voice by centering on Chikako's 'to-be-looked-at-ness' through the police investigation. However, in the final scenes, the camera's point of view and the diegesis as a whole shift to the feminine perspective as Chikako explains her motives to an enraged Ryōichi. After he storms off into the night, the narrative remains focussed on the feminine; on the inside worlds of, first, Chikako's room and then Harue's with only a few minor cuts to Ryōichi walking in the street and then sitting on some rubble at a building site. We do not see his suicide and only learn of it when Chikako and Harue find out. We, the spectators, empathise with his death through the reactions of Harue who is silent and tearful, and Chikako who makes the following statement:

> Ryōichi, until the last you didn't understand me (long pause). To die like this, really (another long pause). You were a weakling (*yowamushi*).

In this way the film ends in discord even in death. It is through this depiction of discord that the film criticises 1930s economically depressed Japanese society. In *Tōkyō no onna*, there are no shots of people acting in unison as in the fishing scenes in *Chichi ariki*. This is because there is no sense of instinctive harmony between characters in this film. Chikako compromises in order to survive in the modern world, but Ryōichi could not bear the dishonour her behaviour brought upon him. In psychological terms he relives the sense of betrayal and hatred a child experiences when that child realises for the first time that his mother has been unfaithful to him by having a sexual relationship with his father. This explains Ryōichi's anger when Chikako asks him if he does not believe in her. His reply, that it is because he did believe in her that he now hates her, confirms this analysis. Therefore, in their dramatic climactic scene, he beats her before his anger implodes and he kills himself.

By giving Chikako and Harue, to a lesser extent, a voice in the narrative, the film does not apportion blame to any one character, but etherealises it, placing it on the society at large and a business economy undermining the legitimacy of the traditional family. The fact that the two households depicted in the film, Ryōichi's and Harue's, are both comprised of brother and sister living together emphasises the breakdown of the traditional family structure which in Ozu's nostalgic idealised world would have had a strong central father-figure who would never have allowed a woman like Chikako, or an adolescent son like Ryōichi, to be placed in such vulnerable situations.

While the central theme of *Tōkyō no onna* is the breakdown of traditional familial relationships between men and women due to the demands of a rapidly changing economic environment, Ozu's 1932 silent film *Seishun no yume ima izuko (Where are the Dreams of Our Youth?)* portrays the breakdown of relationships between men. Within this scenario, Oshige (Tanaka Kinuyo) is reduced to the level of a mere object of exchange between friends.

The structure of *Seishun no yume ima izuko* is again clearly defined in two segments. The first covers the student days of Horino Tetsuo (Egawa Ureo) and his three friends. The second part shifts to the world of the salaryman as Horino inherits the chairmanship of the family business upon the death of his father and his three friends come to work for him. The various incidents which make up the narrative in the first half of the film all work to establish the relationship between Horino and the other three members of the group. Through humour, the film creates a sense of the equality and intimacy that, in a traditionally hierarchical society, is only possible amongst equals or *dōkyūsei* (classmates of the same age and grade). However, even in this utopian world, the economic realities which will threaten the stability of the group in the second half of the film are already evident. Saiki (Saito Tatsuo 1902-1968), a young student from a disadvantaged background, does not enter into the group as fully as the others. Saiki's position on the margins of the group is evident in the first scene. As the others, part of the university cheer squad, go through their routine, Saiki strolls along with his nose in a book. When Oshige asks why he studies so hard and does not join in with the others, he explains that he and his mother live alone and therefore, he has to rely on his ability (i.e. and not patronage) in order to get a good job. Again, as in *Tōkyō no onna* the reason for his disadvantage is linked to the absence of a father.

In the second half of the film, when the four friends enter the modern corporate world, the strains economic necessity places on their relationships become apparent. Horino attempts to continue their relationship as before, helping his three friends, among other things, to cheat in the company entrance examination. However, he gradually becomes aware of the fact that the others are treating him more and more as their boss and not their friend. Oshige, the young girl who worked at the Blue Hawaii Bakery where they, as students, used to meet, becomes the catalyst which sparks off the crisis of the dénouement. Horino had been fond of Oshige since his student days, but, unbeknown to him, she had agreed to marry Saiki. Horino, finding out about the engagement by accident through

Saiki's mother, is deeply hurt by the betrayal of his friends who were not honest enough to tell him of the engagement, letting him continue with his own plans. After confronting Oshige, who tells him that she had dreamt of marrying him, but realising the difference in their social positions, had agreed to marry Saiki, he goes off to confront the three friends in a climactic scene:

Horino: What did you mean when you gave your approval to my marriage to Oshige? Do you think that I am the sort of man who would enjoy stealing his friend's girl? Saiki, stop shilly-shallying about and give me a direct answer.
Shimazaki: Look, Saiki thought he was doing you a favour. Don't you think it's wrong to attack him like this?
Horino: There are a few things I have to say to you both too. Do you consider yourselves my friends? You stand before me like dogs wagging their tails, is that friendship? When did I ever ask you to behave like that? When have I ever been pleased by that sort of behaviour? Where has the feeling of fellowship (*yūjō*) gone that we had as students?
Saiki: Our families' livelihoods are dependent on you. If we offend you, our boss, we risk losing our livelihood *(Horino strikes Saiki).*
Horino: Are you therefore the kind of fellow to just hand over his girlfriend? Idiot! *(He continues hitting Saiki; the others attempt to restrain him.)* I shall beat this servility out of him ... *(They release him.)* This is the clenched fist of fellowship (*yūjō no tekken da*). Let it penetrate into your very being. *(Horino continues hitting Saiki until he sinks to the ground in tears. By this time Horino is also crying. The other two apologise and the three of them embrace. Horino, wiping the tears from his eyes, bends down and asks Saiki to forgive him.)*

The bonds of fellowship thus restored, the camera cuts to a daytime shot of the roof of Horino's office building. The brightness of the open roof space is in sharp contrast to the dark night-time mise-en-scène of the penultimate confrontation. In this final sequence, unison shots predominate as harmony within the group has been restored. First, there is a shot of two office girls sitting on a wall powdering their noses. This is followed by a shot of two men standing in dark suits smoking. The film concludes with a series of unison shots of the three friends as they wave at a passing train taking Saiki and Oshige on their honeymoon.

In films of the pre-war and war periods female characters, whether physically present or symbolically represented (Ryōhei's mother in *Chichi ariki* is represented by the *butsudan*), generally speaking exist purely as functions of the masculine; either as an object of exchange – Oshige in *Seishun no yume ima izuko* is a catalyst around which the inter-relationships between men are deepened – or as a repository of discontent upon which male characters can lay the blame for their own loss of power. Female characters in these early films are thus the embodiment of clusters of meanings – the *moga,* the westernised, economically independent woman is invested with all the negative connotations associated with civilisation, embodying gender ambiguities threatening traditional socio-economic structures, while the traditional woman remained safe and pure within the predetermined sexual identities of mother or sister. In general, female characters have no constitution of their own as individuals; they exist merely within a masculine consciousness and when they transgress traditionally defined roles of the feminine, they are punished as is Chikako in *Tōkyō no onna* and the hapless Miya in the 1937 Shinpa[19] melodrama directed by Shimizu Hiroshi (1903–1966), *Konjiki yasha (The Userer).*

In this romantic tragedy, the hero Kaiichi (Natsukawa Daijirō, 1913–) is spurned in love by Miya (Kawasaki Hiroko, 1912–1976) who chooses to marry the wealthy Toriyama. In an early scene, Miya gives her reasons for rejecting Kaiichi as (a) he is still only a student and it will be another three to four years before he graduates; and (b) in the current economic climate he cannot be sure of getting a good job even after graduation. Kaiichi, who believes that love can surmount all obstacles, says that if she loved Toriyama, he could understand and he would not stand in her way. If, however, she were basing her decision on purely economic reasons, then he would oppose the match. He then offers to give up his studies so that they could be married sooner, but she rejects this saying she does not want to live such a 'miserable life' (*mijimena seikatsu*), at which point Kaiichi strikes her. As he strides off, he knocks her down as she tries to follow him. After Miya's marriage to Toriyama, Kaiichi gives up his studies and begins work in his father's loan company. He becomes totally ruthless, rejecting all human relationships in the pursuit of profit and ultimately revenge, as after many twists and turns in the narrative, Miya's husband becomes indebted to Kaiichi.

Kaiichi's rejection of Miya is acceptable because in the opening scenes we, the spectators, have been made aware of the duplicity of Miya's character. After an evening out with Toriyama, she is shown in the back of his car with him as he drives her home. He asks about Kaiichi only to be told that he is like a brother to her, at which point Kaiichi comes into view through the windscreen, also on his way home. Miya then asks to be dropped off, as she wants to walk the rest of the way. It is as she and Kaiichi walk home together that the true nature of their relationship, and thus the lie, become evident. As such, the film brings her character as 'good' woman into doubt from the first scene.

Just as *Seishun no yume ima izuko* and *Tōkyō no onna*, *Konjiki yasha* also depicts the strains placed upon traditional social textures and conventions brought about by the unparalleled social changes accompanying economic transformations and recession. Miya's body is the site upon which the frustrations of Kaiichi and her husband are vented; both men strike her during the course of the film. In the second half of the film, in several scenes she admits her fault and therefore conforms to the masculine point of view which makes her body the repository of male discontent. In the final sequence, Miya is both punished and confirmed in the traditional family structure. As she pleads with Kaiichi not to foreclose on the loan, she tells him she is pregnant. The return of her husband just as Kaiichi leaves the house reinforces the narrative closure and confines Miya for the rest of her life to a loveless marriage and economic insecurity. Kaiichi, on the other hand, tears up the promissory note and leaves the house and Miya, a liberated man.

In the early 1940s, romance as a theme in film narratives took an overtly political turn with the instant popularity of the Manchurian Film Company's (*Manshū* Film Co.) star Yamaguchi Yoshiko, alias Riko-ran. She was born to Japanese parents living in Manchuria in 1920. Upon joining the *Manshū* Film Co. in 1938, her name was changed to Riko-ran and in the company's publicity material, it was advertised that she was Chinese. As a Chinese film star of the *Manshū* Film Co., she appeared in approximately twenty films between 1938 and 1945. It was only after the war when she reverted to her real name that the truth about her parentage was revealed. As Shimizu (1994) states, this was one of the best kept secrets of the war.

In the films in which Riko-ran appeared during the war, it is possible to discern a discourse of an inter-Asian 'Orientalism' of the kind described by Said (1991b)[20] in that Riko-ran's body is invested with a sexualised image of what China represented to the Japanese at the time of their attempt at colonial expansion. As Shimizu states:

> Riko-ran, through her attractive Chinese style, her captivating singing voice and her fluency in Japanese, embodied an idealised image of China that appealed to Japanese people. (Shimizu 1994:62)

The Japanese male leads who starred alongside Riko-ran – Hasegawa Kazuo and Sano Shūji – similarly embodied the positive characteristics associated with colonial expansion, such as the bringing of civilisation to backward societies. The popularity of Riko-ran and of these films attests to the efficacy of romance as a metaphor for relations between the Japanese and the Chinese and for the policy of an Asian Co-Prosperity Sphere (*Daitōa Kyōeiken*).

In the 1942 film, *Soshū no yoru (Suchow Nights)*, directed by Nomura Hiromasa (1905–1979), Riko-ran plays the part of a young Chinese woman who works at an orphanage in Shanghai. In the early scenes, she is hostile to the young Japanese doctor (Sano Shūji) who comes to examine one of the children. She tells him the child is Chinese and that Chinese people know best how to look after Chinese children. However, after he saves one of the children from drowning in the river, her attitude changes and she apologises for her behaviour. In this scene, while they wait for the child to regain consciousness, she explains why she had hated the Japanese. She tells the young doctor that with the war

> our lives had been thrown into confusion. My home was in the country in Suchow. I lived there with my brother and cousins, we were happy and our world was peaceful. Then the war began and rough Chinese soldiers came and our family scattered. The men went into hiding. Parents and children were separated, it was terrible. I came alone to Shanghai; you wouldn't understand how lonely I was. All I could think of was my mother and all I wanted was to see her again ...

Here the doctor interrupts, explaining that he understands how she feels, but that the Japanese came to China to help the Chinese and that it is the responsibility of Asians to help each other. He continues saying that it is not only people working in the medical profession, but Japanese soldiers, the technicians and the tradespeople; they all came to China to help the Chinese.

The fact that Riko-ran changes her opinion of the young doctor after he has physically intervened to save the child, illustrates how the narrative is completely contained within a Japanese social logic which values actions far more than words. In filmic romantic relations between men and women, love as a sentiment is rarely expressed in the dialogue, but is expressed through the narrative in terms of actions, for example, in the silent era the knitting of socks for a man was often used as an expression of romantic interest.[21] So it becomes logical within this aesthetic convention of the portrayal of male/female relations that Riko-ran should accept his sincerity at this juncture in the narrative.

In keeping with the feminisation of China through the body of Riko-ran, no attractive or heroic Chinese male characters appear in the film. As the child is drowning, some Chinese men look on, but none attempts to save her. The camera dwells on the doctor's body as he swims out to the child, thereby investing his body with all the positive meanings of masculinity denied to the Chinese male characters. Also, Riko-ran's Chinese fiancé is described by his father as a 'weak man'. This is confirmed when he attempts to shoot the doctor in the back out of jealousy. The fact that the fiancé and other Chinese men depicted in the film all wear traditional Chinese dress further feminises them, as they are constantly compared to the smart suits replete with padded shoulders, worn by the Japanese doctors.

Riko-ran's body/femininity is constantly linked to nature and a fertile penetrability. As she works in an orphanage, she is often depicted surrounded by children. In the crucial scene in which the young doctor's feelings for her first move towards romance, the camera, taking his point of view and unknown to Riko-ran, shows her in a vast field bordered by mountains in the distance, singing amidst a flock of sheep. The fact that this scene is repeated in flashback in the doctor's imagination when he is ill and feverish, underlines its significance as an iconic natural/uncultivated landscape full of appealing potential. This scene invites comparison of the vastness and implied fertility of the new colony with the mountainous claustrophobic order of Japanese rural landscape. In both the actual scene and the flashback, the spectator makes this comparison through the desiring gaze of the young doctor as he watches Riko-ran. This investment of Riko-ran's body with connotations of nature/fertility is even more pronounced in the 1943 film directed by Shimizu Hiroshi *Sayon no kane (Sayon's Bell)*, in which Riko-ran plays the part of a young native girl living in an isolated mountain village in Taiwan. Again, she is constantly associated with young children and animals. In both these films, Riko-ran's body/femininity is equated with fertility and nature and displayed as a defining 'other' in relation to an idealised Japanese masculinity that is associated with modernisation and science. The young doctor's ultimate rejection of Riko-ran in the final scenes reaffirms his purity and therefore reconciles an heroic masculine ideal which spurned love (*ren'a*i) with romance, as Itami stated in his comments on *Muhō Matsu*. The doctor's earlier rejection of his Japanese fiancée similarly functions at one level to maintain his purity, but also is significant as a rejection of claustrophobic Japanese social relations in favour of the more open spontaneous ones the film depicts as being possible in Manchuria, thus further reinforcing the iconic significance of the landscape and Riko-ran's body as sites of freedom. The fact that in the final scene the doctor has left the hospital in Shanghai and is on a boat heading inland to some remote clinic wearing a safari hat and carrying a water bottle implies his new-found freedom and the possibility of future adventure. This image of the doctor is contrasted with intermittent shots of Riko-ran's wedding. The film ends with the reinscription (and therefore, taming) of Riko-ran[22] into traditional family relations while the hero remains free to pursue future adventures.

In films of the early 1940s, a distinct narrative trend in relation to the depiction of female characters is evident. In these films, produced to mobilise the home front, the heroine's love for a male character is sublimated to love of country resulting in selfless heroic actions and even death, as in the spy film *Kaisen no zenya* 1943 (*The Night Before the Outbreak of War*).

In the 1942 film, *Aikoku no hana (The Flower of Patriotism)*, directed by Sasaki Keisuke (1901-1967), the heroine (Kogure Michiyo, 1918-), after her father's failed attempt at negotiating a marriage for her, becomes a Red Cross nurse. Aiako's love for the hero Tetsuo (Sano Shūji), the potential groom of the failed negotiations, is thus deflected on to her work and consummated when Tetsuo, now a soldier, is wounded and admitted to a field army hospital where he is nursed by Aiako. The selfless love Aiako feels for Tetsuo, dramatised by the fact that Tetsuo's wound has temporarily blinded him, is heightened as he is unaware of Aiako's ministrations. The theme of sublimated love in *Aikoku no hana* functions in two ways: (a) it is supportive of the view that women in wartime, when men are scarce, can find fulfillment through other means than marriage and children; and (b) it reconciles two potential areas of conflict by linking adult children's duty to the *kokutai* with Confucian concepts of filial piety in much the same way as *Kaigun* and *Chichi ariki* do.

The later film *Otome no iru kichi*, 1945 (*The Base Where the Maidens Are*), directed by Sasaki Kon (1908-), similarly equates the love young girl mechanics feel for individual pilots with their work. As in all Japanese film romances of the pre-war and wartime periods, the expression of love is reflected in the visual narrative through actions not words. In this example, the little doll *masukotto* (mascots) the girls make for individual pilots signify love. In one scene, after a pilot has been killed in an accident, the girls hold a funeral service for him and bury a mascot one of the girls had been making for him. As they are performing the ceremony, by chance another young pilot sees them and after being told what they are doing says, 'We pilots are indeed fortunate (*shiawase*) that you all care so much for us.' This scene becomes even more poignant when, at the end of the film, he leaves as part of a Special Attack Force.

In all the films discussed in this section, love is transformed into sacrifice: the doing of things for people who are unaware of what is done for them. However, it is essential for the dramatic effect of the narrative, and therefore an important site of pleasure in the diegesis, that the recipient becomes aware of what is done for him. Hence, in the scene just described, it is essential that a young pilot inadvertently sees the girls and acknowledges their affection. Similarly, in *Aikoku no hana*, it is important that Tetsuo finds out by chance from a doctor that it is Aiako who is nursing him. Also in *Kaisen no zenya*, the sacrifice of the heroine, a geisha (Tanaka Kinuyo) who helps the *kenpeitai* uncover American spies, is acknowledged after her death in the final scenes of the film. However, these acts do not have to be great to increase dramatic affect. An example from *Kaisen no zenya* illustrates this point. At the height of the drama, the *kenpeitai* officer places his coat over a junior officer who has fallen asleep. When the junior officer wakes, he reverently holds the coat, a shot the camera lingers on, before he replaces it on the hook; the inference being that the junior officer is deeply touched that his superior should be concerned with his welfare.

This chapter was concerned with the dominant historical and socio-political themes which were simultaneously constitutive of and constituted by the early Japanese cinema (pre-1945). The first section was taken up with a discussion of nationalism and the unifying ideologies of the *kokutai*. In this discussion I put forward the view that nationalist ideologies (or the *kokutai*) were propagated as a natural extension of the Japanese people's traditional communitarian nature and that aspects of the individual's rights, e.g. legal rights (essential to the American, French and British modes of nationalism), were denigrated as bourgeois individualism and therefore contrary to Japanese Confucian-based customs. This philosophical conflict was manifested in popular film as a nature/culture binary opposition which the ideologies of popular nationalism - the *kokutai* and the *kazoku kokka* - attempted to reconcile.

The chapter continued with a discussion from within the context of the nature/culture opposition of two dominant themes evident in male-centred films produced in the early 1940s - the quest for the pure-self and the incorporation of the lower echelons of society into the national *kokutai* through a process of 'samurai-isation'. It must be remembered, since the early 1930s and the release of *Shingun*[23] (*Advancing Army*) 1930, these scenarios were seen as liberating - the breaking down of class barriers - and so becoming confused in the popular consciousness with a form of crude Marxism. The films discussed provide good examples of how the conflicting areas of social obligation and duty to the state were conflated into a greatly altered and expanded concept of filial piety and were therefore both formative and reflective of cultural attitudes. I use the word 'formative' because of the cinematic structure of these films which situate the spectator through filmic devices, such as point-of-view shots, in the position of pupil in relation to authoritarian figures. This is a common strategy in films of the period, particularly in *kinen* films (films made to commemorate historical events such as Pearl Harbour). It is still used extensively in contemporary television documentaries.

The third and final section of this chapter traced the early development and the subsequent demise of romance as a theme in pre-war and wartime productions. Generally speaking, these films attempted to resolve problems of gender identity accompanying industrialisation and 'modernisation', by re-inscribing female characters back into traditional roles, or punishing them or both as in *Konjiki yasha*. Alternatively, they were eliminated from the narrative entirely, thus reasserting the father's traditional position of dominance. As Jeffords (1989) points out, women or femininity are the criteria by which masculinity is measured. As such, these films tend to contain female characters within a 'masculine voice' which shored up masculinity at a time of unprecedented economic and social transformation. The films produced by the *Manshū* Film Co. starring Riko-ran worked in much the same way, constructing the colonies as a feminine 'other' against which a Japanese national masculinity could be measured and found superior.

As Horsman and Marshall (1995) remind us, nationalism was one solution to the anomie felt by former peasants living in cities. The sense of alienation city dwellers felt was intensified with the recession following the Wall Street crash of 1929. Ozu's early 1930 films reflect the fissures that occurred in familial relationships caused by economic insecurity. Similarly *Tsuchi (Earth)* 1939, reflects the hardships rural communities experienced at this time. As Sawada Kiyoshi, a left-wing film director of the period, states, after 1932 and the Shanghai Incident, there was a complete political swing from the left to the right.

> The majority of spectators were persuaded that the shortest route out of poverty was the attack on the Chinese mainland rather than hostility to landlords and capitalists. (quoted in Satō vol 1, 1995:289)

The military institutions, as portrayed in films such as *Kaigun* and *Hawai Marē okikaisen (The War from Hawaii to Malaya)*, offered a sense of masculine fellowship and community symbolised in spectacular shots of massed gym exercises and marching formations. Also, in early silent Ozu films such as *Seishun no yume ima izuko*, when Horino confronts his three student friends for betraying their friendship and he strikes Saiki, it is with the 'fist of fellowship' (*yūjō no tekken*) that he strikes and not out of malice. Similarly, in *Konjiki yasha* when Kaiichi transgresses the code of brotherhood, he too is beaten by the 'fists of fellowship' of his former student friends. Both these films are good early examples of the formation of a code of brotherhood that in Tasaka Tomotaka's two films *Gonin no sekkōhei (The Five Scouts)* and *Tsuchi to heitai (Mud and Soldiers)* finds its ultimate expression on the battlefields of China as *sen'yūai* (comradely love), a theme to be taken up in the following chapter.

CHAPTER 2

The Kamikaze *Film and the Politics of the Collective*

Kisama to ore to wa dōki no sakura
Onaji kōkūtai no niwa ni saku
Saita hana nara ochiru no wa kakugo
Migoto chirimashō kuni no tame.
Kisama to ore to wa dōki no sakura
Onaji kōkūtai no niwa ni saku
Ketsuniku waketaru naka de wa nai ga
Nazeka ki ga aute wasurerarenu.

You and I are cherry blossoms flowering
At the same time in the same Air Force garden.
When we come into blossom, we are resolved to scatter (like petals in the breeze.)
Let's scatter splendidly for the sake of our country.
You and I are cherry blossoms flowering.
At the same time in the same Air Force garden.
We are not brothers, but for some reason
We cannot forget each other.
(The song of the Special Attack Forces)

[Close-ups] show the faces of things and those expressions on them which are significant because *they are reflected expressions of our own subconscious feeling.* (Balázs 1979:289) (my emphasis)

There is a force invisible to the eye steadily pulling us into our graves. But they are not easy to enter. (Fukami in *Kumo nagaruru hateni*)

Morimoto (1992), in seeking to give expression to the feelings which compelled the young Japanese naval pilots to 'volunteer' for

– 68 –

THE *KAMIKAZE* FILM AND THE POLITICS OF THE COLLECTIVE

the Special Attack Forces (*Kamikaze Tokubetsu Kōgeki-tai*) from late 1944, turns to a psychological analysis of the nature of the group in Japanese society. He argues that Japanese group-relations function to diminish individual volition. In a person's consciousness, the fate of the individual becomes inextricably bound up with the fate of the group.

> Therefore, *the decision-making power of the group becomes confused with the decision-making power of the individual; group actions are viewed as individual actions*. As the ego (*jiga*) is strengthened in accordance with the group ego (*shūdan-ga*), the insecurity an individual feels when confronted with making a decision vanishes. (Morimoto 1992:39)

Although employed critically by Morimoto, this concept expresses at the ideological level the ideal of Japanese group-relations whereby the individual is totally subsumed within the group, eliminating all potential areas of conflict. Visually, this concept found expression in *Chūshingura* through the display of *chūgi* (loyalty) and the tear-stained cheek of Asano's vassals as they pay their last respects to Asano before his *seppuku*. In the war period, the motif crossed genre boundaries into the war film where it was manifested as *sen'yūai* (comradely love) in, for example, Tasaka Tomotaka's 1938 film *Gonin no sekkōhei* (*The Five Scouts*) and his 1941 film *Tsuchi to heitai* (*Mud and Soldiers*). Satō, in his latest history of Japanese cinema, explains the meaning of *sen'yūai* which pervades these early films:

> The feelings of a community bound together by a common fate, in other words, a group of comrades who share life and death together, this is the intense feeling depicted in these films. Comradely love in itself can be seen in war films of most countries, but it is only in Japan that it has become in itself a central theme. When a comrade is killed, there is the sense that it is only natural that one fights to avenge his death. Once this feeling becomes entwined in the feelings of a community bound together by a common fate, there is no need to question the rights and wrongs of killing the enemy. There is the sense that in war there exists nothing beyond the shared fate of brothers. (1995, vol. 2:8-9)

As the American Occupation came to an end in 1952, the box office success of Imai Tadashi's *Himeyuri no tō* (1953) sparked off a boom in the production of war-retro films. As Satō confirms, the themes of these early post-occupation films were taken largely from the experiential testimony of soldiers or members of the general public who had suffered during the war. A distinct sub-genre of the war-retro film that came to prominence in the 1950s and 1960s, and that grew out of this thematic trend, is the *kamikaze* film. This chapter is concerned with an analysis of these films as sites where wartime *sen'yūai* is renegotiated as part of the post-war *nihonjinron* discourse of the politics of the male collective.

By proposing a utilitarian model of Japanese society emphasising the role of the group as an autonomous mechanism of power, and through an analysis of films made in the 1950s and 1960s based on the Special Attack Forces, this chapter seeks to demonstrate how the utilitarian group ethic was redirected into post-war economic reconstruction. Finally, the chapter will conclude with a discussion of the 1968 film *Nikudan* which, through parody, lays bare in visual terms the contradictions between the ideal of 'sacrifice' central to the Special Attack Forces and the 'realities' of the group as an autonomous mechanism of power alluded to by Morimoto.

The latter half of the nineteenth century saw a shift in emphasis from rule by coercion to rule by consent at the time when the Tokugawa *bakufu* began to lose its hegemony. This coincided with changes occurring in the economic base of the society, namely the shift from feudal structures to economic activities necessitating a higher degree of individual autonomy on the part of the labour force as it became increasingly dependent on paid employment. As has been stated above, Japanese social structures had already entered a prolonged period of change at this time from collective agricultural structures, based on a degree of co-operation necessary for intensive rice production, to what is now often referred to as a group-orientated society (*kumi shakai*) based on competitive affilial relations. The ideology of an harmonious group society, which had its origins in the pre-industrial collective era, became a vehicle presenting an ideal image of Japanese society as uniquely harmonious and group-orientated and not subject to the competitive ethos which characterises western industrial societies. This section will present a utilitarian model of Japanese society based in part on Jeremy Bentham's spatial configuration of power through surveillance, the panopticon which in the Japanese context manifests as the *seken* – the imagined cultural community in which one's reputation is measured (Ikegami 1995). Here, I shall be drawing on Michel Foucault's *Discipline and Punish* (1991) and Ikegami's concept of 'honour culture'. To sum up, this section will attempt a synthesis of these disparate sources to provide an alternative view of Japanese society that emphasises control as a dominant factor over and above harmony.

In *The Myth of Japanese Uniqueness*, Dale examines the historical development and the ideological role in Japanese society of the literature which he defines as 'the *nihonjinron*', and which Yoshino defines as 'secondary nationalism' – 'nationalism which preserves and enhances national identity in an already long established nation' (Yoshino 1995:44), that is,

> works of cultural nationalism concerned with the ostensible 'uniqueness' of Japan in any aspect, and which are hostile to both individual experience and the notion of internal socio-historical diversity. (Dale 1990:l)

Dale points out that these theories act as a palliative by linking an idealised past to an alienating present, sanctifying 'the hollow banalities and estranging dimensions of the profane, contemporary world' (Dale 1990:18). He likens the appeal of these publications to the new religions, which attract city-dwelling alienated immigrants from rural areas, by creating a sense of national community 'as a kind of emotional ersatz for a wanting sense of either real social solidarity or individual selfhood' (Dale 1990:18). He also tells us that

> the post-war literature on identity in this sense is the subtlest of instruments of ideological coercion, and a 'self-fulfilling prophecy' since it reflects and conditions in turn manipulated categories and modes of expression diffused for the discussion of how the Japanese are supposed to perceive themselves. Such an enculturation of political discourse is potentially a more powerful form of social control than pre-war 'thought policing' since, though demonstrably heir to the ideological patrimony of Japanese fascism, the ideological roots of these ideas have been forgotten, while the ideas themselves are hailed as new conceptualisations and ethnological descriptions of Japanese realities. (Dale 1990:17)

Theories of *nihonjinron* and its pre-war precursor *kokutai* stress the submergence of individual identity within the group (calling people by their status position rather than by name is an oft-cited example). This encourages the view that, when compared with people from other industrialised societies, the Japanese are more homogeneous and group-orientated, qualities which, they argue, have grown out of the innately Japanese historical tradition of loyalty and consensus.

Mouer and Sugimoto, in *Images of Japanese Society* (1990), criticise the 'consensus or group model of Japanese society' which they assert became the dominant model in western academic circles in the 1970s with the translation of such works as *Japanese Society* by Nakane (1972) and the *Anatomy of Dependence* by Doi (1973).[1] They criticise this model on three grounds: its failure to acknowledge social and political conflict; its failure to examine the structures of power and authority in Japanese society; and finally, its failure to examine social inequalities. The emphasis of this model on the homogeneous nature of Japanese society and its concomitant failure to acknowledge conflict as part of the dynamic process of social and political change has meant it is extremely difficult to explain changes in the power structure rationally. Hence, the inability of this model to deal adequately with the student unrest of the late 1960s, the anti-pollution movements, the Narita airport citizens' protest movement,[2] and the women's movements of the 1970s.[3]

Both the earlier pre-war ideologies of *kokutai* and its post-war counterpart *nihonjinron* negate change, elements of which are simply absorbed into the *kokutai* and explained as having been there all along. Yoshida's commentary to the Diet on the revised constitution (25 June 1946) is an example. Here, he explains that American concepts of democracy 'had always formed part of the tradition of our country and was not – as some mistakenly imagined – something that was about to be introduced with the revision of the Constitution' (Yoshido 1961:139).

Mouer and Sugimoto go on to examine an alternative model of Japanese society based on Marxist class-determined conflict. They state that this model emphasises social conflict generated by economic inequalities, but as I have argued elsewhere,[4] income is not a definitive factor in the delineation of social division in post-war Japanese society. On the contrary, there is a polarity of occupation status determined by access to education and is reflected in, for example, the existence of two contemporary youth sub-cultures, the *bōsōzoku* (members of car and motorcycle gangs), a manual working-class youth sub-culture with a high disposable income reflected in the cost of their vehicles; and college students, the *dokushin kizoku* (unmarried aristocrats) youth culture.

Mouer and Sugimoto go on to say that there is also a need to study the obverse side of social conflict, that is, the mechanisms of coercion and their inter-connectedness to sanctions both juridical and, more importantly for this study, social. In post-war Japanese society class cannot be defined in traditional late nineteenth- and twentieth-century western terms. However, it must be acknowledged that Japanese society is fragmented, as the existence of youth sub-cultures, students and women's movements attests. But equally it must be recognised that there are common ideologies and myths bridging these different interest groups and that there are strong social mechanisms for control negating outright opposition except in the most extreme cases. It is to these mechanisms of control that I now wish to turn and to suggest an alternative model to the two discussed briefly above – a utilitarian model that I shall refer to as the panoptic model.

The move towards an industrial economy was accompanied by an increasingly fragmented and unstable society necessitating a change in the mechanisms for social control. Also, the demands of industry for a more mobile and autonomous labour force required a move from coercive forms of control to an emphasis on social mechanisms whereby the individual becomes the agent for his/her subjugation. Put another way, the individual gives the law unto him/herself. I suggest this occurs through two interactive forces of control. The first is the establishment of a shared internalised belief system bridging differing interest groups as discussed in the preceding chapter. The second, with which this section is concerned, is the group or the *seken* (society at large) which I argue forms a spatial configuration of power not unlike the disciplinary schema designed by Jeremy Bentham.[5]

Ikegami (1995), in her historical study of the 'honour culture' of the samurai, argues that since the medieval period (eleventh century) there was a slow shift in emphasis in samurai culture from the seeking of honour (*na*) – through aggression and competition, to the desire to avoid shame (*haji*) – through conformity. It is this process which she argues brought about the ultimate 'taming of the samurai' during the Tokugawa period.

Ikegami argues that the avoidance of shame led to 'an intense concern for one's social appearance, associated with one's status in the eyes of the *seken*, ... [which] seems to lie at the heart of the modern Japanese sentiment of honor' (Ikegami 1995:18). This panoptic role of the *seken* as an 'imagined community', Ikegami argues, had clearly emerged by the late Tokugawa period and was carried over into the Meiji period forming the ideological basis for Japan's modernisation.[6]

I would suggest that the group or *seken* in both pre-war and post-war Japanese society forms the same configuration of power through unverifiable and constant visibility as the panopticon. However, in Japan this mechanism of control functions not as Bentham and Foucault have argued on the body, but at the psychological level – in the 'imagined community honour' (Ikegami). Hence the comment made by Fukami, a *kamikaze* recruit, in *Kumo nagaruru hateni*, 'there is a force invisible to the eye steadily pulling us into our graves' (*me ni mienai ōkina chikara ga, bokutachi o hakaba no naka e gungun, hikikonde iku n desu*). Ikegami in her exposition of the honour culture of the samurai reinforces this utilitarian view of group relations in the Tokugawa period:

> honor by definition respects values derived from the public opinions of a social group (the imagined community of honor), whereas universalistic religions inculcate the supremacy of values beyond the boundaries of normative systems of human social groups. Universalist religions did not pose serious challenges to the ethical system of the Japanese samurai, ... Buddhism or Shintoism in Japan did not develop a powerful single institutional centre that could represent an independent "public power" strong enough to oppose secular power ... Japan neither developed indigenous elitist counter-ideologies nor imported those of Western Europe (such as Christianity or Enlightenment humanitarianism), which might have modified the moral roots of the honor culture. (Ikegami 1995:335)

The Japanese ideological emphasis on a common ethnicity, cultural homogeneity and the group-orientatedness of their society, combined with the lack of a metaphysical code of behaviour in Japanese religions to which individuals could appeal over and above the immediacy of the society, has meant that this 'technology of power' has reached a degree of sophistication.

Foucault identifies two images of discipline which he defines as 'techniques for assuring the ordering of human multiplicities' (Foucault 1991:218); the first, an extreme form, 'the enclosed institution, established on the edges of society' (Foucault 1991:209), for example, the military institutions of the industrial age and the juridical power of the *han* in the pre-industrial era of Japanese society. The other image of discipline is the panopticon, which allows for a lighter, less direct form of control through generalised surveillance. Foucault goes on to make the point that the formation of a disciplinary society follows an historical trajectory from extreme enclosed disciplines to the more general and open panoptic schema evident in the post-war period. Historically, in Europe (in particular France and Britain), he identifies the seventeenth and eighteenth centuries as the periods which saw the 'formation of what might be called in general a disciplinary society' (Foucault 1991:209). He explains that in Europe the emergence of disciplinary societies grew out of a desire on the part of the ruling élites to 'neutralize dangers, to fix useless or disturbed populations' (Foucault 1991:210), and to make them into useful individuals through education which gradually developed into one of the dominant disciplinary mechanisms for social control of the latter type.

In Japan, the formation of a utilitarian control-disciplinary society occurred at an historical conjuncture in the late nineteenth century when there was a threat of colonisation by western powers. The other aspect of the conjuncture was the need of industry, which was rapidly developing to increase output and efficiency, to enable Japan to compete with the west and so maintain her own autonomy and increase profits. By now, as Beasley has argued, the residual feudal structures were incapable of dealing with these two factors. Ideologically, with the 'samurai-isation' of the lower orders, the ethic of the 'honour culture' became more pervasive.

The Meiji oligarchs encouraged the development of a group ethos to unify the country against the western threat and to consolidate their position as the rulers of Japan. This group ethos has continued to develop as the economic and political situations have changed until the present day. As a disciplinary body for the control of a multiplicity of individuals, the group or *seken* has developed as a procedure for social partitioning, not only along hierarchical lines, but also between individuals of the same level. The 'honour' element of the ethos, encouraging aggressive inter-group competition, effectively increases the utility of each individual by means that are fast and cost-effective.[7] The introduction of timetables, collective training exercises and surveillance also improved individual productivity and social control. And so disciplines

> [increased] the effect of utility proper to the multiplicities, so that each is made more useful than the simple sum of its elements: it is in order to increase the utilizable effects of the multiple that the disciplines define tactics of distribution, reciprocal adjustment of bodies, gestures and rhythms, differentiation of capacities, reciprocal co-ordination in relation to apparatuses or tasks. (Foucault 1991:220)

In this group structure, the dynamics of power (honour and shame) work discreetly from within the very texture of the group and not from some external source as in feudal societies. Nakane provides an example of the dynamics of power within the group in regard to the post-Meiji Japanese family.

> ... although the power of each individual household head is often regarded as exclusively his own, in fact it is the social group, the 'household', which has the ultimate integrating power, a power which restricts each member's behaviour and thought, including that of the household head himself. (Nakane 1972:14)

Viewed historically, the development of Japanese society along panoptic lines can be traced back to the Meiji period in which the military institution was open to all levels of society and became a model for civil life. The disciplinary structures of the military honour code were absorbed through a process of 'samurai-isation' into schools, the work-place and even the family, and this led to the virtual abolition of the distinction between soldiers and civilians in the 1930s and early 1940s. Corporal punishment and surveillance combined to allow more flexible forms of control. These included social mechanisms, for example, the establishment of the *koseki* (family register) as part of the Civil Code (1898) which defined in clear terms the structure of the family and the legal responsibilities of each member within it. Also, numerous other groups and organisations were formed outside the work place, school and home to regulate and control free time (Sims 1991). Then there were the state control mechanisms, for example, the formation of the *kenpeitai* (gendarmerie).

In the post-war era, the emphasis shifted from physical coercion to an even greater emphasis on observation and visibility as dominant mechanisms for social control. The threat of physical coercion became a secondary form of control to be used in more extreme cases, for example, physical violence has been used against the protest movements of the 1960s and 1970s. According to Amnesty International, the police still resort to violence and torture to extract confessions.[8] However, their main function, as the familiar term for the police, *omawari-san*, implies, is to circulate in their respective neighbourhoods and gather information through observation. The post-war period has seen a further shift in the emphasis on outright physical coercive mechanisms to gathering information as a means of social control.[9]

The fluid spatial design of Japanese architecture, emphasising floors and ceilings rather than walls (Ashihara 1992:15), is the architectural configuration of visibility and control. There are few permanently installed inner walls, space is partitioned by sliding doors and removable panels, often made only of paper.[10] The open office plan of Japanese companies, where the section manager works together with his juniors and not alone in a separate office is another example. Ozu's films provide a wonderful example of the fluidity of space in the traditional family home and the open office plan.[11]

To summarise: the power configuration of human relations existing in groups within Japanese society, whether they be the family, company quality circles, school clubs or *fujin-kai* (married women's associations), exist inside the very texture of the group itself becoming an anonymous internalised instrument of control. The separation of people into groups enables the basic standard of the 'normal' (*seken-nami*) to be calculated and measured through classification devices. The norm becomes 'an average to be respected or an optimum towards which one must move' (Foucault 1991:183). With the decrease of rank and privilege as indices of status in the industrial era and under the unifying ethos of homogeneity and classless society, desirable norms as part of the disciplinary process were established through such instruments of classification as the examination. The mechanisms of normalising judgements measure 'in quantitative terms and hierarchizes in terms of value the abilities, the level, the "nature" of individuals' (Foucault 1991:183). The establishment of norms serves two purposes; it at once classifies people according to ability and imposes homogeneity as each individual attempts to achieve the norm. 'It is easy to understand how the power of the norm functions within a system of formal equality, since within a homogeneity that is the rule, the norm introduces, as a useful imperative and as a result of measurement, all the shading of individual differences' (Foucault 1991:184). As Lebra has explained the 'norm' or *seken-nami* also functions to ensure the maximisation of human output in economic terms.

> It is [the] possibility of being passed by one's peers, or worse yet by a junior entrant, that mid-career employees fear most. Paradoxically, the seniority rule, which should function to minimize internal competition, in fact throws peers into ferocious competition and leaves the losers totally demoralized. The losers in career competitions are face-losers in the eyes of their families, friends or *seken* as a whole. (Lebra 1994:108)

The group ethos or *seken* as social control is reflected in the spatial dynamics of power in Japanese architecture which, according to Ashihara (1992), was never designed to be seen as, for example, were the more ostentatious European palaces. He tells us that traditional Japanese architecture emphasised the interior in relation to the lives of the individuals. Ashihara attributes this development to the 'unique' climatic conditions of Japan. I suggest that it is, in fact, the architectural configuration of the structures of power evident in the group as a utilitarian mechanism for social ordering and control through the minimisation of privacy and the maximisation of visibility.

Fallen Blossoms

Thematically, mainstream *kamikaze* films made in the 1950s and 1960s are concerned with an exposition of the dynamics of power at work within the texture of group relations. These films subordinate the greater discourses of war responsibility on to narratives centering on the individual's relationship to the group. As such, these films focus on the affinities between males in a homosocial sub-text reaching a climax just before the deaths of the heroes. While ostensibly adopting a pacifist position through a critique of wartime ideologies that was manifested in the dialogue, the visual image reaffirms the centrality of a code of brotherhood (*sen'yūai*) as both a mechanism for control and a site of pleasure. This aspect is perhaps best expressed through a term used by Rosalind Miles (1992) as the 'tyranny of male bonding'. Therefore, at one level these films conform to the general formula of most war films both western and Japanese, that war is pleasurable, as it allows men to express an intensity of emotion prohibited in society under more 'normal' conditions; while at another level, they expose the negative aspects of this bonding which, in the case of the Special Attack Forces, demanded the death of the individual as a solipsistic act of group identity divorced from its wartime ideological meaning as an expression of patriotism (as per Satō's definition of *sen'yūai*, refer p 69).

Both *Kumo nagaruru hateni*[12] (*Beyond the Clouds*) 1953, directed by Ieki Miyoji (1911-1976) and *Ningen gyorai kaiten* (*The Sacrifice of the Human Torpedoes*) 1955, directed by Matsubayashi Shue (1920-) are set in the last desperate stages of the war and cover the period of time when the young pilots and submarine operators, respectively, wait before departing on their final missions. This period of time is prolonged and tension maintained as missions are postponed and comrades die during training exercises, forcing the survivors to face the reality of their own impending deaths. It is in the depiction of the heroes' inner psychological struggle that these post-war films differ from the wartime productions such as *Kaigun* and *Hawai Marē okikaisen*. The emphasis in these post-war films is on character development rather than plot. Unlike the wartime productions, the plot is contrived in such a way as to develop the characters' 'interiority'. This is achieved through dialogue, flashbacks into memory, flash-forwards into imagination, voice-over narration, close-ups, reverse and point-of-view shots. On the other hand, films produced during the war rarely used flashbacks or close-up shots. 'Voice-of-god' narration was used in wartime productions to describe historical events and the passage of time, often cast over images of newspaper headlines or actual newsreel footage of the events described. In post-war *kamikaze* films, through these various filmic devices, the spectator is given access to the 'interiority' of the characters explaining their psychological motivations. In both these films, it is through the dialogue that the spectator is made aware of the hero's scepticism of wartime propaganda. As one young pilot in *Kumo nagaruru hateni*, mimicking the voice of a senior officer, declaims during a drunken evening 'Students of Japan, the fate of the historic Imperial Navy rests on your innocent shoulders. Pilots of the Imperial Navy, rouse yourselves ...[13] After pausing and reverting to his normal voice, he concludes, 'It's all a lot of bunkum (... *tena koto wa detarame de aru*)' at which point the others all laugh. On a more serious note, Noguchi, reflecting on his childhood days says:

> When I was younger, I also wondered about the rights and wrongs of war, so I asked the minister outright – that German missionary, well, I respected him – Do you think God would forgive people for killing each other? He gave a really third-rate reply: 'The Americans are bad, it is right to destroy them, therefore, God will forgive the war.'

After a pause, Noguchi continues, 'From then on, I grew to despise that minister.' In another scene, an orderly looks at the sleeping Matsui and muses, 'Is this the face of a living God?' While in *Kumo nagaruru hateni*, this scepticism is often expressed subtly through humour, in the later film *Ningen gyorai kaiten*, it is discussed openly amongst the submarine operators.

Despite the general assumption that all sailors and airmen of the Special Attack Forces died during their mission, many in fact returned. This was particularly the case with the submarine operators who were sent out as part of the general armory of the mother submarine and during the voyage were kept on constant alert. If, as was sometimes the case, they were not required, they returned to base with their mother submarines. The 1956 film *Ningen gyorai shutsugeki su* (*The Human Torpedo's Sortie*), directed by Furukawa Takumi (1917–), deals specifically with this subject. However in the following two scenes taken from *Ningen gyorai kaiten*, this situation of the return of two submarine operators becomes a context in which to question the use of 'human bullets' (*nikudan*) and the wartime propaganda surrounding their image. Tamai (Kimura Isao, 1923-) is rebuffed in the following dialogue when he greets the young Kitamura who returned with his ship.

Tamai: Kitamura, it is great that you came back.
Kitamura: No, it is a disgrace.
Tamai: Do you really think so?
Kitamura: Yes.
Tamai: But your single death won't affect the outcome of the war.
Kitamura: If we all hit our targets, Japan is certain to win.
Tamai: I would like to think so.
Kitamura: Ensign Tamai, although you are an officer, you don't have the martial spirit (*gunjin seishin*).
Tamai: You are probably right. But I am not speaking to you now as an officer, but as a brother - a troubled brother... I have changed, and you will probably change too. But if you are allowed to live, don't take lightly the feelings of those who secretly prayed for you. If your mother were here, what would she say?

In a later scene, a young recruit confronts the more senior Murasei (Utsui Ken, 1931-) who also returned due to a fault in his submarine.

Matsumoto: Your return was a great shame as now I have been taken out of the formation.
Murasei: Do you really want to die so much?
Matsumoto: Yes, I want to die for the Emperor and have my spirit enshrined at the Yasukuni Shrine.
Murasei: Yes, I see. How old are you?
Matsumoto: Eighteen. ... Ensign Murasei, let me go ahead of you.
Murasei: Fool! Tonight, write a letter to your parents, and live at least until you reach my age.

In these scenes, the film opens up the contradiction between filial piety and loyalty to the *kokutai* that wartime films such as *Chichi ariki* effectively masked through the conflation of the public and private spheres of the individuals' lives.

In scenes such as these, the films question established wartime discourses which equated the death of individuals with sacrifice and patriotism, distancing from wartime propaganda the meaning the films attribute to the deaths of the heroes. This then begs the question: if the pilots and submarine operators of the Special Attack Forces did not offer their lives as a gesture of patriotism, then what was the motivation for their sacrifice? The answer lies partly in an analysis of the two characters played by the actor Kimura Isao and their relationship with other members of the group.

In both these post-war films, Kimura Isao plays the part of the young pilot-submarine operator who, through a superficial wound in *Kumo nagaruru hateni* and because of the unexpected return of Murasei and Kitamura in *Ningen gyorai kaiten*, entertains the vague hope that he might just survive. In each of the narratives, he represents a 'weak' side to masculine nature that the films link to his relationships with women. It is only in the final scenes when he rejects the feminine and rejoins the male group that his character is redeemed. As Rosalind Miles describes in *The Rites of Man* (1992), for the male to achieve the desired status of 'manliness', he must break with his mother upon whom he was totally dependent as a child. Miles suggests this struggle is the hardest in a man's life. It is further aggravated in Confucian-based social systems where the mother is so totally dependent on her first-born son for her social position and status and as such, she resists these attempts to break away in a desperate bid to prolong his dependency. Miles continues, the gang, and I would suggest in Japanese society, the male group, functions to switch the male's 'primary allegiance from the single female mother to the group male'.

> From the riddle, the nuisance, the threat and the danger of woman, where should the young male recoil but back into the bosom of the gang? So the move towards individuation in reality serves only to reinforce group loyalty and the tyranny of male bonding. (Miles 1992:274)

Both films depict this rite of passage to manhood and self-definition through death that the two characters, played by Kimura Isao, must pass along in order to rejoin the male group. They must make a physical break with their lovers which also becomes a symbolic break with their own feminine natures. In both films, an ideal masculine type is depicted to counter the character played by Kimura. In one sense, these two characters come to represent the two oppositional aspects of masculine nature constructed in each film. In *Kumo nagaruru hateni*, Otaki, played by Tsuruta Kōji (1924-), represents the stoic male who, as first son, was destined to inherit the patriarchal authority of the father. This becomes apparent in flashbacks depicting him in the centre of the family. In one poignant scene he is shown as an adult sleeping between his parents. It is the letters of Otaki to his parents, read in voice-over that provide the frame within which the narrative is placed. In the opening shots, as the camera pans along the line of dozing airmen lying in the sun, it stops at Otaki who has a gentle smile on his lips. The peacefulness of this image is contrasted with the voice-over as he ironically tells his parents, 'I am well and don't expect to die until it is time to die.' Later in the film, it becomes apparent that, apart from his mother and sister, he disdains women. As he tells Matsui who is on his way to pay a final visit to his prostitute-lover, 'I thought a woman would be more beautiful . . .' And finally, on the night before his suicide mission and after his 'passion on the mountain' when in the darkness of the night all the inner struggles of the previous days depicted through his feminine other, Fukami, spill out in a flood of tears, he swims naked in the lake. The camera lingers on his powerful body, reminiscent of the rescue scene in *Soshū no yoru*. In this scene, Otaki symbolically cleanses himself of the feminine and the domestic. Just as the young men who participate in the *Shintō kenka matsuri* (festivals of fighting, where *mikoshi* portable shrines are rammed into each other) must bathe and be purified with salt, so too Otaki purifies himself before battle in a scene which glorifies the young male body about to be mutilated.

In *Ningen gyorai kaiten*, Tamai's alter ego, Asakura, played by Okada Eiji (1920-), is more problematic. Following on from his role in *Mata au hi made (Until the Day We Meet Again)* 1950, directed by Imai Tadashi, in which Okada Eiji plays the part of the hapless young student out of step with the militarised society, in *Ningen gyorai kaiten*, he is a student of western philosophy who on his final night chooses to read Kant's *Critique of Pure Reason* rather than attend the farewell party. As the film progresses, it becomes evident that, in exploring western thought, he believes in an individualistic ethos based on 'humanism'. Thus, using Kantian moral rationalism as his theoretical base, he openly criticises the military institutions and the utilitarian principles of moral relativism used to legitimate the establishment of the Special Attack Forces. Like Kaji, the hero in *The Human Condition* (dealt with in detail in the following chapter), Asakura is seeking to define an alternative morality valuing human life and existing independently of everyday social relations. Therefore, on his final night during a long conversation with an orderly who before the war had been a university lecturer, he says:

> If you become a lecturer again, please lecture on *The Critique of Pure Reason*. The next generation must become better and stronger than we were, they must have more courage.

The introduction of Kantian philosophy into the discourses of the film attempts to challenge wartime ideologies on two counts. First, rationalism is set up in opposition to nature as defined in the ideologies of the *kokutai*; secondly, it seeks to establish an 'humanitarian' morality that values human life above the needs of the social unit and therefore rejects the concept of the sacrifice of the few for the 'greater good'. These two themes come together in a scene in which Asakura intervenes on behalf of two elderly orderlies who are being beaten for carrying out their duties in a relaxed non-military manner. After dismissing the orderlies, he confronts the self-appointed disciplinarians.

Non-commissioned officer A: I have been in the Navy for ten years.

Non-commissioned officer B: We understand the Navy's tradition and spirit well.

Asakura: I see; I have only been in the Navy for one and a half years, therefore I am probably not as familiar with these things as you are. But I think this tradition and spirit are wrong. What are the Special Attack Forces to you? Who are the officers who go on these missions, you?

A & B: No.

Asakura: In the name of the Special Attack Forces, I shall discipline you. Stand firm! (He raises his fist in readiness to strike, then gently lowering it, he continues:) If it is the tradition of the Imperial Navy not to treat human beings as human beings, then it is gravely mistaken. From time to time remember these words – the last words of an officer of the Special Attack Forces who is about to leave on his final mission.

In this dialogue, Asakura directly challenges the nativist concept of a 'unique' Japanese spirit (*seishin*) through his appeal to humanism reinforced by his reluctance to use physical violence (*yūjō no tekken*-the fist of fellowship) against the two non-commissioned officers. Nevertheless, despite these arguments against wartime ideologies, the film is structured in the final dialogue that Asakura has with the former lecturer to reaffirm the very utilitarian principles that had earlier been criticised. In this scene, Asakura searches to find a reason for his imminent death.

Asakura: We shall die so that people will realise the senselessness of war. Then if weaker people protest, that will be good. Violence must have a limit.
Tanabe: I have been passive, passive to a frightening degree. Why, I don't know.
Asakura: Strong people do exist.

Asakura's rationalisation of his impending death in these terms serves only to deflect the goal from the desire for victory to a pacifist stance - so that other 'weaker people realise the senselessness of war'. The fundamental utilitarian principle - the sacrifice of the few for the greater good - remains unchallenged. Tanabe's responses, his realisation of his passivity and therefore his complicity in the establishment and maintenance of the industrial military system only reaffirms the effectiveness of Asakura's sacrifice - his death will not have been in vain. Tanabe's role as a former university lecturer is significant as many teachers and lecturers were criticised in the early post-war period for the propagation of wartime propaganda amongst their students and for not resisting the war.

In the film, Asakura's relationship with the wider group is problematic. In the second half of the film when his philosophical opposition to the military institutions and the war becomes apparent, he physically separates from the group. On their final night, while the others sing the *sakura* song (quoted above) at their party, he stays behind in the barracks. At first, Tamai wants to stay with him, but when he realises that Asakura intends to read alone, he becomes angry at this rejection and leaves to rejoin the main group. Tamai is also isolated from the group. This is evident at the farewell party when he sits alone and refuses to take part in the customary poetry writing, arguing that he does not want to lie on the night before his death (see figures 1 and 2). While Asakura's isolation is based on an intellectual rationalist opposition, Tamai's is grounded in the emotional, in nature, physically symbolised in his relationship with Sachiko, his girlfriend, played by Tsushima Keiko (1926–). Tamai's isolation can therefore be cast off with his maturation and by his acceptance of death as point of entry into the masculine world. In the last scenes, both Asakura and Tamai accept the inevitability of the forces at work on them and accompany the group to go to their deaths. However, the film adds one final twist in the last scenes which further negates the Kantian argument. Tamai and his two comrades, despite their doubts, resolve them during the film and come to represent the embodiment of the Japanese spirit as their submarines explode on target destroying the enemy ships. In contrast, Asakura, whose objections and doubts were based on western philosophical grounds, fails in his mission and drowns in his submarine. One possible reading of this final scene is that his spirit was contaminated by western culture and was therefore lacking the purity idealised in the wartime film *Muhō Matsu no isshō*.

The obverse side of social relations based on the panoptic role of the *seken* and depicted in these films through the 'interiorisation' of the heroes, is the individual's concern with what Lebra has defined as the 'presentational self'.

> The presentational self involves the surface layer of self, metaphorically localised on the person's face, visible or exposed to others either in *actuality or imagination*. The person's self-awareness is sharpened as the object of attention, inspection, and appraisal by others around. This

Figures 1–2: *Ningen gyorai kaiten* 1955

self-awareness is labeled '*kao*' '*mentsu*', '*taimen*', '*menboku*', '*teisai*', '*sekentei*'. These terms might be translated as honor, self-esteem, dignity, reputation, and the like, but such translations do not fully convey the self's sensitivity to interactional immediacy and vulnerability entailed in the Japanese terms. (Lebra 1994:106) (my emphasis)

The importance actual *kamikaze* pilots attached to their 'presentational selves' is evidenced in the diaries and letters gathered in various memorial collections. One example, taken from a book published by the Yasukuni Shrine to commemorate the fiftieth anniversary of the great call-up of students in 1944, is a diary of a young Waseda student who confided:

> In the next room they are drinking and making a noise. Before death a person should observe a period of abstinence (*shōjin*), in particular, the officers of the Special Attack Forces who are representative of the Japanese spirit (*Yamato damashii*). Until the last I am determined not to do anything to shame the name of the Special Attack Forces. (*Izasaraba Ware wa Mikuni no Yamazakura* 1994:96)

Tamai and his comrades are similarly conscious of their 'presentational selves' as the return of Murasei in an early sequence demonstrates. On returning, he is most concerned that the others in his immediate group believe him when he tells them his submarine had engine failure and that he was not a coward. This theme is reinforced when an officer commenting on Murasei's return says, 'It isn't a respectable way to die going out two or three times.' Another officer concurs, 'For Murasei's sake, he should be sent out again as soon as possible.' Even Asakura, who in turning to western philosophy sought an alternative ethic based on metaphysical concepts of good and bad, could not resist the utilitarian imperative of the collectivity that demands the sacrifice of the few for the greater good.

In *Kumo nagaruru hateni*, the Otaki-Fukami relationship is foregrounded within the depiction of the wider group relations. In the first scene, during the bombing raid on their Kyūshū airfield, it is Otaki who helps Fukami when he is wounded, shielding him with his body and dressing his wound before taking a machine gun and firing at the enemy. Similarly, when it becomes apparent that, because of his wound, Fukami will be exempted from the forthcoming mission, Otaki goes over to where Fukami is sitting – symbolically separated from the main group, a position of ostracisation (*mura-hachibu*) he occupies until the final scene – and says, 'I thought we would be together until the end'. Later, when there is a suggestion that Fukami is a coward, it is Otaki who attempts to defend him. In this scene, the camera cuts to a close-up reaction shot of Otaki's face as Fukami, after rejecting Matsui's reconciliatory cup of *sake*, storms off. This close-up shot of Otaki identifies Fukami as the object of his gaze just as did earlier close-up shots of Michiko, the young school teacher (see figures 3 and 4). As the narrative progresses and as the dialogue between Otaki and Fukami becomes more open and honest, the camera marks this progression by moving into extreme close-ups and reaction shots. Thus stylistically the camera links the two conflicting relationships motivating Fukami's inner struggle; his growing love for Michiko, representative of his desire to live and therefore seen as weakness, and his love of Otaki, representative of a process of maturation culminating in the acceptance of the adult world of sacrifice and death.

The film centres Otaki's private life on his family while Fukami's private life concentrates on his relationship with Michiko. This latter relationship is established within the first few minutes of the film through a series of reverse shots as the pilots return to their barracks, a converted school house, after the bombing raid on their airfield. Fukami's acknowledgement of her look, verified through a reverse-cut shot, is in marked contrast to a similar scene in the wartime production of *Kaigun* when Takao's young sister looks affectionately at Makoto only to be rebuffed in the return shot. At

Figures 3–4: *Kumo nagaruru hateni* 1953

this point, Fukami leaves the male group to exist on the fringe with Matsui who is also involved with a woman. Fukami's ostracisation is represented physically as he sits away from the main group while they gather around the table. Otaki, as representative of the ideal male, is highlighted by his white shirt as he sits centre right at the table. His centrality to the group is constantly emphasised throughout the film by means of spatial positioning, by his white shirt against a mass of khaki uniforms and by lighting. In this early scene, the officer reads out the names of the pilots selected to take part in the following day's mission. Fukami has not been chosen; his separation is complete. After the officer leaves, the other pilots stand before the improvised *butsudan* (Buddhist altar) and offer a cup of *sake* to Akita who died during the air raid. Fukami's face is just visible as he remains isolated, seated against the wall watching the proceedings. The others conclude by singing the *sakura* song, a communal act of bonding – 'We are cherry blossoms flowering at the same time in the same Air Force garden.' While they are singing, Fukami rises, but remains apart from the group. The camera then cuts to a rear view shot of the group and it becomes noticeable that Matsui is also sitting alone. He pours himself some *sake* and then, going over to Fukami, takes him aside to tell him that he is slipping out to visit his girlfriend. The film thus spatially links Fukami and Matsui as separate from the main group due to their relations with women.

After the death of one of their group in a training accident, Fukami and Otaki are confronted with the crash and their own impending deaths. Fukami asks:

Fukami: What do you think of the Special Attack Units? Can you really agree with these methods? Airmen of the Special Attack Forces are certain to die. This isn't a war strategy!
Otaki: Certain death, certain death for a certain kill; Japan is in a desperate situation. Fukami, war is not logical, it burns up people's lives, it is fundamental to human nature, it is a passion, it is no longer a question of victory or defeat ... it is to live only for the eternal great cause. It is a national passion in which the individual transcends life and death and all are equal. Our lives have been entrusted to the Emperor. Fukami, you are in love with a woman and now you want your life back.
Fukami: No, these are two different issues.

Otaki: No they aren't.
Fukami: Otaki, this accident. There was nothing left of him. That's what frightens me.
Otaki: Fukami, you have changed.
Fukami: At the time I broke my arm, I thought just maybe I might survive. From that moment on, I began to lose confidence. I shan't deny that I love Michiko, but that is unconnected to my fears. Otaki, honestly, don't you want to live? That's what I want to ask.

In this dialogue, Otaki angrily makes the direct connection between Fukami's doubts and his relationship with Michiko. Despite Fukami's protestation to the contrary, this dialogue only reinforces an earlier scene in which Fukami and Michiko are stopped on a country road by an officer who beats Fukami, reprimanding him for being out with a woman. After this, there is a close-up shot of Michiko's face as she bursts into tears and runs out of the frame, leaving a close-up profile shot of Fukami as he watches the officer's car disappear into the distance. After a brief pause, he turns into the camera in an extreme close-up frontal shot of his face as he calls out her name, thus rejecting the officer and following Michiko (see figures 5, 6, 7 and 8). When he reaches her, they embrace, and Michiko, voicing Fukami's inner thoughts says, 'Don't go. Let's just die here. I want to get away from here, take me away, take me away!' Fukami continues after a pause,

> I want to get away from here too. It's not just you. But I can't. *There is a force invisible to the eye steadily pulling us into our graves.* But they are not easy to enter. When we crash into an enemy ship, our flesh and bones, even the last hair on our heads, will disappear. Even now we have no human affection, no human will, all traces of our humanity are gone. For the sake of the war, we have become expendable objects. That is what I have been reduced to. (emphasis mine)

In this passage, Fukami refers directly to a panoptic force of the *seken* 'invisible to the eye' pulling him into his grave, that is, in this case, the ostracisation (*mura-hachibu*) which has been at work on him both in the dialogue, through Matsui's accusations of cowardice and Otaki's disapproval of his relationship with Michiko, and visually, through his physical separation from the group. These

THE *KAMIKAZE* FILM AND THE POLITICS OF THE COLLECTIVE

Figures 5–8: *Kumo nagaruru hateni* 1953

scenes are reinforced by earlier flashbacks into Fukami's past in which it becomes obvious that, as a young student, he joined the Navy and then the Special Attack Forces out of his desire to be with Otaki. In the dénouement in which Fukami reaches maturity and is reintegrated into the group, his impending death is distanced from wartime ideologies of sacrifice and linked instead to a homosocial ethic which the film presents as being the force that binds the male group. This scene is worth examining in some detail as it is through the use of filmic devices such as camera movement and lighting rather than dialogue or plot that the intensity of the relationship between Fukami and Otaki and their wider relationship to the group are conveyed to the spectator.

In the preceding scene, Fukami throws off his sling and goes into the senior officers' mess and asks to be allowed to go on the mission. After his return to the barracks where the others are writing their final letters, Fukami still exists in the shadows, dressing on the fringes of the group. Otaki, as representative of the true male, is constantly highlighted by the key light, a motif used throughout the film which locates him in the centre of the group.

When Fukami, in the next shot, walks from the centre background into the lit foreground, he says 'I want to die with you'. Thus his physical and emotional reunion with the group are marked symbolically through both the motif of the lighting and the mise-en-scène. For the remainder of the sequence, Fukami occupies a central position with Otaki in the group. The lighting in these early shots is organised to create a sense of depth, thus clearly defining the space within the frame, separating the group gathered around the candle-lit table from the dark background out of which Fukami walks.

The use of extreme close-ups in reverse shot sequence, while Otaki cross-examines Fukami in order to ascertain his motives, is justified by the confrontational nature of the exchange. Then as Fukami says 'I thought I was the only one who was troubled. Then I realised that each one of us is suffering in his own way', the camera pulls back to emphasise Fukami's spatial centrality to the group before moving into a series of reaction shots of the pilots and finally holding an extreme close-up of Otaki's eyes, followed by one of Fukami's tear-stained cheek. Both these shots are held for much longer (approximately 120 and 96 frames respectively) and are focussed on the eyes rather than their faces as a whole. Neither speaks in these two shots, all hint of conflict that had masked the erotic component of the earlier extreme close-up sequence has gone, leaving only the love between the two, expressed through the camera's penetrating focus on their eyes and the direct eyeline match (see figures 9 and 10). This scene culminates in their physical embrace.

The last shot of the sequence, in which the pilots sing the *sakura* song and embrace, is a long shot from a high angle, the lighting is behind the *butsudan*, throwing all the foregrounded

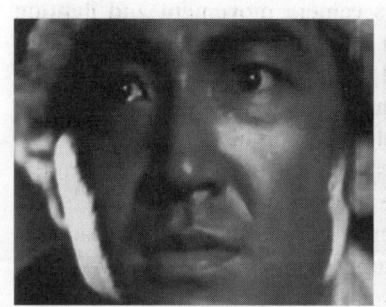

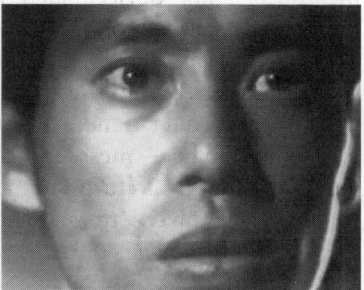

Figures 9–10: *Kumo nagaruru hateni* 1953

figures into silhouette, and it becomes impossible to distinguish one from another (see figure 11). In this way, the lighting and the camera position establish the total reintegration of Fukami within the group. The preceding shot of the *butsudan,* (see figure 12), introduces the theme of death again and in the final shot, it is the *butsudan* at the back of the frame and not the table in the foreground, symbolic of food and life, that is thrown into prominence through the lighting. The pilots who anonymously sing and embrace move about in the space between these two motifs. They are neither dead nor are they a part of the living world.

Visually, this scene draws on filmic conventions established during the war period in, for example, Tasaka Tomotaka's *Gonin no sekkōhei*, as a comparison of figures 9 and 10 with 13 and 14 will demonstrate. This latter scene occurs towards the end of the film when the last of the five missing scouts returns to camp. He is welcomed back into the group by his fellow soldiers and his greatly relieved senior officer. During the war period, the visual expression of *sen'yūai* was not confined exclusively to men. There are many scenes in women's films depicting the devotion of young girls to their factory work group and their reluctance to leave work due to ill health or family obligations. One example would be Kurosawa Akira's 1944 *Ichiban utsukushii (The Most Beautiful)*. However, after the war, this theme was quickly abandoned as women were reintegrated into traditional roles as wives and mothers and has only recently reappeared in the late 1980s in for example, yakuza films (*Gokudō no onna-tachi-Yakuza Women* series).

Both *Kumo nagaruru hateni* and *Ningen gyorai kaiten* attempt the impossible; the reconciliation of an anti-war imperative and an acknowledgement of the 'heroic' sacrifice of the young officers in

Figures 11–12: *Kumo nagaruru hateni* 1953

Figures 13–14: *Gonin no sekkōhei* 1938

the Special Attack Forces. These films, in endeavouring to portray their deaths as heroic, recast their sacrifice in order to orientate the spectator towards the future. In *Kumo nagaruru hateni*, this is achieved through Otaki's opening and closing letters to his parents and the constant juxtaposition of shots of the school children – a motif for the next generation – with the young pilots. *Ningen gyorai kaiten* is similarly framed within a voice-of-god narrational sequence at the beginning and end of the film. These sequences clearly situate the spectator in the present (i.e. 1955) in relation to the events portrayed. Ivan Morris' study suggests that the actual *kamikaze* pilots seemed to be aware of Japan's inevitable defeat, but this did not deter them. As Vice-Admiral Ōnishi, who was responsible for the establishment of the first squadron of Special Attack Forces in the Philippines and Taiwan, said 'even if we were defeated, the noble spirit of the *kamikaze* attack corps will keep our homeland from ruin. Without this spirit, ruin would certainly follow defeat' (quoted in Morris 1980:284). These films similarly contribute to this discourse as Otaki expresses the same sentiments in his letters, urging his parents to believe in Japan's ultimate victory and to live long lives. In *Ningen gyorai kaiten*, this sentiment is expressed by Asakura who, in rationalising his own death, says that others will come to realise the senselessness of war. Both films are excellent examples of the wider post-war discourse of defeat which co-opted the image of the *kamikaze* as a symbol of the spirit of post-war regeneration. Surviving *kamikaze*, such as Sakai Saburō, and the military establishment represented at the Yasukuni Shrine Museum among others, had a vested interest in contributing to, and encouraging this hegemonic image which gave meaning to the deaths of the young officers despite the failure of defeat. *Kumo nagaruru hateni* and *Ningen gyorai kaiten* contribute to this discourse by displacing the wider discourses of war responsibility through the 'tragic hero' on to themes of spiritual regeneration, and through the homosocial sub-text, a reassertion of the primacy of the male group. As one *kamikaze* is reported as saying, 'a nation had to suffer and be purified every few generations, so that it could become stronger by having its impurities removed' (quoted in Morris 1980:314). This sentiment echoes that expressed in a poem composed by Vice-Admiral Ōnishi Takijirō:

Sugasugashii	Refreshingly
Bōfū no ato ni	After the violent storm
Tsuki kiyoshi	The moon rose radiant.

(quoted in Iguchi and Nakajima 1958:187)

In giving this new post-war meaning to the deaths of the young officers, through the visual sub-text of homosocial bonding, both films reconfirm the underlying principles upon which the ideologies of the *kokutai* are predicated; this occurs despite their apparent challenge to wartime propaganda through the dialogue. They can therefore be viewed as a nexus where wartime ideologies of the *kokutai* are renegotiated and emerge as their post-war variant *nihonjinron*. Satō confirms this reading in his essay on 'The Genealogy of the Anti-War Film' when he states:

> After *Kumo nagaruru hateni* many films based on the Special Attack Forces were made, but for the most part they stayed within this established format. Filmmakers probably intended to emphasise the misery of war due to the portrayal of the enforced death of personable young men out of a sense of comradely love and love of family. However, if we alter the perspective slightly, if these young men are only capable of comradely love and love of family, we can probably say they were incapable of opposing the war. Films made during the war to promote a fighting spirit did not depict the enemy as a monster to stimulate hatred, instead they depicted men rich in comradely love and love of family. (Satō 1989:133-134)

Satō goes on to argue that for films to present a truly anti-war stance, they need to effect a 'wider field of vision', for example, the portrayal of the enemy as human beings similar to ourselves.

Both films follow the early post-war convention of giving their heroes a private life and a psychological depth through which the films challenge wartime propaganda. This was in part achieved through the creation of a feminine alter ego in the two characters portrayed by Kimura Isao. While at one level acknowledging a feminine aspect to male nature (which must ultimately be disregarded), these characters also served to deflect this aspect away from the principal heroes who are constructed as pure, masculine, ideal types. Socially, the depiction of a feminine alter ego is acceptable as in both films the characters portrayed by Kimura are established as secondary sons. A tension has always existed around the position of secondary sons in Confucian-based social organisations. Their position is problematic in their relation to the sameness of their biological male status, but equally their difference as non-hereditary possessors of the symbolic order of the father, the phallus. Hence, the position they occupy in the family and in the wider social relations of the male group is somewhere between the feminine and the masculine.[14] The slight build and delicate features of the actor Kimura support this image in these roles, and the soft lighting used to create a soft focus effect further emphasises his intermediate status. However, both films uphold a heterosexual imperative as the two characters portrayed by Kimura are involved with women. Kimura Isao's type-casting in these roles is also evident in Kurosawa Akira's *Shichinin no samurai (The Seven Samurai)* 1954, in which he plays the youngest of the seven and the only one to be involved with a woman, and in the 1965 adaptation of Kawabata's novel *Yukiguni (Snow Country)* in which he plays the lead opposite Iwashita Shima.

On the contrary, the 1956 Nikkatsu production *Ningen gyorai shutsugeki su* discards entirely the feminine aspect of masculinity. This film operates at two levels. First, in building on the earlier box office success of *Taiyō no kisetsu (The Season of the Sun)* 1956, also directed by Furukawa Takumi, in which Ishihara Yujirō (1934–1987) made his debut, it incorporates elements of the rebellious *taiyōzoku* (suntribe) sub-culture into the war narrative. As such, in this film at least, the hero Kurosaki (Ishihara Yujirō) becomes a rebel with a cause.[15]

The late 1950s and early 1960s *taiyōzoku* sub-culture was in part a reaction to the American occupation and the powerlessness felt by youth after the failure of the AMPO demonstrations.[16] It was therefore based on a reassertion of an image of masculinity combining a curious mixture of Japanese elements with a James Dean-like image of nihilistic rebellion. Ishihara Yujirō, the actor, came to symbolise these elements. In keeping with the generational conflict inherent in 1960s *taiyōzoku* discourse, the character Kurosaki, played by Ishihara in *Ningen gyorai shutsugeki su*, is distanced from his family. There are no farewell visits nor is there the customary final letter, his only contact with his family is through his younger sister. The inclusion of a relationship between a young officer and his younger sister is a generic convention established in the earlier two films maintaining an opposition between women as lovers and the 'pure' image of women as mothers and sisters. As the *taiyōzoku* male hero's masculinity is predicated on hedonistic action, Kurosaki's character is denied any real psychological depth or 'interiority'. This is reflected filmically as there are very few close-up shots of him. He is constantly held in long and medium shots emphasising his body as the site of action. In fact, one of the aspects associated with the Ishihara image is that of his long legs repeatedly thrown into prominence by low-angle shots showing him standing with his legs slightly apart.

On the second level, *Ningen gyorai shutsugeki su* frames a critique of the mechanisms of power at work on Kurosaki and on the other young officers in his group within the wider popular discourses of the war. The film links the use of 'human torpedoes' to the atom bomb attack on Hiroshima and Nagasaki and in so doing poses the utilitarian question of how one can equate the life of one individual against the thousands who died in those cities. This question is then juxtaposed at the first level within the personal narrative of Kurosaki who, in the final scenes, as a 'human torpedo' sacrifices himself to save the mother submarine. The film opens in a courtroom in which the submarine captain, Hashikawa, is being interrogated by an American naval attorney on the sinking of the United States warship *Indianapolis*. He asks the captain, 'When did you learn of the fact that the *Indianapolis* was carrying atomic bombs to the Tinian Islands?' The captain replies, 'When I returned to base.' The scene immediately shifts to a press conference where an American reporter asks the captain how he felt when he learned that the bombs were used on Hiroshima and Nagasaki. The captain replies that he was saddened and is further prompted to speculate that, if he had sunk the *Indianapolis* before it had delivered its cargo, the people of Hiroshima and Nagasaki would have been saved. Another reporter then follows with a question on the captain's use of 'human torpedoes'. Thus, in the opening scenes, the film poses the following hypothetical question: if the captain's submarine had met the *Indianapolis* before it had delivered its cargo, would he have been justified in sacrificing the life of one young officer in order to save the thousands killed in the attacks on Hiroshima and Nagasaki? The film then proceeds in flashback through the captain's memory to recount the voyage and, in so doing, to answer the above question in the affirmative through analogy played out in the micro-narrative of the 'tragic hero' Kurosaki's personal experience which in turn criticises the social mechanisms of power at work on the young submarine operators.

In an early scene, a senior officer upbraids the four young officers of Kurosaki's group during a briefing by making a direct attack on their 'presentational selves'.

Senior officer: Aren't you ashamed of yourselves! Listen carefully! Some in your group have sortied two, even three times, and due to engine failure or some such reason, returned to port. Generally, when officers sortie, one or two come shamefully back. It is because these officers have the wrong attitude. They tie their *hachimaki* (headband) on before they leave, waving their swords above their heads as the whole base comes out to send them off. They leave full of pride and then they fail. When they reach the battle zone, the screw propeller won't rotate or some such ...

Later, Kurosaki and his friends discuss the effect this speech has on them, making them determined not to return, come what may.

Kakida: That was a really harsh thing to say, but I expect that is what they truly think. This time I am definitely going to die. I don't care what goes wrong with the sub. I won't be called a coward.
Kurosaki: (*Framing the discussion within the terms of the 1960s generational conflict.*) Can those fellows who have never been themselves and who just keep harping on and on about the same thing, can they understand how one of us feels?
Kakida: At any rate, this time let's do our best and not give them the opportunity to say anything. Kurosaki, I know

they affect even you. We must do our utmost to make this sortie a success.
Kurosaki: But will they understand?

Later in the film, when it becomes evident that one of the minisubmarines has a fault, the two remaining officers, Kurosaki and Imanishi, beg the captain to let them go together in the same minisubmarine. Their motivation is therefore expressed in terms of shame and fear of exposure to the censuring panoptic gaze of the senior officers and is totally unconnected with patriotism and the war effort. The film thus deflects their motivation away from love of country and on to the pressures placed on them by the *seken*. However, unlike *Kumo nagaruru hateni* and *Ningen gyorai kaiten*, in this film, the censuring panoptic gaze emanates, not from within the young officers' immediate group, but from the wider *seken*, the senior officers back in Japan. In this way, the film uses the *kamikaze* experience as an historical mise-en-scène in which to play out the generational conflict inherent in the *taiyōzoku* subcultural discourse.

All the films of the *kamikaze* genre discussed so far attempt to give meaning to, and, in the case of *Ningen gyorai shutsugeki su*, to justify the deaths of the young officers of the Special Attack Forces. The only film still readily available in the public domain that negates this hegemonic image of the officers as 'tragic heroes' is the 1968 black comedy *Nikudan (Human Bullet)*[17] directed by Okamoto Kihachi (1924-). *Nikudan* is an iconoclastic film exaggerating and distorting the generic conventions of the earlier *kamikaze* films, turning them into farce. The film distances the spectator emotionally from the hero who is constructed as a stereotypical representation of the iconography that has become associated with the image of the *kamikaze*. The film encourages the spectator towards a critical response to this image and the role of the *kamikaze* and their significance in the late 1960s.

In *Nikudan*, the hero's character is constructed to connote all the qualities, such as youth, sexual innocence and purity of spirit (*makoto*) that the iconography of the actual *kamikaze* officers has come to represent. His age is determined in the first few shots as the narrator, using statistics on age and longevity, subtracts the average age of death for Japanese males in 1945 from that for 1968 and arrives at the hero's age, 21.6 years old. His youthfulness is further established by his friendship with a young boy of about ten and his relationship with the young high school girl in her sailor suit with whom he falls in love while helping her with her algebra. His sexual innocence, commented on by the old man and the *kenpeitai* officer who both immediately recognise his virgin status, is also brought out in his horror of the women who work in the prostitute quarter. Finally, his purity of spirit is depicted in his determination to carry out his mission despite his awareness of Japan's impending defeat. However, through the exaggeration of generic conventions established in the earlier films, *Nikudan* succeeds in parodying these qualities, turning the hero's experiences into a black comedy. His status as a representative *nikudan* is symbolised through his anonymity - throughout the film he is simply referred to by the narrator as *aitsu* (that fellow). The actor who plays the part of Aitsu is Terada Minori (1942-). When asked by the officer for his name and rank, he answers that his name is *Sakura*, which is a play on the phonetic appropriation of the Chinese characters with which his name is written. *Sakura* also means 'cherry blossoms' which became a metaphor for the Special Attack Forces.

Until the final scene, the narrative is solely motivated by the hero's recounting of events told in flashbacks and voice-over. In the early scenes, the flashbacks are sequentially linked through the use of continuity devices in a backward flow as Aitsu remembers his initial training and his inclusion in the Special Attack Forces. Here the narrative moves forward ultimately returning full circle to 1968, the year in which the narrator calculates Aitsu's age in the second scene in the film. Through the narrative, the film constructs a complex series of comparisons. In the early sequences, the status of the new recruits who are brutalised and treated like animals is contrasted with the god-like status of the officers of the Special Attack Forces. Later, a distinction is made between prostitutes and 'pure' women. This comparison is further extended to connect the hero's first sexual encounter to his impending death. And finally, a contrast is drawn between the young *kamikaze* officers and the hedonistic *taiyōzoku* youth of the 1960s.

The physical appearance of the hero, Aitsu, is similarly iconoclastic. He is a frail bespectacled figure. During his initial training, told in flashback and voice-over, he is naked except for his glasses and soldier's cap[18] (see figure 15). He is representative of the civilians conscripted in the last desperate stages of the war to defend the home islands. His nakedness connotes vulnerability (his

Figures 15: *Nikudan* 1968

own as well as Japan's) and is contrasted with wartime images of the young brothers who swim naked except for a white loin cloth in the sea in *Hawai Marē okikaisen* and with the heroic nakedness of his 1953 predecessor, Otaki, in *Kumo nagaruru hateni* who purifies himself by swimming naked in the lake on the night before his death.

In the early scenes, the exaggerated use of extreme close-ups visually parodies such scenes as the penultimate one in *Kumo nagaruru hateni* discussed above. By subverting the homosocial sub-text in these scenes, *Nikudan* negates this aspect of male bonding and pre-empts the sense of isolation felt in the second half of the film set on a beach where Aitsu makes his preparations for his solitary attack during an anticipated invasion by the United States army. In reality, the sacrifice of the officers of the Special Attack Forces was a solitary affair. Whether in planes, in minisubmarines (*kaiten*) or in speedboats (*renrakutei*), they all went to their deaths alone. Therefore, despite the surrealistic nature of the scenes in *Nikudan*, the feeling evoked of the hero's solitary existence is perhaps closer to the actual reality of the young officers' experiences than the earlier films which gave priority to the group nature of their sacrifice in order to orientate the spectator towards the future. To fully appreciate the iconoclastic nature of the film, it is worth examining one scene occurring early in *Nikudan* between Aitsu and the senior officer.

The camera cuts from an outdoor scene in which the officer is beating the hero to a flashback of an interior scene of the storehouse in which Aitsu is also being beaten. The beating provides the continuity.

1. Medium close-up. The officer beats Aitsu across the face from left to right.
   Officer: Stand up! [264 frames]
2. Cut to close-up of a rat. [34 frames]
3. Long low-angle shot of Aitsu, having regained his feet and standing to attention.
   Officer: Name and rank? [72 frames]
4. Long high-angle shot from opposite end of the room.
   Aitsu: Army Engineers Special Military Cadet, Third Company, Third Platoon, Third Division, Sakura, sir. [264 frames]
5. Cut to a close-up from behind Aitsu
   Officer: Cadet Sakura, give me the reason why four bags of dried noodles were stolen from the food stores while you were on night duty? [108 frames]
6. Reverse-cut, extreme close-up of Aitsu's bruised and swollen face.
   Aitsu: Three bags, sir. [24 frames]
7. Extreme close-up reverse-cut of officer's face.
   Officer: The reason? [48 frames]
8. Cut to extreme close-up of the officer's boots as he steps on the tail of a rat. [24 frames]
9. Medium close-up shot of Aitsu.
   Aitsu: To stay my hunger, sir. [48 frames]
10. Extreme close-up reaction shot of officer's face.
    Officer: What, you were hungry? At Guadalcanal, it was rats. [60 frames]
11. Extreme close-up of officer's boots as the rat bites at his heel trying to free its tail. [48 frames]
12. Extreme close-up of officer's face.
    Officer: Give me a more detailed explanation. [48 frames]
13. Medium close-up shot of Aitsu.
    Aitsu: There are many reasons, sir.
    Officer: I don't care. The reasons!
    Aitsu: The cadets of our section have become cows, sir. [240 frames]
14. Close-up reaction shot of officer.
    Officer: A cow? With horns and that moos? [168 frames]

15. Medium close-up shot.
    Aitsu: Yes, that's right. The cadets and all the lower ranks have started to chew the cud, sir.
    Officer: Just a minute! What do you mean, 'chew the cud'? [216 frames]
16. Medium close-up shot of Aitsu.
    Aitsu: Chewing the cud is when one regurgitates food already swallowed and chews it again and then swallows. That is chewing the cud, sir. Animals such as cows do it. [288 frames]
17. Cartoon drawing of a cow. [48 frames]
18. Cut to long-shot of soldiers cleaning their boots and chewing the cud. [24 frames]
19. Medium close-up shot of a line of soldiers at the latrines, chewing the cud. [24 frames]
20. Medium close-up shot of a line of soldiers doing their washing and chewing the cud. [24 frames]
21. Medium close-up shot of a line of soldiers mending their clothes and chewing the cud. [24 frames]
22. Medium close-up shot of the officer.
    Officer: Just a minute! Is that technically possible? [72 frames]
23. Close-up of Aitsu's face.
    Aitsu: With practice, it is possible, sir. [72 frames]
24. Close-up reverse-cut shot of officer's face.
    Officer: I don't believe it. Demonstrate! [96 frames]
25. Close-up of Aitsu's face.
    Aitsu: Demonstrate, sir? [24 frames]
26. Close-up of officer.
    Officer: Yes, demonstrate!
    Aitsu turns to the left, bringing his profile into an extreme close-up to the right of the frame as he begins to chew the cud. This profile shot emphasises the movement of his cheeks and throat. [576 frames]
27. Medium close-up shot. Aitsu turns towards the officer.
    Aitsu: I have chewed the cud, sir. [48 frames]
28. Extreme close-up shot of officer.
    Officer: I suddenly feel quite ill. Are you human? [144 frames]
29. Extreme close-up of Aitsu.

Aitsu: No, a cow; I would like to return to being a human again. Permission to express an opinion, sir. [264 frames]

30. Medium close-up high-angle shot.
Officer: You want permission to express an opinion? I'll listen. [120 frames]

31. Medium close-up low-angle reverse-cut shot.
Aitsu: Cadet Sakura will state his opinion. All the cadets at this moment are hungry. Two thirds of the cadets are malnourished. Out of them, one third are confined to barracks, one third are resting from drill and one third are in the infirmary. In relation to myself, before I joined the army, I was 135lbs; after six months, I have reduced to 98 lbs. [552 frames]

32. Close-up of officer's face.
Officer: That's because your method of chewing is ineffective, it has nothing to do with army rations. Army rations are more than adequate. The other day the company commander addressed the cadets on that very subject. [336 frames]

33. Medium close-up of company commander sitting at a dinner table.
Company commander: Chew each mouthful forty-eight times. If you chew each mouthful forty-eight times, the food in front of you will turn into blood and muscle. I shall demonstrate. Begin eating! [576 frames]

34. Close-up shot of the back of the officer's head and shoulders. Aitsu's face is partially visible over the officer's right shoulder.
Aitsu: But two thirds of the cadets are malnourished. Out of them, one third are confined to barracks, one third are resting from drill and one third are in the infirmary. [144 frames]

35. Extreme close-up of officer's eyes and mouth.
Officer: Shut up! What on earth are you trying to say? [72 frames]

36. Reverse-cut extreme close-up shot of Aitsu's eyes and mouth.
Aitsu: The food storehouse. [48 frames]

37. Reverse-cut extreme close-up shot of the officer's eyes and mouth.
Officer: What about the storehouse? [24 frames]

38. Reverse-cut close-up of Aitsu's eyes and mouth.
Aitsu: The storehouse is full of food. [24 frames]

39. Long shot high-angle looking down on the two figures standing amid the boxes and bags of food.
    Officer: This food is for the men who will fight the final battle.
    Aitsu: The cadets won't look after the food until the final battle. [168 frames]
40. Medium long shot.
    Officer: What! Do you remember New Guinea, Attu, Lady Island, Guam and Saipan? ...
    Aitsu: Iwojima, Okinawa, I remember them all. All lost. [312 frames]
41. Medium close-up shot.
    Officer: What are you trying to say? What are you trying to say? What are you trying to say? [96 frames]
42. Close-up of a gramophone, the needle has become stuck, a hand nudges it on. [96 frames]
43. Extreme close-up of the officer's eyes and mouth.
    Officer: What are you trying to say? [72 frames]
44. Close-up of Aitsu's face.
    Aitsu: I am hungry.
    The officer turns to the left of the frame, his profile comes into an extreme close-up position, the camera pans left keeping him in the frame as he walks away from where *Aitsu* is standing.
    Officer: No, this is not about your stomach! Iwojima, Okinawa, what do you think about them? I want to hear. Iwojima, Okinawa ...
    The officer turns into the camera in an extreme close-up. The camera pans right keeping him in the frame as he walks back to where Aitsu is standing. **Aitsu:** Next it will be Kyūshū, and if Kyūshū falls, then we will all be lost. [432 frames]
45. Medium close-up shot. The officer is standing opposite Aitsu.
    Officer: If you think like that, does that mean you will run away?
46. Extreme close-up, the back of the officer's head in the left foreground. Aitsu's face is visible on the right of frame over the officer's shoulder.
    Aitsu: No, I won't run away. There is nothing for it but to fight. Japan is an island nation. I'll fight, but I can't do battle on an empty stomach [288 frames]

47. Reverse extreme close-up shot of the officer's face.
    Officer: Yes, you can. If you have the right spirit (*seishin*), you can endure hardships and privation ...

In both *Kumo nagaruru hateni* and *Ningen gyorai kaiten*, dialogue is subordinate to the images. This is evident in the climactic penultimate scene described earlier. However, in *Nikudan*, this is reversed; the images are rhythmically matched to give priority to the dialogue. This occurs throughout the film – the extensive use of the narrator whose voice-over operates not as the 'voice-of-god', but as soliloquy, conveying the 'interiority' of Aitsu's subjective thoughts. In *Kumo nagaruru hateni* and *Ningen gyorai kaiten*, it is the images, the close-ups of facial expressions, where the thoughts and emotions of the characters are manifested. In the example scene from *Nikudan* discussed above, the editing pace of reaction shots and reverse-cut shots are subordinated to the internal rhythm of the dialogue. As a result, in this sequence, the editing rhythm is manipulated to climax at two points. The first can be seen in shots 6 to 9 (see figure 16, shots 6 and 7); and the second from shots 36 to 39. As a result, the preceding and intervening shots have no fixed pattern of length, being determined by the length of each line of dialogue. It is only in shots 13, 15 and 44 where the two characters exchange dialogue within one shot. However, once the initial construction of the scene has been established in these early and intermediate shots, Okamoto builds up the rhythmic acceleration of the sequence to correspond with, and thus underline, the central points of the dialogue – in shots 6 to 9, this is the fact that Aitsu is hungry; and in shots 36 to 39, that there is plenty of food available in the storehouse. Visually, the camera marks these

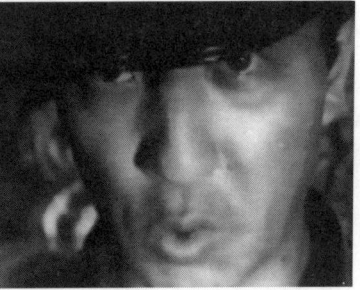

Figure 16: *Nikudan* 1968

THE *KAMIKAZE* FILM AND THE POLITICS OF THE COLLECTIVE

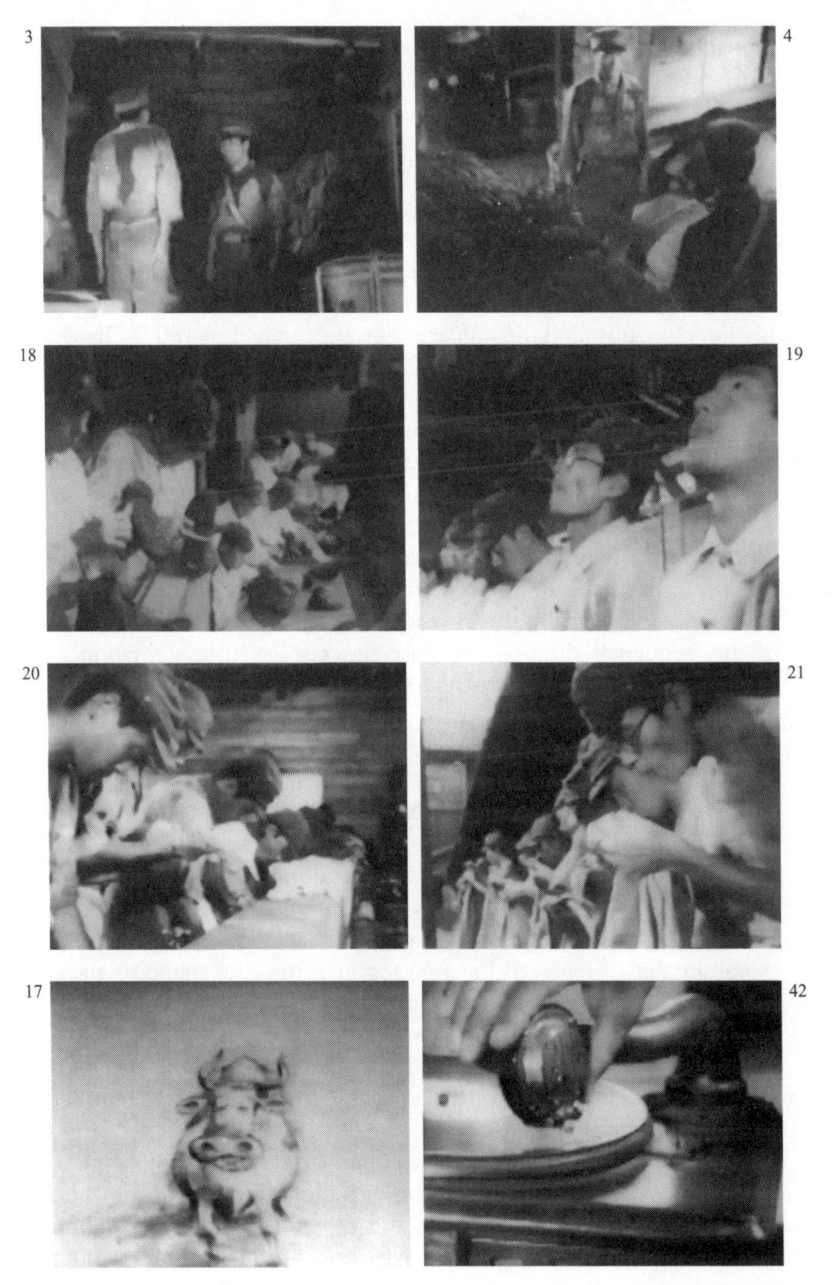

Figure 16: *continued*

climactic points, as the description shows, by moving into extreme close-ups. After each of these two climaxes, the shot length increases, breaking the acceleration and providing a pause until the next point of confrontation between Aitsu and the officer.

In this montage sequence, all the cinematic conventions of reverse-cut, point-of- view and direct eye-line matches are observed creating a narrative unity and potential points of empathy for the spectator. However, the absurdity of the dialogue emphasised through the editing technique; the images of Aitsu's bruised and battered face, held in close-ups; and the officer's ugly appearance played by Tanaka Kunie (1932-); all negate a deep empathetic response, turning the sequence into farce. It is these absurdities that the scene highlights through the structured opposition of the cinematic conventions observed and the subject matter of the scene. Any homosocial component, as in the penultimate scene in *Kumo nagaruru hateni*, is further masked by the confrontational nature of the exchange. This aspect is also reinforced by the editing style which takes its initial rhythm from the beating which linked this montage sequence to the preceding one. Visually, this rhythm is accentuated in the early shots of this sequence through the mise-en-scène by the alternation of diagonal lines of action constructed in the frame. In shot 1, Aitsu is beaten from left to right, with the officer in medium close-up foregrounded left, this is then reversed and the officer is foregrounded right. A similar framing pattern is established in shots 3 and 4 (see figure 16, shots 3 and 4), only this time the high and low camera angles support the hierarchical positions of subordination and domination. In shots 6 and 7, a diagonal eye-line match is maintained. And finally, in shots 18, 19, 20 and 21 (see figure 16, shots 18, 19, 20 and 21), diagonal lines of soldiers are depicted 'chewing the cud'. The establishment of diagonal lines of action across the frame in these shots and the other Brechtian alienating devices employed, such as the insertion of cartoon drawings (see figure 16, shot 17) and the gramophone (see figure 16, shot 42) all serve to remind the spectator of the constructed nature of the images, further distancing him/her from an emotional response.

The construction of ideal masculine types (i.e. Muhō Matsu, Otaki, Kurosaki) in Japanese popular film narratives is, in the majority of cases, predicated on the rejection and denial of the feminine aspects of male nature. Symbolically, this is built into the narrative through the negation of women completely as in the wartime productions *Chichi ariki* and *Muhō Matsu no isshō*, or, as in the post-war cinema, in the rejection of lovers as seen in *Kumo nagaruru hateni* and *Ningen gyorai kaiten*. However, there is an inescapable conflict built into this definition of masculinity. As masculine power is symbolised through possession of the phallus, it is socially expressed through the sexual act and procreation, both of which require contact with a female. Therefore, there is always a contradiction inherent in the construction of these ideal characters. One of the devices used by films produced during the war period to mask this contradiction was the construction of virgin fathers, later to be reintroduced in popular cinema in the yakuza genre in the 1960s with the creation of a hyper-masculine image around such actors as Takakura Ken, and in the hedonistic *taiyōzoku* male anti-hero who uses his young heroines as sex-objects to be cast aside after his desire has been sated. This usually results in the death of the heroine at the end of the film. However, in the early post-war films which construct the image of the young officers of the Special Attack Forces as heroic, this contradiction becomes problematic. One device used to overcome this was, as discussed above, the creation of a feminine alter ego to complement the ideal masculine hero. A further device was to reassert a distinction between women as 'pure' (i.e. mothers, and younger sisters as future mothers) and women who are simply used for the satisfaction of male desire. As Mishima, in his exposition of the *Hagakure* explains:

> Until the war, youths were able to distinguish neatly between romantic love and sexual desire, and they lived quite reasonably with both. When they entered the university, their upper-classmen took them to brothels and taught them how to satisfy their desire, but they dared not lay a hand on the women they truly loved. (Mishima 1977:30)[19]

It is this ability to 'distinguish neatly between romantic love and sexual desire' that these post-war films reintroduced as one of the characteristics of the ideal male. This masked the contradictions between the need to reject the feminine and the social need to reassert and reaffirm male phallic power through the sexual act. Romantic love if undeclared is hidden from social view; sexual desire is satisfied through women who are cast aside after use and therefore are not a threat.

This distinction is represented by the female characters appearing in these films. In both *Kumo nagaruru hateni* and

Ningen gyorai kaiten, the young officers spend their final night carousing at the local geisha house cum brothel. These women in the narrative are then set up in opposition to the women who are the love interest of the two characters played by Kimura Isao. In *Ningen gyorai kaiten*, at the farewell party, Tamai is offered the services of a geisha whom he rejects, saying, 'I thought a woman would be more beautiful,' thus echoing Otaki's description of his young sister in *Kumo nagaruru hateni*. Later, in *Ningen gyorai kaiten*, Tamai's true love interest comes to the geisha house and is brought into direct contrast with the prostitutes. As she runs from room to room searching for Tamai, the horror of what she sees is registered in her facial expression increasing this distinction. When she finally finds Tamai, the two spend the night together on the beach. In both these early films, the beach is a motif for a 'pure' love and is contrasted with the drunken atmosphere of the geisha house. On the following day, as Tamai's submarine leaves, Sachiko watches from the beach before walking into the sea and drowning herself, thereby proving her virtue by following her lover into death.

Nikudan constructs a similar distinction between the female characters in order to give Aitsu the same masculine attribute of being able to 'distinguish neatly between romantic love and sexual desire'. However, by parodying this generic convention, *Nikudan* turns Aitsu's first sexual encounters into a masculine rite of passage reflecting the adolescent male's often unsuccessful and therefore painful first experimentation with a woman. 'For the young beginner, this crucial, inescapable rite of manhood can often seem ... bizarre, distasteful, and threatening ...' (Miles 1992:106–107). The solitariness of Aitsu's first sexual encounter is then linked to the solitariness of his impending death through the editing technique and the soundtrack.

Before proceeding to the prostitute district on his final leave, Aitsu first goes to a secondhand bookshop where he meets the old man (Ryū Chishū) who lost both his arms in an air-raid. As a result of these injuries, the old man is totally dependent on the help of others, even to urinate. Aitsu obliges him by helping him in the latrine. During the course of the conversation, the old man, recognising Aitsu's virgin status, proceeds to give him advice on the great importance attached to a man's first experience.

Old man: ... the first time is most important, you can climb to heaven or you can descend to hell. ... If it goes wrong, the shock can be terrible. You feel desolate (*sakubaku*). Yes, that's right, desolate. At any rate, you need an angelic-like girl. You need a woman like the Goddess of Mercy (*Kannon*).

The irony of this situation – an old man with no arms, symbolically castrated by the war, giving Aitsu advice on matters sexual – is further underlined when Aitsu comments on the splendid nature of the old man's appendage (*rippana mon desu ne*).

In the scene set in the prostitute quarter, Okamoto again uses the rhythm of the editing to match the soundtrack. However, unlike the earlier montage sequence described above, in this sequence, the camera adopts a purely subjective position – Aitsu's point of view. After the establishing shots of the bustling street, the camera moves into medium close-up shots of Aitsu as he takes shelter from the rain under an awning. Here, the editing rhythm begins to accelerate. This occurs after his escape from a prostitute who tries to pull him in through an open window under which he had taken shelter. Each time he stops to shelter, the face of an unattractive prostitute, framed within an open window, is held in close-up. The series of point-of-view shots that follow increases in speed and reflects Aitsu's exclamations of 'witches!' (*obake*) as he flees from one point to the next (see figures 17, 18 and 19). The close-up shots of the faces of the prostitutes are punctuated with medium close-up shots of another prostitute with a mortar and pestle grinding grain between her legs (see figure 20). The soundtrack emphasises this rhythmic grinding over which farmyard animal noises are superimposed to match the close-ups of the prostitutes. This sequence concludes with Aitsu's summation, 'They are all witches!', as he walks away. Eventually, when he does find a safe place to shelter, he sees a young girl in a sailor suit through an open window and he exclaims 'A Goddess of Mercy!' (*Kannon sama da*!). He offers to help her with her algebra homework. At this moment, the length of the shots increases allowing for a pause until the next climactic sequence inside a brothel. Mistaking the young girl for a prostitute, he enters the house only to find out, when it is too late and he is confronted with an old hag of a prostitute, that the girl is in fact the 'madam'. Her parents were both killed in a firebomb attack so she has taken over the running of the house. The camera reflects his horror at the old prostitute through a freeze-frame. As she takes off her gown, the camera freezes on her bare knees – symbolically

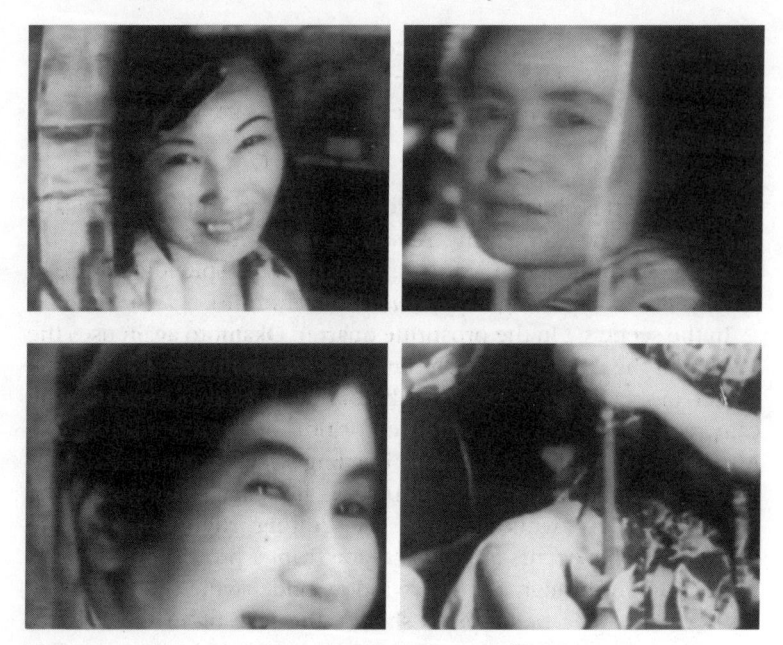

Figure 17–20: *Nikudan* 1968

connoting female genitalia and the shock the inexperienced male receives when first confronted with the naked female form (see figure 21). There follows a subjective shot taken with a hand-held camera in a backward tilt as the prostitute descends on top of Aitsu. This then cuts to a side-on close-up of Aitsu's head as he is smothered by a large breast (see figure 22). The scene then cuts to outside and shows Aitsu leaving the house. Again the camera freezes as the narrator says in voice-over, 'Desolate! Completely desolate! If you drew a picture of desolation, this is how it would turn out!'

This sequence contrasts sharply with the scenes in the geisha house of the earlier *kamikaze* films where the geisha are given a grace and elegance despite being contrasted with the 'pure' woman. On the other hand, this scene in *Nikudan* is constructed as a parody which makes explicit the sense of 'desolation' often felt by young men after their first sexual encounter with a woman. The fact that the young girl who, in the film represents the 'pure' woman, is a brothel madam further distorts these conventions. The film holds the war responsible for the distortion of 'normal' social

THE *KAMIKAZE* FILM AND THE POLITICS OF THE COLLECTIVE

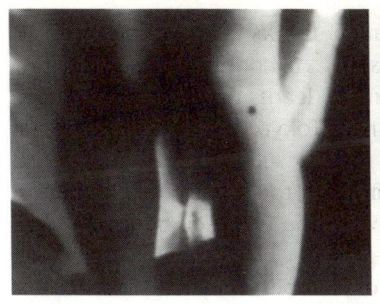

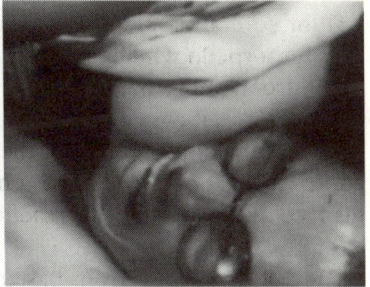

Figure 21–22: *Nikudan* 1968

roles and conventions. This is also reflected by the shot as Aitsu enters the brothel and is given an umbrella to use inside to shelter from the drips that fall through the roof. Cinematically, the freeze-frames held on the prostitute's knees and on Aitsu as he leaves the house are linked to two earlier freeze-frames of the atomic bomb blasts on Hiroshima and Nagasaki. The camera thus visually links these events parodying films produced during the war, such as *Kaigun* which conflated the public and the private.

Aitsu's first successful sexual encounter with the young girl is similarly constructed cinematically to make the connection between orgasm and death. Meeting her again, they both take cover from the rain in an air-raid dugout. They take their clothes off to dry and shelter under blankets. During the conversation, it becomes apparent that her elder brother also went to his death as a *kamikaze*. This directs the conversation to Aitsu's own future role. He becomes affected by the thunder and lightning and, taking up an old wooden crate, he runs naked from the dugout. In a mock death charge, he flings himself under a broken-down truck as the thunder and lightning on the soundtrack intensifies. The young girl imitates his performance, and the soundtrack climaxes as she flings herself under the truck. Later, when they return to the dugout, they embrace and the sound of thunder climaxes once more, linking the two acts. In this sequence, the motif of the rat, first introduced during Aitsu's conversation with the officer, reappears. Aitsu was born in the year of the rat and the young girl in the year of the rabbit. Rat and Rabbit become their pet names for each other, reintroducing the animal/god contrast.

In the final scenes of the film after Aitsu has been floating in the sea in a forty-four gallon tin drum attached to a torpedo (see figure

– 113 –

24) for several days, he sees what he thinks is an enemy ship; he fires his torpedo which promptly sinks. He continues alone, floating in his drum, until a barge passes and he learns that the war has been over for several days and that he is in Tokyo Bay. The barge owner offers to tow him to port, but the rope breaks and again Aitsu is set adrift. At this point, the camera moves into an extreme close-up of his face as he sums up his reaction to the war (see figure 23).

> He said the war is over. Bastards! Rabbit! They say Japan has been defeated. Open brackets XY square plus 2A close brackets, brackets, brackets, brackets ... That's it ... Rabbit plus Rat equals zero. Rabbit and I are nothing, aprons and old books all equal zero. Everything equals zero ... Japan is a good country, a strong country, it is the first country of the Gods. Rabbit, the fifteenth night of the eighth lunar month ... Fools! Rat was a fool, Rabbit was a fool!

After this monologue, the scene and the soundtrack suddenly change as a title *'Shōwa 43 Natsu'* (Summer of 1968) is superimposed over a long shot of a crowded beach. In a series of shots rhythmically matched to a jaunty soundtrack, the camera moves into medium shots of bathers and then into a rapid succession of medium and close-up shots of people playing in the surf. The camera then picks up on a motor boat and water skier. The skier falls off and the motor boat, held in a long shot, circles a floating tin drum before speeding off. The music then reverts to Aitsu's theme tune as the camera gradually moves in towards the tin drum, cutting to a series of close-ups inside the drum of Aitsu's skeleton, his mouth wide open as his echoed voice-over yells out,

Figure 23–24: *Nikudan* 1968

'Rabbit, we were fools, we were all fools!' The camera then freezes on a close-up of the skeleton's head over which the credits are superimposed.

This last scene brings the film full circle back to the present (1968) connecting up all the motifs that had developed through the film – statistics, animals, algebra as the points of common interest that brought Aitsu and the young girl together. Finally, the visuals contrast the affluent lifestyle of the 1960s youth with Aitsu's frail skeleton. The film thus makes the powerful statement, as Aitsu himself recognises in his final monologue, that the war and the sacrifices the Japanese military institutions called upon young men to make were all in vain.

The two mainstream 1950s *kamikaze* films *Kumo nagaruru hateni* and *Ningen gyorai kaiten* while, at one level attempting to distance their heroes from overt wartime propaganda, at another level, stay within a filmic discourse of group relations established in the late 1930s war film by the director Tasaka Tomotaka. The use of close-up reverse- cut reaction shot sequences constitutes the visual realisation of the loyalty motif evident in *Chūshingura*. In Tasaka's wartime productions, this motif was extended to incorporate loyalty as *sen'yūai* (or comradely love), as the male group formed a microcosm of the *kokutai*, the officers representing the patriarchal authority and concern of the Emperor. The two post-war films break this connection through the dialogue which questions wartime slogans and propaganda while, nevertheless, maintaining the group ethos. Therefore, in both these early post-occupation films, the allegorical meaning of death as sacrifice is distanced from patriotism, becoming instead part of a rite of passage whereby the young male reaches maturation by accepting his death as point of entry into the adult male collective. This rite of passage has symbolic meaning beyond the *kamikaze*, as for example, in contemporary society it is not unlike that undertaken by blue-collar youths who join *bōsōzoku* gangs (motorcycle and car gangs–speed tribes). As part of their entry into the male group, they are compelled to go through extremely dangerous death-defying manoeuvres on their bikes or in their cars. Similarly, as Kondo pointed out in her ethnographic study of artisans working in a cake factory in Shitamachi, the *totei seido* (apprenticeship system) ensures great hardship. But, for the qualified artisan, the mere fact he survives these hardships defines his sense of himself as an artisan and marks his entry into the brotherhood of artisans.

On the surface, [Kondo's informant] decries the *totei seido*, apprenticeship system, as exploitative. But the condemnation is ambiguous. For an artisan's claim to special powers of endurance and fortitude – and, therefore, a special claim to maturity and toughness – is also heightened thereby. (Kondo 1990:237)

However, to return to the specifics of the *kamikaze* film, the above analysis leads to a further question: why, in Japanese popular discourse, was there a need to distance the meaning attributed to the sacrifice of the young officers away from patriotism? This chapter has in part answered this question by demonstrating how these films orientated the spectator towards the future. In the case of *Kumo nagaruru hateni* and *Ningen gyorai kaiten*, this was done in a positive sense through a reaffirmation of the centrality of the collective in Japanese life and the co-opting of the *kamikaze* image as symbolic of post-war regeneration. Therefore, in order to answer this question from the perspective of the wider discourses of the politics of defeat, it becomes necessary to turn to an analysis of the War Crimes Trial and, in particular, its depiction on film.

All the films discussed in this chapter are extremely complex and reflect the political and ideological confusion following defeat. The problems posed by the desire, on the part of filmmakers, to salvage the *kamikaze* as cultural heroes from the mires of defeat while at the same time projecting an anti-war imperative, led to an often contradictory mix of sub-texts, as for example, in *Ningen gyorai shutsugeki su*. In this film, the meta-narrative is concerned with a justification of the use of 'human bullets'. This is linked to ethical questions in relation to the American atomic bomb attacks on Hiroshima and Nagasaki, while the micro-narrative, formed around Kurosaki and his group, condemns a system of panoptic social relations compelling the young officers to 'volunteer'. The generational conflict depicted in this sub-narrative, although grounded in the *taiyōzoku* sub-culture, also carries wider meanings in terms of social discourses about the war which blamed 'uniformed politicians' for Japan's entry into the war and ultimate defeat; a point that will also be taken up in the following chapter.

The ideological confusion surrounding the reception of these films was taken up in an anonymous article in *Kinejun* in 1953. The author quotes from the reactions of a youth after seeing *Kumo nagaruru hateni*.

The film depicts the pilots of the *kamikaze* Special Attack Forces gathered on the front-line before leaving on their missions. These officers struggle with questions of life, death and love before going to an heroic death. (*Besuto obu Kinema Junpō* 1950-1966:225)

The article goes on to question whether this youth was in fact feeling a sense of 'nostalgia' (*nosutarujia*) for Japan 'as a country of the Gods rather than being conscious of the anti-war elements of the film'. As the above quotation confirms, the 'tragic hero' structure of these films plays on the nostalgia for a past promising male camaraderie and as such it inherently criticises the individualism and materialism of modern society. This critique of contemporary society is a dominant theme carried over into the yakuza genre from the 1960s to the present day.

In contrast, *Nikudan* parodies the 'romanticism' (*romanchikku*) of these early post-occupation films by turning established generic conventions into a black comedy. Satō (1968), in an article addressing the harsh criticism some established Japanese film critics levelled at Okamoto Kihachi for making humorous films about the war, explains that, for the generation of young men represented by Aitsu who were in their early twenties at the end of the war, there was an element of self-scorn (*jichō*). At the outbreak of war, they were small children who grew to political consciousness after the anti-socialist purges of the 1930s. They therefore, had no organised intellectual framework through which opposition to the war could be reasoned. Satō suggests that these youths often went to the war believing the slogans and rhymes, all evident in the film, which were learnt by rote in schools. Ozaki Hideki, a critic who was himself a young conscript during the final stages of the war, made the following comment about Aitsu:

> Aitsu's existence appears comic to the generation who did not know the war. He is an insignificant human being, laughable and pitiful to the extent that he makes one weep. But Aitsu comes close to the truth in his complete emptiness (*kyomenka*).[20] (Ozaki 1968:13)

Satō suggests that these young men, like Aitsu in the film, focused meaning for their impending deaths on the belief that they would save their families and loved ones, and that after defeat, they felt a sense of self-scorn as their world-views collapsed. It is this sense of tragedy combined with self-scorn that Okamoto, himself a twenty-one-year-old army cadet at the end of the war, captures so well. Ozaki describes the feeling of despair from within the context of the film which many Japanese of his generation felt at the end of the war.

> What is the fatherland to Aitsu?
>
> What does death mean to Aitsu?
>
> What is the period of youth (*seishun*) to Aitsu?
>
> He carries these questions around with him; he understands the hopelessness of the situation (*naraku*)[21] in which he finds himself and in which he cannot find the answers to these questions. A hopeless situation, in which on that summer's day, [15 August 1945] all one knew was that one was alive; one fell into a bottomless abyss. (Ozaki 1967:13)

Nikudan, by contrasting this generation with the 1960s *taiyōzoku* generation who as Ozaki points out were ignorant of the significance of the war, and by invoking a sense of tragedy and self-scorn, succeeds in depicting the pointlessness of Aitsu's death. The film thus directly challenges the hegemonic, allegorical meaning of death as sacrifice as Aitsu himself concludes, 'We were fools, we were all fools!

CHAPTER 3

Uniformed Politicians: The Enemy Within

Ningen o, ningen toshite atsukau. Treat human beings as human beings. (Kaji, in *The Human Condition*)

The discourse itself is the actual combination of facts and meanings which gives to it the aspect of a specific structure of meaning that permits us to identify it as a product of one kind of historical consciousness rather than another. (Lévi-Strauss 1962:107)

The analysis of mainstream *kamikaze* films in the previous chapter drew attention to a dominant theme inherent in post-occupation war-retro films, that is, the potential for conflict between the interests of the individual and the needs of the group. These films all questioned the utilitarian nature of group relations which in the war setting required the ultimate sacrifice of the individual, death. However, despite their questioning of wartime ideologies and the politics of the collective, as the above analysis has shown, these mainstream films (unlike *Nikudan*) stayed within a filmic discourse of group relations established in the late 1930s war film.

During the war period, this discourse reproduced pseudo-filial relations within an affiliative structure by conflating the public and the private. This occurred as part of a wider process whereby the *kokutai,* an 'imagined community', came to fill an 'emotional void' left by the disintegration of 'real human communities', accompanying the economic and social transformations of society.[1] The conflation of the public and the private, discussed above in relation to films such as *Chichi ariki* and *Kaigun,* masked a process whereby the shift from filial to affilial relations was accompanied by a lessening of the importance of the individual. The individual is less important than the 'transhuman' institutions to which he or she belongs and whose maintenance and continuance becomes the *raison d'être* of the individuals living and working within a given institution. The individual is affiliated first and foremost to the institution and not to the other individuals comprising its membership. As such, within the family it is possible to rank family members according to their importance to the institution, hence the alienation felt by many secondary sons.[2] Also, since the Tokugawa period up until the early Shōwa period, poor families were able to justify selling their daughters into prostitution to help the family as an institution. Similarly, during the war period the sacrifice of young men in the Special Attack Forces could be rationalised on utilitarian grounds, of the sacrifice of the few for the greater good of the collective – to cite just a few examples.

With defeat and the War Crimes Trials, western concepts of the rights and responsibilities of the individual, independent of the group, were brought into sharp conflict with Japanese utilitarian concepts of the primacy of the group. This chapter, through an analysis of *The Human Condition* which marks a clear delineation between the public and the private worlds of its hero, and films such as *Watashi wa kai ni naritai* (*I Want to be Reborn as a Shellfish*) based on the War Crimes Trials, will demonstrate how this clash of ideologies formed another dominant theme of many post-occupation war-retro films. Finally, this chapter will conclude with a discussion of why, and in what manifestations, the 'tragic hero' mythic form was adopted as the dominant figurative structure in the visual media (both film and television) around which Japanese people could interpret the events of the war.

The nine hours thirty-eight minute epic *Ningen no jōken* (*The Human Condition*) 1959–1961, directed by Kobayashi Masaki (1916–1996), was based on a six-volume best-selling novel of the same title by Gomikawa Junpei (1916–1995). In 1978, he won the *Kikuchi-kan* literary prize for his war novels. The film, the first two parts of which were released in 1959, was listed fifth in the *Kinema Junpō* top ten films for that year and the final part was listed fourth in the year of its release, 1961. The continued popularity of the film is evidenced by its availability in most suburban video rental shops. To coincide with the fiftieth anniversary of the end of World War II it was re-released for sale as part of the *Shōchiku Best Selection* series in the summer of 1994. *The Human Condition* is a complex film which, from an intuitive 'humanitarian' perspective systematically examines and ultimately condemns three of the great 'isms' of the twentieth century – industrialism, militarism and Stalinism – through the conscience of its main character, the 'tragic hero' Kaji, played by Nakadai Tatsuya (1932-). In *The Human Condition*, two narratives are interwoven around Kaji: his public role as a supervisor in a Manchurian mine, then as a soldier in the last stages of the war and finally, as a prisoner in a Soviet labour camp; and his private role as husband and friend. It is this secondary private narrative, in which Kaji is given a psychological depth often denied to wartime heroes, that attempts are made to challenge the pre-war and wartime ideologies of the *kokutai* and the ideal masculine image projected in wartime productions. This is most evident in the depiction of his relationship with his wife, Michiko, played by Aratama Michiyo (1930-). However, as the following analysis will demonstrate, the overall ideological organisation of the 'tragic hero' mythic structure in the end negates this challenge through the primary, public narrative formed around Kaji. Furthermore, the film attempts (and I would suggest, by its continued popularity, succeeds) to explain and heal in part the contradictions that arose in Japanese society as a result of defeat and a foreign-imposed sense of guilt generated by the Tokyo War Crimes Trial (29 April 1946 – 23 December 1948). At the same time, the film reaffirms the role of the individual in relation to the group. Therefore, the following discussion will be divided along these two narrative lines, Kaji's private role in his relationship with Michiko and his public roles as supervisor, soldier and prisoner.

The Post-war Rebirth of Romance

> Narrative is not a machine for producing desire in texts and in spectators. Rather, the systematic and normative dispositions of aesthetic work should be understood as historically specific attempts to shore up ideological representations against the entropic nature of desire. (Rodowick 1991:xi)

As argued in chapter one, the underlying text, inherent in the images of masculinity dominating the cinema of wartime Japan, was a discourse of sexual repression. Reflected in these films was the conflation of private and public, a natural consequence of the panoptic nature of social relations. This fusion affected the way Japanese manhood was perceived. The films depicted masculinity in terms of nature, such as the primitive masculinity of *Muhō Matsu*; in terms of men's interaction with the community, such as the father's role as head of the household, teacher and factory worker in *Chichi ariki*; and the role of sons as inheritors of the family business and as sailors and soldiers in *Rikugun* and *Kaigun*. The conflation of social roles and family relations integrated the private into the political as the family was made to represent the smallest unit of the *kokutai*. As such, the family was primarily a unit of production. Foucault has pointed out that in such situations, sex becomes repressed, 'because it is incompatible with a general and intensive work imperative' (1990:6). Under this system, affection (*aijō*) between family members is converted into duty and obligation.

While Foucault identifies the seventeenth century and the emergence of capitalist relations of production as the period in European history when sexuality became increasingly linked to procreation rather than pleasure, I would suggest that in Japan it was first linked to the emergence of the warrior class between the twelfth century and seventeenth century. This was finally codified into political discourse through the adoption of Confucian principles of primogeniture which were partly a reaction to the increase in population and the scarcity of arable land. The system of primogeniture gives priority to the relationship between parent and child, in particular, mother and first son, thereby shifting the emphasis of conjugal relations on to the procreative. Ivan Morris makes the point that women of the Heian period 'enjoyed a favourable position in love'. This he links to the Fujiwara system of 'marriage politics'.

> [the Heian legal codes] guaranteed her right to inherit and keep property (the custom of unitary male inheritance was not established until much later)... Daughters of the provincial-governor class appear to have been particularly well provided for, usually receiving a share of the inheritance in the form of real property or rights in manorial estates, and being entitled by law to keep their own houses. (Morris 1978:205-206)

It was only as land became scarce with the increase in population and the non-economic viability of continually dividing land up was acknowledged, that there was a gradual move towards a Confucian structure which first excluded women from inheritance and finally secondary sons. This change greatly affected the role of women in the family and by extension the way sex was perceived, gradually shifting the emphasis from pleasure (as depicted by Murasaki Shikibu and Sei Shōnagon) and on to procreation and filial duty.

In the 1890s, when the Japanese government needed a system of values to promote production and help create model citizens, they turned to those values that proved effective since the Tokugawa period, inscribing them into the Rescript on Education and the Rescript for Soldiers and Sailors. This process was intensified during the crisis of the 1930s and was related to the filmic representations of virgin fathers in *Muhō Matsu no isshō* and *Chichi ariki*.

In the films of the war period, women were cast primarily as mothers or alternatively, as in *Aikoku no hana* (*The Flower of Patriotism*) 1942 and *Kaisen no zenya* (*The Night Before the Outbreak of War*) 1943, as heroic women whose love for the hero is sublimated into love of country resulting in selfless heroic actions and even death, as in the latter film. It was only this maternal and sublimated love-patriotism that was acknowledged by the hero. Romantic love (*ren'ai*) was spurned, as the hapless young girl who is infatuated with Makoto in *Kaigun* experiences. Any deviation from these two roles of mother and patriot brought censure from the authorities, as was shown by the harsh criticism the final scene of *Rikugun* received. 'If sex is repressed, that is, condemned to prohibition, non-existence, and silence, then the mere fact that one is speaking about it has the appearance of a deliberate transgression' (Foucault 1990a:6). One of the reasons for the popularity of the reintroduction of romance in films, such as *Mata au hi made* (*Until the Day We Meet Again*) 1950, directed by Imai Tadashi (1912-) and *Kimi no na wa* (*What is Your Name?*) 1953, directed by Ōba Hideo (1910-) in the early post-war period, was related to this sense of transgression; not only a moral, but more importantly a political transgression. Furthermore, certain post-war directors such as Kobayashi Masaki in *The Human Condition*, Ōshima Nagisa in *Senjō no merii kuriisumasu* (*Merry Christmas, Mr Lawrence*) 1983 and Suzuki Seijun in *Kenka erejii* (*Elegy to Violence*) 1966 used romantic love as a vehicle to criticise the pre-war and wartime ideologies of the *kokutai*, making a direct link between wartime excesses of violence and sexual repression.

The first scene in *The Human Condition* juxtaposes visually the two spheres of Kaji's life, the private and the public. In the war situation, these are incompatible and will provide the psychological conflict that motivates the narrative for the following nine hours of the film. Kaji and Michiko are standing in the snow in front of a shop window, behind them an endless column of soldiers is marching past in time to a martial tune. In the centre of the window is a small reproduction statue of Rodin's *The Kiss*[3] (see figure 25). In his mind, Kaji is trying to reconcile his desire for Michiko, established through a series of reverse shots between Kaji and the statue, and a sense that, because of the war, they will have no future as he could be conscripted into the army at any time and, like the soldiers behind him, march off to war. Michiko, who throughout the film represents in Kaji's mind an ideal of humanism (*hyūmanizumu*) by her almost blind, innocent love, asks, while looking at the statue, 'Don't you want me?' Kaji clearly does, but in this instance, his concern for the future is stronger than his desire. Through the iconography of the statue, signifying sexual pleasure, this first scene bases Kaji's and Michiko's love in the physical, thus defying the pre-war and wartime ethos that sought to limit sex to procreation within the institution of marriage for the good of the nation. It similarly challenges the definition of love presented in the *Hagakure* as undeclared and unrequited. Later in the film, when asked by a nurse, 'Who is Michiko, is she your lover or your wife?', Kaji replies that she is both, thus merging the two previously separate and oppositional female roles into one woman.

The film continues this theme of the physical union between a man and a woman through 'structuring absences' as described by Richard Dyer (1993), that is, the film's refusal to equate Kaji's and Michiko's relationship with the wartime institution of marriage and

Figure 25: *Ningen no jōken* 1959-1961

procreation for the good of the household (*ie*).[4] There is no mention of the involvement of either Kaji's or Michiko's families in the wedding, nor is there any hint of the traditional pre-marital negotiations (*miai*); theirs is a simple decision as individuals, divorced from family concerns, to be together. After the scene in which Kaji is told of his transfer to the Manchurian mine, he simply asks Michiko if she will go with him. The scene then cuts to their arrival at the mine, where they are shown kissing and embracing in the back of a truck, thereby denying any sense of the public nature of marriage as a social institution.[5] In addition, as their union is childless, their sexual relationship centres on pleasure rather than procreation. Themes related to the traditional extended family were central to films such as *Hawai Marē okikaisen* (*The War from Hawaii to Malaysia*) 1942. Their 'absence' in *The Human Condition* is clearly structured into the narrative and becomes a transgression.

Throughout the remainder of the film, the relationship between Kaji and Michiko provides the reference point against which all other male-female relationships are measured and found wanting. According to the film, the wartime ideologies distorted men by sublimating a 'natural' sexual desire (as defined by the Kaji and Michiko relationship) on to violence. This then results in the abuse of the weak, whether in the humiliation which leads to the suicide of the soldier, Obara, or in the cynical use of 'comfort women' by the manager of the mine to keep his Chinese labourers docile and compliant. Violence in such circumstances becomes purely functional to obliterate fear of weakness associated with the feminine in the perpetrator. This is obvious in the scene in part three of the film when Michiko visits Kaji at the training camp. The officers are hostile in their attitude to her; she is entering a masculine world systematically designed to deny the feminine. Even so, she is allowed to spend one night with Kaji. In this scene, the film again reasserts the physical nature of their union when Kaji asks Michiko to stand naked in the soft light from the window. This is the last time they meet and it is this naked image of Michiko that Kaji will carry in his mind through the subsequent battle and his wanderings in Manchuria. The next morning during *kendō* practice, he is severely beaten. In the final part of the film a 'comfort woman' who has resorted to sleeping with Russian soldiers explains to Kaji, 'There is no hope of going home is there, or of meeting my husband again. We don't even know how long we can stay alive. It's the same for everyone. Our lives have been wrecked (*mecha mecha*). All that concerns us is eating and keeping our strength up.' Kaji again refuses to give in to this moral decay. Whereas the other members of his group avail themselves of the prostitutes, Kaji prefers to sleep outside alone, clinging to his belief in Michiko.

The Human Condition depicts the disintegration of the ideologies of the *kokutai* which were based on utilitarian panoptic social relations. There was no alternative metaphysical morality against which people could measure their actions since the social mechanisms for control had broken down and, as the 'comfort woman's' speech implies, a feeling of hopelessness pervaded all, hence the emphasis on the epizeuxis '*mecha mecha*' which is onomatopoeic for 'wreck, destruction or mess'. This word is repeated over and over in Kaji's mind in voice-overs as the camera pans through the house where soldiers lie in the embraces of the prostitutes. The picture this scene portrays is Hobbesian in its bleakness; the meaning of life has been reduced to the satisfaction of bodily needs at the lowest level.

Despite the fact that the relationship between Kaji and Michiko is portrayed as liberating and an ideal against which all other male–female relationships are measured and found wanting, the character of Michiko is constructed within a regressive 'masculine point of view'. The few examples of female role differentiation which had crept into some wartime productions, such as *Aikoku no hana*, *Ichiban utsukushii* and *Otome no iru kichi*, disappeared in the war-retro film, as women were re-inscribed into stereotypical roles based on the Confucian precept of 'good wife and wise mother'.[6]

The female characters who provide the love interest of the heroes in *Kumo nagaruru hateni* and *Ningen gyorai kaiten* are similarly contained within the masculine consciousness of the heroes. The flash-forward into the imagination in *Ningen gyorai kaiten* functions to enhance the sense of Tamai's sacrifice. In the early morning before his departure on the mission, Tamai imagines that he and Sachiko are walking barefoot along the beach at Enoshima just ten days after their marriage. In this scene, Sachiko's character is constructed from within Tamai's imagination and is symbolic of the domestic world he must relinquish. After having spent the night with Tamai, Sachiko's suicide redeems her ascribed status as 'good woman' from within the Confucian and *bushidō* precepts that require a wife to remain celibate after the death of her husband. Similarly in *Kumo nagaruru hateni*, Michiko is constructed not as a character in her own right, but as a vehicle through which Fukami can express his inner doubts.

The very nature of the subject matter, - war as an activity of male endeavour - and the structure of these films as first person experiential accounts, ensures that female characters are portrayed from within a masculine consciousness. It is only in rare cases, such as in Imai Tadashi's *Himeyuri no tō*, that female characters are given a voice through which attempts are made to challenge the stereotypical representations of women perpetuated in the more mainstream war-retro films.

As a war film, *The Human Condition* shows not so much a conflict between the Japanese and the enemy, but an internal conflict between the Japanese themselves. There is a clear dichotomy between the 'good' characters, Kaji and his few friends who are opposed to the war, and the 'bad' characters who represent the inhumanity of the system. In earlier Japanese films set in Manchuria the camaraderie (*sen'yūai*) between men was emphasised, such as in *Tsuchi to heitai* and *Gonin no sekkōhei*. *The Human Condition* reverses this trend by giving prominence to Kaji's relationship with Michiko, which is portrayed as the only constant and satisfying relationship in the film. In contrast, Kaji's relationships with men are unsatisfying. In his defiance of authority and in his refusal to accept the status quo, Kaji rejects his place in the social order and so does not accept the personal identity imposed on him by the community; instead, his subjectivity is defined in relation to Michiko and his humanitarian beliefs. As a result, in the public world, he occupies an isolated position midway between the authority of the various institutions with which he comes into contact and the physically weaker men he tries to help. In the first section, he intervenes between the *kenpeitai* (gendarmerie units) and the Chinese labourers; in the second section, between the senior soldiers and the new recruits; and in the final section between the Russian authorities, Japanese collaborators and the exhausted Japanese labourers in the prison camp. It is in this middle ground that reason prevails and it is this middle ground that the film privileges. In each incident, Kaji attempts to negotiate a more liberal humanitarian way of operating within the hegemonic institutions, but, as 'the nail that sticks out', he is beaten for representing a different and more humane masculinity that challenges brutality.

The Individual Versus an Anthropocosmic World-View

In his public life, Kaji follows a moderate conservative colonial policy first framed by such scholars as Nitobe Inazō and Yanaihara Tadao in the early 1900s. These scholars recognised 'that the welfare and happiness of colonized peoples were linked to the nation's reputation as a responsible colonial power' (Myers and Peattie 1984:92). As Nitobe explained:

> Do we govern an unwilling people for their sake or for our own? As to the general unwillingness of any colony... to be governed by a power alien to it, there is little doubt. A colonial government has received no consent from the governed. Nor is there much reason to believe that a colonial power, white or brown, bears the sacrifice simply to better the lot of the people placed in its charge. The history of colonization is the history of national egotism. But even egotism can attain its ends by following *the simple law of human intercourse - 'give and take'. Mutual advantage must be the rule.* (quoted in Myers and Peattie 1984:93) (my emphasis)

However, as Peattie points out, despite this ideal held by various Japanese bureaucrats and scholars, the reality was very different as often 'overbearing officials, callous policemen and rapacious traders' exploited the powerless position of the colonised.

Like these early scholars, Kaji wrote a thesis entitled *Shokuminchiteki rōmu kanri no shomondai* (*Various Problems with the Management of Labour in the Colonies*) in which he tried to balance the two concerns set out by Nitobe above; the needs of Japan for raw materials and increased industrial production, and a concern for the moral implications of colonial policy. He was thus sent by the company to the mine in Manchuria to put theory into practice and, as an individual who wanted to alter the status quo, he immediately fell foul of the group work ethos based on seniority, not merit. Kaji arrives at the mine just in time to participate in a meeting in which the topic of discussion is the sudden fall in the number of Chinese labourers. He suggests improving wages and conditions and altering the organisation of the work group. As Kaji explains to one of the more belligerent foremen at the mine, 'It is stupid to try to compare humans with ore. If you treat people with care, the ore will be mined.' He at once comes into conflict with Okazaki and Furuya, the foremen, who, throughout this first section of the film symbolise the corruption and exploitation of the industrial system. At this meeting, they ridicule Kaji, pointing out that theory and reality are not the same. They express a racist attitude to the Chinese indicative of a colonial ethos that justifies exploitation in the name of civilising backward peoples (an ethos found not only in Japan, but also in Europe and America).

Kaji represents an individualist ethic influenced by the west that views man as a self-motivated agent capable of effecting change.[7] In the mine, in the army and later in the Soviet labour camp, Kaji, as the embodiment of individualism and a sense of humanism, is pitted against a Japanese 'anthropocosmic' world-view upon which the ideologies of the *kokutai* were predicated. This world-view legitimated utilitarian panoptic social relations by linking the 'norm' to the Way and Truth, therefore negating change.

Kaji is thrown into this anthropocosmic world-view defining man in a fixed place in relation to the world and the cosmos. Ooms (1989) has argued that it was in the seventeenth century that Japanese scholars first constructed this world-view placing man in harmony with the universe. Such scholars as Yamazaki Ansai (1618–1682) merged Neo-Confucian teachings and *Shintō* mythology into an innate Confucian ethic that became the ideological mainstay of the Tokugawa hegemony, being re-appropriated by nationalist ideologues such as Kita Ikki (1884–1937) in the 1930s and 1940s.[8] Yamazaki believed that the Truth existed in the world before men and that man's role was that of transmitter and not creator of the Way. 'The Way transcends all ages, was not man-made but Heaven ordained – *tenri no shizen* – and regulated the life of man and the universe' (Ooms 1989:200). Yamazaki's method of extrapolating the Truth was simple; he looked for latent significations in the exegesis of Confucian texts and in the early chapters of the *Nihongi* through native readings (*kun yomi*) of Chinese characters.[9] The exposition of the 'Truth' embedded in these texts led to the emergence of what Ooms has called an 'anthropocosmic' world-view, that is,

> the refusal to recognize separate realms of reality that respond to different laws of formation ... These parallels all point to the political order that is therefore presented as an instance of the cosmic coherence of things. In this mental construct, through 'gulliverization' and 'gigantization', *tench*i (Heaven

and Earth) becomes an intimate substance and man coterminous with the universe ... Not analysis, but identification of similitudes is the explanatory procedure. This procedure decenters man, even if he is *analogum princeps*. He finds himself in the projected unity of the world and cosmos. *This discourse refuses to recognize man as a source of initiative other than for action confirming that general order.* (Ooms 1989:94-95) (original emphasis)

It is Kaji's attempt to challenge this state of affairs through his belief in a morality, an intuitive humanitarian sense of justice as fairness which extends beyond the utilitarian reference point of the 'norm' and which, despite its ideologically implied fixity, is, as the film depicts, unstable and constantly subject to change and redefinition. In each of the three sections of the film, Kaji intervenes in the name of humanism on behalf of the physically weak, that is, people who fail to fulfil the requisite standards of the 'norm'. He challenges the utilitarian explanations of his superiors which are based on the greater good, the needs of Japan and the war effort, demanding instead the rights of the individual. When Kaji insists that Okazaki be brought to trial for the murder of one of the Chinese labourers, the mine manager tells him that, 'If Okazaki is excessive in his use of violence, who is at fault? What is wrong is the fact that I have to fulfil strict orders for the increase in iron ore production.' He goes on to say, 'This is war. When you consider the greater purpose, what is one small mistake?' Kaji similarly endeavours to intercede on behalf of the Chinese when the *kenpeitai* decide to make an example of seven labourers who tried to escape after provocation from Okazaki. He objects to the *kenpeitai's* arbitrary use of power and the officer's refusal to investigate the circumstances. For the *kenpeitai* officer, the Chinese are mere objects upon whom his sergeant can practise *kendō*. In both these instances, either Okazaki or Furuya was the cause of the problem. Earlier, Furuya had deliberately manoeuvered a situation with the Chinese labourers in order to vindicate his own use of despotic violence and defeat Kaji's liberal theories. The struggle here is between two Japanese extremes, the mine manager and his foremen on the one hand, and the humanitarian Kaji on the other; the Chinese are incidental. The *kenpeitai*, the highest source of power, are brought in to mediate between the two extremes. It is, of course, Kaji who suffers and is beaten and tortured by the *kenpeitai*.

This first section of the film tends to put the blame for the cruelty of the labour camp on to the sadistic impulses of individuals thus limiting the challenge to the institutional mechanisms of power which prompted the individuals to comply with the brutality of the regime. As characters, Okazaki, Furuya and the *kenpeitai* officers are representative of 'evil' while Kaji, with whom the audience is encouraged to identify, is representative of 'goodness'. It is through this identification with Kaji that the audience maintains a psychological distance from the brutality of the *kenpeitai* and later, the army. It is the depiction of characters such as the mine manager, struggling to fulfil ever increasing production quotas, that the mechanisms of power are made more explicit; a power which caused individuals to act against their own intuitive humanitarian impulses. As such, unlike Kaji, the mine manager is more representative of the majority in wartime Japan who were forced to compromise in endeavouring to preserve their own positions.

In the second part of the film, after Kaji has been released from the *kenpeitai* guardhouse and been drafted into the army, he again intercedes when one of his fellow recruits commits suicide. Obara, played by Tanaka Kunie, is a frail man whose glasses symbolise his inadequacy. He is constantly the object of the company leader's homophobic violence which in the end, leads to his suicide. In attempting to place the blame for Obara's death elsewhere, the officers accuse his widow, who had been quarrelling with his mother, of not providing a stable home for him. As one officer tells her, 'Non-reliable soldiers come from non-reliable families.' Kaji, who from the onset of their training together had tried to help Obara, demands that the company leader be court-martialled and punished. The officer, like the mine manager before him, can see the 'truth' of Kaji's argument, but is unwilling to become involved. Kaji is, however, allowed to see Obara's widow after the cremation when he tries to explain why Obara took his life. He tells her that she was partly to blame and that he too was at fault and did not help Obara enough during the long route march the day before he died. At this point in the conversation, the officer orders Kaji to leave the room. It is in the following scene when Kaji is being interrogated and beaten by the officers for having spoken so frankly to Obara's wife, that it becomes clear he really places the blame for Obara's death on the army. He regards the army as an institution encouraging the brutalisation of the weak by those who have achieved or surpassed the standards set by the 'norm'; standards which, like masculinity itself, are constantly subject to redefinition. Therefore, there is a need for those who achieve its standards to regularly revalidate their status position, usually through their harsh treatment of the weak.

After his training, Kaji is sent to another camp and is reunited with an old friend who was also opposed to the war, but had accepted conscription and was now an officer. Defying traditions of seniority, he puts Kaji in charge of training a group of new recruits. This gives Kaji another chance to put theory into practice and again he gets caught in the middle ground between the sadistic pleasures of the more senior officers and the new recruits. As he tries to explain, 'I don't think that people become strong through discipline alone.' This attitude leads to his metaphorical rape as a slipper is stuffed into his mouth by one of the senior soldiers. Just as Obara was made to play the courtesan, so too the senior soldiers try to feminise Kaji. He is only saved from continued beatings when his company is sent to the front to dig trenches.

In the final section of the film set in a Soviet labour camp, the conflict motivating the narrative is between the Japanese prisoners themselves rather than between the guards and the prisoners. In one instance, a Soviet guard intervenes on behalf of Terada, a sickly young soldier who is being beaten by the sadistic Japanese group leader, Kirihara. Kaji again mediates on behalf of Terada and the weaker prisoners. This leads to his classification as a 'fascist samurai' (*fashizumu no zamurai*) when he is accused of being obstructionist (*sabotāju suru*) by the Soviet authorities. Their opinion of him is further impaired when they discover that he had worked in the Manchurian mine. This is perhaps the greatest irony of the film and a theme taken up repeatedly in subsequent films about the War Crimes Trials; it was so often the 'good' Japanese like Kaji who became the victims of the immediate post-war period of retribution and revenge while the 'bad' Japanese were in many instances incorporated into the new regime.

The Individual and the Multifarious Relations of Power

Ore ga nihonjin datte koto wa, ore no tsumi ja nai.
Shikashimo, ore no tsumi no ichiban fukai no wa, ore ga nihonjin datte koto nan da.

The fact that I am Japanese is not a crime. Nevertheless, my greatest crime is that I am Japanese. (Kaji, *The Human Condition*)

The central psychological theme motivating the narrative of *The Human Condition* is the individual's relationship to power and his conscience, not as in the *kamikaze* films at the psychological level of the 'imagined community of honour', the *seken*, but at the level of the physical. This power is not only portrayed in the negative terms of institutional disciplines and the hierarchical authority found in the *kenpeita*i, the army and the labour camp with its ability to prohibit and punish, but the more subtle 'manifold forms' of power which Foucault describes in *The History of Sexuality*.

> ... power must be understood in the first instance as a multipicity of force relations immanent in the sphere in which they operate and which constitute their own organization; as the process which, through ceaseless struggles and confrontations, transforms, strengthens, or reverses them; as the support which these force relations find in one another, thus forming a chain or a system, or on the contrary, the disjunctions and contradictions which isolate them one from another; and lastly, as the strategies in which they take effect, whose general design or institutional crystallization is embodied in the state apparatus, in the formulation of the law, in the various social hegemonies. (Foucault 1990a:92-93)

Within the film's narrative, power relations are examined at their lowest point of application in the social hierarchy. The individual within this conception is portrayed as an active element in the articulation of power relations and not the mere passive target acted upon by institutional forms of power. This is self-evident in the panoptic nature of social relations, where the individual is the agent of his/her own subjugation while simultaneously functioning as an agent for the control of other individuals.[10] 'The individual is an effect of power, and at the same time, or precisely to the extent to which it is that effect, it is the element of its articulation. The individual which power has constituted is at the same time its vehicle' (Foucault 1980:98). However, in *The Human Condition*, the individual, here represented by Kaji, does not always consent to his role as a vehicle in the application of power. Within the film's 'anthropocosmic' discourse, despite Kaji's conscience and his active resistance, he becomes a mere pawn in the greater movement of power relations. He is forced through circumstances beyond his control to go against his own intuitive humanitarian principles. He becomes an instrument suppressing the Chinese labourers, kills Russian soldiers and Chinese peasants and near the end of the film, deliberately and brutally murders a Japanese collaborator in the Soviet labour camp. Within the film's view of power relations, individual choice is clearly limited. This raises the question: to what extent can the individual be held responsible for his actions?

In the first part of the film, in the scene where Kaji and Okijima take delivery of the conscript Chinese labourers from the *kenpeitai*, Kaji is forced to take the whip and beat the half-starving Chinese when they attack as a mob and try to reach the grain cart. In their weak condition, the raw grain would have made them ill. This scene follows an earlier one in the mine when he reprimands one of Okazaki's subordinates for beating a labourer with a whip for allegedly being lazy. The juxtaposition of these two scenes visually represents Kaji's dilemma in all his subsequent dealings with the Chinese labourers who, through their refusal to compromise, are set upon a course of apparent self-destruction despite Kaji's good intentions. The ironic twist of this first third of the film is that, after the Chinese attempt unsuccessfully to escape, Kaji is forced to act as the official witness at the resulting execution and thereby to represent the very institutional authority he had fought against.

Prior to this execution scene, Kaji has a long conversation with one of the older Chinese labourers who acts as the voice of Kaji's conscience in this part of the film. He tells Kaji that he (Kaji) is standing at a 'momentous crossroad' in his life and that the fate of the seven prisoners is intimately connected to Kaji's belief in himself as a human being. He goes on, 'If you fail at this moment, no one will believe in you as a human being again, moreover, you won't be able to believe in yourself anymore.' He then proceeds to clearly state Kaji's choices:

> Kaji, you and I have both committed small errors and mistakes, but if we corrected them, they were forgiven. However, if at a decisive moment, we make a mistake, it will become an offence which can never be forgiven. The way I see it, there is a contradiction between your beliefs and your job. Yet you keep hoping that some means to correct this situation will appear. Today, in the coming moment, there are no such means. It goes without saying, this moment is the crossroad. Will you just wear the mask of humanism, while

being an accomplice in these murders, or will you restore the beautiful name of humanity?

Michiko, his wife, representing the constraint to male freedom of action imposed by the family, takes the counter argument, forcing Kaji to face the consequences of his actions if he were to help the seven prisoners. She points out that their life together would be destroyed, which indeed is the actual outcome of the incident. This scene with Michiko concludes with her realisation of what she has done, 'I am probably wrong. Afterwards, you will come to hate me for having stopped you [from helping the prisoners]. You will stop loving me.' In the film, these two scenes have been placed in the reverse order to which they appear in the original novel. The film thus emphasises Kaji's compromise in the execution scene when, after the mishandled and painful death of Takao, he does eventually intervene, helped by the watching Chinese labourers, and saves four of the seven prisoners.

This part of the film depicts not only how Kaji is forced to face this 'crossroad', but also how the Chinese themselves are instrumental in bringing Kaji to this point. After the first escape attempt, Kaji and Okijima, his only friend at the mine, take five representatives of the labourers to dinner to try to explain that they, Kaji and Okijima, are in fact the lesser of two evils. If the Chinese persist in their escape attempts, then the *kenpeitai* will be brought in. Despite the scepticism of the Chinese after the murder of one of their members and the failure of the company to prosecute Okazaki for the deed, Kaji wants the Chinese to trust him again. Hence, after the final escape attempt when the prisoners ask Kaji if they are to be turned over to the *kenpeitai,* Kaji confronts them, 'You didn't believe me in the past, it is probably better not to believe me now. The *kenpeitai* have power. I have none.' In one sense then it becomes clear that the Chinese labourers, through their own actions, have thwarted Kaji's humanitarian efforts to help them and therefore they are partly the cause of their own deaths. This is especially evident in the case of Takao who forms an attachment with one of the prostitutes whom he has promised to marry after the war. Takao sees Kaji as a Japanese and not as an individual and therefore rejects his advice outright thus leading to his own execution by the *kenpeitai*. In this sense, Takao refuses to be helped and is therefore an accomplice in his own eventual execution and, more importantly from the Japanese perspective, he and the other Chinese labourers are in part held accountable in the film for causing Kaji's suffering.

The manifold circulation of power relations is also apparent amongst the Chinese themselves. This is demonstrated in the conversation Takao has with one of the thirty 'comfort women' brought to the camp to service the six hundred labourers. Takao first confronts Kaji with the fact that they are being given the women to keep them compliant and docile. In turn, the prostitute says, 'It is useless to object. It is the same with you labourers.' Takao then asks her if she is not ashamed, she replies that she was not asked, but told to come. Again she makes the point that the labourers were also there against their will. 'Do you enjoy digging ore out of the ground?' The exploitation is cyclical - Chinese women involuntarily become part of the mechanism of control helping to ensure the docility of the labourers and the production of ore for the continuance of the war of which they and their fellow Chinese are but one group of victims. Ironically, both Takao and the prostitute attack Kaji for their predicament despite the fact that he was opposed to conscript labour and the use of 'comfort women'. In this case it is his symbolic representation as a Japanese which is attacked. Hence Kaji's lament, 'The fact that I am Japanese is not a crime. Nevertheless, my greatest crime is that I am Japanese.'

It is in the final third of the film that the ultimate irony is played out. After deserting the battlefield, and after many hardships, Kaji and his small band of deserters surrender to the Russians and are taken to a Soviet labour camp. Terada, a young soldier who under Kaji's influence has undergone a rite of passage in their long journey together, is severely malnourished and becomes ill. In

Figure 26: *Ningen no jōken* 1959-1961

trying to get medicine for him, Kaji is brought before the camp commander who is sitting at a large desk framed in the background by a giant portrait of Stalin (see figure 26). Here, Kaji undergoes a mock war crimes trial. It is in this scene that all the threads of the previous eight hours are brought together in a dramatic climax, as Kaji becomes the victim upon whom all the crimes of the Japanese military industrial system are heaped. Within the first few moments of the interview, it is revealed that Kaji had worked at the Manchurian mine and that, after deserting from the army, he had killed Soviet soldiers and Chinese peasants. The commander states, 'These two reasons alone are sufficient for you to be condemned as a war criminal.' However, from the opening scene with Kaji and Michiko in front of the shop window, the film has been constructed to refute visually the arbitrary nature of this judgement. In this final section of the film, and during Kaji's dazed wanderings in Manchuria, through the use of flashbacks and freeze-frames reflecting Kaji's pained conscience, the spectator is reminded of all the main reasons behind his actions. The killing of the Soviet soldier to enable his group to cross the road is contrasted in flashback with scenes of the battlefield; and later, as he passes through a field where the corpses of Japanese soldiers lie rotting in the sun, he remembers the Chinese executions. The fact that the Soviet camp commander bases his judgement on factual information alone is thus shown to be unjust and is reminiscent of the refusal of the *kenpeitai* officer to investigate the circumstances of the Chinese labourers' attempted escape and their arbitrary condemnation and execution. Kaji makes an impassioned speech accusing the commander of not recognising the brutal behaviour of his own troops towards Japanese refugees. 'You don't acknowledge these things because if you did the authority and ideals of the Soviet army would be weakened. I acknowledge what I have done. I want to show you what you are doing.' In this speech, Kaji is referring to scenes he has witnessed on his journey through Manchuria of the rape of Japanese women by Soviet soldiers and other atrocities. He is also referring to the use of Japanese collaborators as gang leaders in the labour camp, whose brutality has aggravated Terada's weak condition. Kaji's plight in this interview is further intensified as the Japanese translator has mixed feelings towards him and misinterprets what he is saying thus sending the commander into a rage in which he proclaims, 'Germans are the worst, and next comes fascist Japs like you.' At this point the film has come full circle. The

Soviet commander's inability to see Kaji as an individual beneath his symbolic representation as a Japanese is likened to the *kenpeitai* officer's view of the Chinese as an inferior mass to be exploited. The brutality of the Stalinist labour camp, despite 'humanitarian' socialist ideals, is similarly condemned and compared with the Manchurian mine. The three 'isms': industrialism, militarism and Stalinism are exposed as corrupt. Justice does not exist except as a concept of ideology; revenge is its actuality. It becomes obvious that Kaji has accepted this fact when, in the next few scenes, and going against all his former beliefs, he feels compelled deliberately and brutally to kill the collaborator, Kirihara, who was responsible for the death of Terada. After Kaji escapes from the camp, he in turn becomes the object of the revenge of the Chinese peasants, finally dying of exposure and starvation somewhere in the bleak landscape of Manchuria.

The Human Condition depicts situations in which the individual becomes locked into a series of power relations which often force him to act against his own beliefs, therefore, in such situations, all become victims. First, Chinese are exploited by a military industrial system that is in turn shown as causing the suffering of Kaji and Michiko. Therefore, in this situation, Japanese exploit Japanese, Chinese exploit Chinese. In the army, the enemy is incidental, the conflict is the institutionalised internal rivalry between divisions of soldiers. As Kaji states, 'The enemy is not the senior soldiers. It is here, it is the army itself.' In the labour camp, the conflict is between collaborators, who exploit their position, and prisoners of war with a few 'good' Soviet guards, who, taking over Kaji's former role, try to intervene on behalf of the weak. During Kaji's wanderings in Manchuria, he meets Japanese 'comfort women' who find the Soviet soldiers more agreeable than their former Japanese patrons. They are later contrasted with the Japanese refugee who is raped and then discarded and thrown from a moving Soviet army truck. Similarly, Takao's relationship with the Chinese prostitute, a relationship based on love and mutual respect, is contrasted with the rape and murder of a former Japanese 'comfort woman' by Chinese peasants. As such, the film is a critique of war that implicates humanity in general and not the Japanese in particular. The Japanese are victims just as are the Chinese. All are simultaneously shown as victims and perpetrators, locked into situations of power relations in which their actions are predetermined. Within this 'anthropocosmic' world-view in which individuals operate in a fixed position in relation to society, it becomes obvious that in Foucault's words, we all to a certain degree 'fight each other. And there is always within each of us something that fights something else.' (Foucault 1980:208)

Therefore, *The Human Condition* succeeds as a pacifist statement through its depiction of war as being based on manifold relations of power reducing everyone in varying degrees to the levels simultaneously of both victim and perpetrator. Secondly, unlike most Japanese war films, it destroys all illusions of death as either glorious or beautiful. Obara's furtive suicide takes place in the middle of the night in the latrines and is the result of bullying and not in any way an expression of sacrifice or 'purity of spirit' (*makoto*). His act is within the dominant western conception of suicide as a form of escape. His death is further degraded by the fact that his first few attempts fail; it is only when he has decided that he can die at any time so he might as well go on living that the gun goes off by accident, killing him. The execution of the Chinese labourers is treated in the same manner as a negation of beauty. The camera takes Kaji's point of view with the skewed camera angles reflecting his emotional and physical revulsion at the killings (see figures 27 and 28). Similarly, during his wanderings in Manchuria, he is haunted by recurring images of death on the battlefield and by his hand-to-hand killing of the Soviet guard. Kaji looks at his bloodstained hand in horror and wonders how this hand that had caressed Michiko's body could now be stained with the blood of the Soviet soldier. War is condemned because it negates life.

Finally, while in some instances *The Human Condition* does represent war as a male rite of passage, it does so through typically unheroic figures who do not survive the war to pass on their wisdom to their sons as does, for example, the hero in Oliver Stone's *Platoon* (1987). During his time in the army, Kaji is put in charge of a division of new recruits representing the dregs of the remaining male population who have been conscripted in the final desperate stages of the war. It is the experiences of this division on the battlefield that are recounted in the film. Fear is the dominant emotion as they wait, each in his lone bunker, for the Russian tanks, speculating on who will be alive after the battle. During the fighting, the camera adopts their point of view. In one very subjective shot, Kaji just grasps the wounded Terada and pulls him into his bunker as a tank rolls over the top of them. In other shots, a severed arm lies abandoned on the ground; wounded soldiers are

Figure 27–28: *Ningen no jōken* 1959–1961

blown up struggling to take shelter in their bunkers; others are shot while passing ammunition to their comrades; a shell-shocked Japanese soldier attacks Kaji in a moment of madness after the battle; late, during the night, Soviet foot soldiers return to kill off the Japanese wounded; Kaji and the remnants of his division barely escape death by hiding in their bunkers. The only heroic action depicted is that of a soldier running forward with a grenade towards an on-coming tank which ends tragically in his death and the tank's continued advance. Terada, the young soldier who began his military career full of ideas of a glorious death for Emperor and country, comes to see the futility of war under Kaji's tutelage. Tragically, this occurs just before his death.

The 'anthropocosmic' world-view presented in *The Human Condition* automatically acknowledges multifarious power relations at work on the individual. The very concept of a *Rambo*-like hero who takes on a problem and victoriously solves it is alien, if not impossible to conceive within this world-view which disavows change. Hence, the certain death of the hero in the final unravelling of the plot of this drama. The 'technologies' of power at work on the individual are so great that not even the exceptional strength, both physical and moral, of Kaji can withstand them. All that the individual can do is acknowledge his complicity as an unwilling vehicle of these mechanisms and make restitution in death. 'It is not a crime that I am Japanese, but my greatest crime is that I am Japanese.' Within these lines, repeated twice in the film by Kaji, lies the core of the dilemma. Birth, over which the individual has no control, condemned Kaji, despite his own beliefs in a 'humanism' which were at odds with the current social ethos. Thus his life became a contestation between two opposing ethos – the only possible solution is his death as the 'technologies' of power operating upon him are too great for human life to withstand. The ideological conception of an 'anthropocosmic' world-view places man in a predetermined and fixed position in relation to the world, and the cosmos. This conception is based on harmony (*wa*), while the actual multifarious relations of power are based on conflict and control both between and within individuals. It is the workings of these relations of power that *The Human Condition* narrativises in the character of Kaji. Thus the film, despite its strong pacifist stance, presents a bleak world-view in which the individual is powerless to alter the circumstances that govern his/her life, thereby legitimating the position of the majority who in wartime often compromised their ideals for the perceived 'greater good'. It is for this reason, I would suggest, that the film was so popular with early post-war audiences who were confronted not only with defeat, but also with a foreign-imposed sense of guilt that accompanied the War Crimes Trials.[11]

I Want to be Reborn a Shellfish and the War Crimes Trials

Kondo umarekawaru naraba, watashi wa nihonjin ni naritaku wa arimasen. Iya, watashi wa ningen ni naritaku arimasen. Ushi ya uma ni mo umaremasen, ningen ni ijimeraremasu kara. Dōshitemo umarekawaranebanaranai no nara, watashi wa kai ni naritai to omoimasu. Kai naraba umi no fukai iwa ni hebaritsuite nan no shinpai mo arimasen kara. Nani mo shiranai kara, kanashiku mo ureshiku mo naishi, itaku mo kayuku mo arimasen. Atama ga itakunaru koto mo naishi, heitai ni torareru koto mo nai. Sensō mo nai. Tsuma ya kodomo o shinpai suru koto mo naishi, dōshitemo umarekawaranakereba naranai no nara, watashi wa kai ni umareru tsumori desu.

If I am to be reborn, I do not want to come back as a Japanese person. No, I do not want to come back as a human being. I do not want to become a cow or a horse because people bully them. If I have to be reborn, I think I shall become a shellfish. If I become a shellfish, I would live attached to a rock deep in the sea and have nothing to be anxious about. Because I would not know anything, there would be no sadness or happiness, nothing at all to worry about. There would be nothing to make my head ache and I could not be conscripted into the army. There would be no war. I would not have a wife and child to be anxious about. If I have to be reborn, I intend to come back as a shellfish. (Katō 1994:27)

Watashi wa sensō no saikō no sekininsha de aru. Watashi wa sensō hanzainin de wa nai.

I am the person most responsible for the war. I am not a war criminal. (Tōjō Hideki in *Daitōyō Sensō to Kokusai Saiban* 1959)

Sensō no shinjitsu o anata wa shitte imasu ka. Do you know the truth about the war? (From the video cover of *Watashi wa kai ni naritai*.)

In the final third of *The Human Condition*, Kaji undergoes a mock war crimes trial during which, due to superficial evidence, the Soviet camp commander arbitrarily condemns him. In this scene all the complexities of Kaji's life are reduced to limited factual information: (a) he worked in a forced labour mine in Manchuria, and (b) after deserting from the Japanese army he had killed Chinese peasants and Soviet soldiers. All the mitigating circumstances in which we, the spectators, have been immersed during the preceding eight hours (poignant scenes of which are given in flashbacks throughout the final third to remind those who have seen the film in stages) are rejected by the Soviet officers. This scene therefore offers a sharp critique of a system of 'victor's justice' that relied on purely factual evidence to convict 'war criminals' without reference to the social and political specificities of the situation in which the 'crimes' were committed.

Onuma (1993), in his book on the Tokyo War Crimes Trial and war responsibility, argues that the trial raised the question of the individual's moral responsibility of 'conscientious refusal' versus the individual's social duty to follow the directions of his/her government representatives. In the following quote, Onuma explains the principle upon which the War Crimes Trials (both in Nuremberg and Tokyo) were based and which became established in International Law as a result, that is, 'the duty of the individual to disobey illegal orders' (*Ihanna meirei e no fufukujū no kannen*). In his article 'The Tokyo Trial: Between Law and Politics', he states:

> In today's world, all countries, even the most dictatorial, subscribe in principle to democratic forms of government. Thus, on a formal level the leaders of a country derive their authority from the will of the people. Therefore, it is necessary that the people not cooperate in illegal acts in order to establish grounds for arraigning government leaders – and not the people – for such acts. One cannot escape responsiblity for cooperating in wars of aggression or genocide by arguing that one was acting under orders. This means a repudiation of the idea that, as one member of the state, the individual is completely subsumed in the state. (Onuma 1986:50)

This view, first published in the charters for the Nuremberg and Tokyo Trials,[12] totally rejects the Confucian 'anthropocosmic' explanation of the individual's place in society as fixed. In the Japanese version of his article, Onuma continues:

> These concepts of the responsibility of leaders and the concomitant duty of the individual to disobey illegal orders were set forth at the Nuremberg and Tokyo Trials.It is clear that there are many problems with the actual implementation of these concepts. Most people are ordinary citizens and not heroes. To disobey an illegal order is to call for heroic actions, something one cannot unconditionally demand of people. (Onuma 1993:52)

He goes on to explain that, even if an individual acknowledges the need to resist government directives, it is not always wise or prudent to do so. The people connected to one, family and friends often suffer retaliatory repercussions. He therefore suggests that, even though an individual may acknowledge the moral need for resistance, the social (*shakaiteki hakugai*) and legal forces at work on the individual will in the majority of cases compel conformity. It is these social forces or, in Foucault's terminology, 'the technologies of power', that the *kamikaze* films, discussed in the preceding chapter, and *The Human Condition* have narrativised through the 'tragic hero' mythic structure. In this section, the following analysis will be concerned with how this theme was manifested in relation to the depiction of an actual war criminal as portrayed in the TBS remake of the television drama *Watashi wa kai ni naritai* (*I Want to be Reborn a Shellfish*). This drama was first aired in October 1994 and released for sale and rent in early 1995. As such, I feel that its distribution technique, and the fact that the original highly acclaimed 1958 TBS version was remade as a film in 1959, justifies its inclusion into what is primarily a film study.

Watashi wa kai ni naritai is loosely based on the prison writings of Katō Tetsutarō. It is a semi-factual account of Katō's experiences in Sugamo Prison portrayed through the fictional character, Shimizu Toyomatsu (Tokoro Jōji-Georgie), who, according to the plot, was conscripted into the army in the spring of 1944. Acting under orders from a senior officer, he was involved in the execution of two American airmen shot down during a bombing raid over the home islands. After the war, Shimizu was arrested and tried at the Yokohama Military Court along with several officers and found guilty of the wilful execution of the airmen. He was given the death sentence which, after the failure of various appeals, was duly carried out.

The character, Shimizu, represents the antithesis of the heroic 'tragic hero' as depicted in *The Human Condition* by Kaji. Shimizu is representative of the silent majority who, after the war, argued that they had conformed to the requirements of the rule of law despite their intuitive sense that it was perhaps wrong to do so. Katō Tetsutarō (1994), on whose prison writings this drama is loosely based, argues that a distinction should be made between the concepts of the law (*hō*) and morality (*dōtoku*). Here it should be born in mind that *dōtoku*, translated into English as 'morality', is defined in modern Japanese, not in terms of metaphysical commandments, but, as has been argued in the previous chapter, on the utilitarian principle of the social interaction of individuals within the group. Therefore *dōtoku* in the Japanese-Japanese dictionary (*Kōjien* 1991) is defined as:

the criterion by which, in a given society, members of that society mutually make judgements on right and wrong conduct. *It is the complete set of norms to which all give their consent.* Unlike the law, it is not accompanied by external sanctions, but is an internal principle held by the individual. (emphasis mine)

As Katō argues, in social life, the law and concepts of morality are often brought into conflict. This is a point divergent to western political theory in which social principles of justice should ideally form part of the individual's conception of 'right' (Rawls 1973:335). Therefore, Katō's distinction forms part of the nature/culture divide (i.e. nativist Confucian morality/western-influenced concepts of the rule of law). Katō elaborates:

Due to justice and humanity (*giri-ninjō*), a law (*okite*) is often violated and, in order to uphold the law, *giri* and *ninjō* are at times abandoned. This is the cause of many of society's tragedies and is one of society's great contradictions. In so far as we are war criminals we have become the leading characters in this tragedy... The law, namely society's power of coercion, that at times openly manifests as violence, this inescapable coercion and our morals (*moraru*) are in many instances antithetical. When morality and the law came into conflict and we had to make a choice, we chose to violate morality. (Katō 1994:51-52)

It is this philosophical dilemma, the conflict arising between the individual's legal duties and obligations and his moral principles, that the drama *Watashi wa kai ni naritai* narrativises through the 'tragic hero' structure. Kaji, in *The Human Condition*, faced a similar dilemma, however, he attempted to find a middle ground through which a compromise could be reached between morality and the law. Shimizu, in *Watashi wa kai ni naritai*, as the unheroic 'tragic hero', succumbs to the coercive forces operating on him and violates his own principles of morality. As Katō says, 'In so far as we are war criminals, we have become the leading characters in this tragedy.' This drama is in keeping with established docu-drama cinematic conventions for television dramas and films of this genre. There is an inherent contradiction in the claims of these films to 're'-present 'reality' and the cinematic techniques employed which direct the spectator to an empathetic, rather than an analytic response. The extensive use of documentary footage reinforces the drama's claim to reveal the 'truth' about the war. As the question on the video jacket asks the potential spectator, 'Do you know the truth about the war?' This claim to 're'-present the 'reality' of the war is in contrast to Katō's more modest statement opening the section of his book upon which the drama is ostensibly based.

> A citizen, a former war criminal, wrote what follows. I would not like to say that it is based entirely on fact, but I would be distressed if the reader were to think it entirely fiction. In due time, the events described in this volume may throw light on the period. (Katō 1994:13)

Unlike the 1959 film *Daitōyō Sensō to Kokusai Saiban* (*The Pacific War and the International Tribunal*) directed by Komori Kyoshi (1920–) and the 1983 *Tōkyō Saiban* (*The Tokyo Trial*) directed by Kobayashi Masaki, both of which offer varied and at times conflicting positions on the trials, *Watashi wa kai ni naritai* is contained within conventions that appeal purely to the emotions and therefore negates a critical response.

From the opening sequence, Shimizu is cast as an inconsequential figure caught up in world events. The opening shots of Shimizu with his wife and child collecting drift-wood on a beach are merged through super-impositions over the sea of a series of iconic documentary still photographs taken from major wars. The first is taken from the Gulf War of 1990 symbolised by shots of oil-coated sea-birds, followed by scenes from the civil war in Sudan in 1984, the Vietnam War of 1965, represented by a shot of a military helicopter and peasants, the Korean War of 1950 with shots of refugees and soldiers, ending finally in a résumé of the major events of World War II as depicted in newsreel documentary footage. The effect of this opening sequence is threefold: first, it provides, through a chain of signifiers, an historical trajectory taking the spectator back to the events of World War II while linking us to Shimizu as the point of identification. Secondly, it forms part of a post-war discourse referred to colloquially as *gojūppo-hyappo de aru* (six of one, half a dozen of the other) in which it is argued that the countries that sat in judgement on Japan in the Trial did themselves betray the ideals of civilisation for which the Military Tribunals were designed to safeguard. During the war period this included the United States' use of the atomic bombs,[13] the United States and British histories of colonisation and the Soviet Union's disregard for the neutrality pact with Japan of 1941 (Onuma 1993:26). In the post-war period, Onuma (1993:9) argues that popular discourse points to the Soviet Union's violation of human rights in Hungary, Czechoslovakia and Afghanistan; the United States involvement in Vietnam; and the British and French involvements in Egypt. Kobayashi's 1983 documentary compilation film *Tōkyō Saiban* makes a similar statement in the final scenes when a list of wars since 1945 is superimposed over documentary footage of President Truman driving through the streets of Washington to cheers from onlookers after his re-election in 1948. Finally, the opening sequence of *Watashi wa kai ni naritai* places Japanese 'war crimes' within a wider global perspective that relates to the Japanese national concern with their 'presentational selves'. In this way, Shimizu's 'war crime' can be viewed from a perspective relative to other countries that have been guilty of similar offences at different historical periods.

The documentary footage taken from the Shanghai Incident of August 1937 to the Battle of Midway of June 1942 is Japanese archival film; that used after Midway, including newsreel film shot at Guadalcanal in August 1942, is taken from American archival sources. This latter footage is shot from behind American lines and depicts United States' soldiers with flamethrowers and the fields of Japanese dead. This use of American footage and also the subsequent use of American archival material of the United States landing on Iwojima in February 1945 and the Tokyo fire bombings of March 1945, establishes the Japanese, and by implication Shimizu, as victims. Within the narrative *Watashi wa kai ni naritai*, Shimizu is depicted as a victim on two counts: first, he is a victim of the brutality of the army and secondly, as a victim of the Allied Military Courts. In the early scenes after Shimizu's conscription into the army, we see the brutality of the military institution as the sergeant singles out Shimizu for beatings. It is this same sergeant who, in the execution scene, vindictively selects Shimizu as one of the two to carry out the bayoneting of the airmen. This execution scene therefore builds on the victimisation theme, as we, the audience, are aware of the sergeant's dislike of Shimizu. Through filmic devices such as point-of-view shots and the subjective use of slow motion, our sympathies are directed away from the airmen and on to Shimizu. Earlier documentary footage of the fire bombings of Tokyo also helps to anaesthetise spectator feelings for the unconscious airmen. Documentary footage of the Hiroshima and Nagasaki bombs is inserted immediately following the execution scene. The inclusion of these shots at this crucial juncture in Shimizu's narrative draws on established iconic meanings. As Onuma (1993:45) explains, with the dropping of the atomic bombs there was a sense that Japanese war responsibility or 'guilt' was wiped out for it could be argued that the victor nations were just as 'guilty' as were the Japanese (*gojūppo-hyappo*).

In the execution scene, a distinction is drawn between the 'good' Japanese, represented by Shimizu and the other soldiers whose demeanour expresses a reluctance to carry out the order, and Captain Hideka who is symbolic of the young fanatical officers. Captain Hideka tells Shimizu and the other private, 'Those two [referring to the American airmen], they burnt your houses and killed your wives and children.' After a pause, looking them intimidatingly in the eyes, he asks, 'Don't you hate them?' It is at this point that Shimizu is forced to choose between his intuitive moral sense (*ninjō*) and his obligation to obey orders. As Katō (1994) states, 'When morality and the law came into conflict, and we had to make a choice, we chose to violate morality.' When Shimizu hesitates and after being beaten by the sergeant, Captain Hideka asks:

Captain Hideka: Why did you stop? (Pause) What do you think an officer's order is?
Shimizu: (After a moment's reflection) An officer's order is like that of the Emperor.
Captain Hideka: (Raising his voice) Yes that's right. An officer's order cannot be rejected, it is an order from the Emperor. (*Meirei wa tennō no meirei da*).

Just as in *The Human Condition*, the scene depicting Shimizu's trial contrasts the factual evidence, upon which he is ultimately convicted, with the 'reality' of the execution scene as depicted earlier in the drama. The musical score similarly connects the two scenes with an ominous repetitive beat. Just as Kaji's explanations were mis-translated by a Japanese collaborator, Shimizu's answers are often inaccurately translated. The fact that a large proportion of the dialogue in this scene is in English without sub-titles encourages non-English speaking spectators to empathise with Shimizu's confusion. During his cross-examination, an American judge asks Shimizu in English, 'Did the accused regard such an order as lawful?' The interpreter simply translates this as 'Did you think it was a good order?' (*Anata no kimochi sono meirei ga yoi da to omoimashitaka*). Shimizu is incredulous, not quite understanding the question. The interpreter repeats the question and Shimizu answers, 'It was neither good nor bad. An officer's order is an order from the Emperor. I had to obey.' (*Ii mo warui mo arimasen. Jōkan no meirei wa tennō meirei de arimasu, zettai fukujū shinakereba*.) This the interpreter simply translates as, 'There was nothing I could do, as it was an order from the Emperor.'

This scene builds on *nihonjinron* discourses encouraging the view that Japanese customs and culture are so different from western practices that foreigners are unable to understand. Certainly, as Onuma (1993:10) has argued, there was resentment at the treatment metered out to B and C class war criminals based on the fact that the Allied judges were unfamiliar with Japanese society and culture. However, the philosophical differences underlying the misunderstandings dramatised in this scene are ignored. It is clear from the questions of the judge and prosecution lawyer that they are basing their arguments on western concepts of the inalienable rights of the individual and not on a Japanese 'anthropocosmic' world-view.[14] This is particularly evident when the judge asks Shimizu, 'An order of any superior officer can be rejected if it is improper. Why did the accused not reject the order?' The fact that this is spoken in English and inadequately translated by the interpreter encourages non-English speaking spectators to empathise with Shimizu's confusion rather than making a critical appraisal of the different arguments. This emotive response is further reinforced through the spectators' memories of the earlier execution scene in which it was apparent that had Shimizu rejected the order, as he says in court, 'it would have been suicide'.

The construction of the character of Captain Hideka, as the young fanatical officer in the execution scene, picks up on themes of the 'enemy within'. His character provides a contrast against which General Yano (Tsugawa Masahiko 1940-), the heroic 'tragic hero' of the drama, can be measured. The court sequence opens with a medium close-up pan from right to left along the line of defendants sitting in the dock. The camera thus visually traces the chain of command through which the order to execute the airmen passed, progressing from General Yano at the top end to Shimizu at the bottom. Captain Hideka is missing from this line-up and it is revealed, again only in English thereby encouraging spectator confusion, that when Japan was defeated, he committed suicide, thus confirming his fanatical status. During the cross-examination of General Yano, it becomes apparent that Captain Hideka interpreted General Yano's original order in its most extreme form. General Yano states, 'I said that the prisoners were to be dealt with appropriately (*tekitō ni shochi suru*). I was not aware that I gave an order for their execution. However, because I was the commanding officer at the time, I do feel a deep responsibility for their deaths.' During this scene, the unexplained (in Japanese) absence of Captain Hideka, who the drama constructs as the real villain of the piece, increases the general sense of the injustice of the verdict handed down to Shimizu by the court.

The construction of General Yano's character as the 'good' and responsible army officer forms part of a wider and extremely complex post-war debate. Films, such as *Kumo nagaruru hateni* and *Nikudan*, expressed a cynical attitude towards senior military officers. In *Kumo nagaruru hateni*, a young pilot mimics the morale-boosting speech of a senior officer (see page 80 above). Also in the final scenes after the pilots have taken off, actual documentary footage of *kamikaze* planes being shot down, crashing into the sea and missing their targets is inserted into the narrative, the implication being that no one in Otaki's and Fukami's squadron hit their targets. All died in vain. After these shots, the camera cuts back to the communications room at the airfield as two officers listen to the report. One says, 'It was worse than I had expected', to which the other replies, 'They were still inexperienced (*giryō mijuku*).' The first officer then cynically says, 'What! There is any number of *kamikaze*.' The camera then cuts to a shot of one of the classrooms in the school where the pilots had been billeted. Rows of young boys are sitting in their desks singing. The camera thus links the officer's remarks to the boys whom the film designates as the next generation of Special Attack Forces. The cynicism that comes through in these films for senior military officers or the 'uniformed politicians', in Yoshida's terminology, relates to a general feeling which Onuma describes:

> Already during the war, as the situation worsened, Tōjō had become a secret object of resentment. This became fixed when, after defeat, the Japanese began to see themselves as

victims of the war. In this, the Tokyo Trial provided unquestionable proof that Japan's former leaders were responsible for all the hardships the people had faced. (Onuma 1993:154)

Watashi wa kai ni naritai forms part of an alternative discourse portraying a positive image of Japan's wartime leaders. This theme developed as part of a backlash reaction against the criminalisation of Japan as a nation during the trials. Therefore, in many popular films based on the Pacific War and the trials, there is a tendency to frame the roles of Japan's wartime leaders within the 'tragic hero' narrative structure. The spectator is therefore encouraged to extrapolate from the individual subject hero to the nation as a whole. This tendency can be seen in *Nippon no ichiban nagai hi (Japan's Longest Day)* 1967 in the construction of the character of General Anami and in *Daitōyō Sensō to Kokusai Saiban* and *Dai Nippon Teikoku (The Great Japanese Empire)* in relation to General Tōjō. In both the latter films, Tōjō Hideki is cast within a 'tragic hero' narrative structure linking his trial and death to sacrifice, a sacrifice that saved the Imperial institution and by extension the *kokutai*.

In western historical accounts, it has been put forward that General MacArthur bowed to political 'expediency' (Beasley 1990) in deciding not to indict the Emperor on charges of war crimes. Minear states that there was a report to the effect that during the Tokyo Trial, 'at one point in his testimony [before the tribunal] ... Tōjō commented that no Japanese ever opposed the imperial will. In consternation at the ramifications of that statement, Chief Prosecutor Keenan requested the Imperial Household to exert its influence on Tōjō to change his testimony' (Minear 1971:113-114). Onuma (1993:35) would appear to concur with this view when he states that Keenan, in his cross-examination of Tōjō, structured his questions to ensure that Tōjō's replies would exonerate the Emperor. However, both the above-mentioned films distance Tōjō's narrative away from American policy, implying instead that Tōjō and his advisors agreed, prior to the arrival of MacArthur and the Occupation Forces, that Tōjō should take full responsibility for the war and thereby offer himself up as the victim of the courts, thus saving the Emperor and the *kokutai*. In *Daitōyō Sensō to Kokusai Saiban*, this is implicit in Tōjō's statement at the time of his arrest when he says, 'I am the person most responsible for the war, but I am not a war criminal' – a statement he reaffirms later in the film during the trial scenes. It is this distinction the film centres on; Tōjō's acceptance of full responsibility for Japan's involvement in the war and his refusal, and by implication Japan's refusal, to accept the guilt being imposed upon him by the trials. Tōjō's status as the heroic 'tragic hero' who saves the Emperor is reinforced by the casting of Arashi Kanjurō (1903–) as Tōjō in *Daitōyō Sensō to Kokusai Saiban*. The star persona of Arashi Kanjurō carries strong intertextual connotations, as Arashi had starred in the swashbuckling *chambara Kurama Tengu* series of approximately twenty-eight films made between 1927 and 1957. In this series, as the 'masked avenger', he fought against the *Shinsen-gumi*, a militia comprised of *rōnin* and established in the late Tokugawa period (1863) to preserve order in Kyōto for the *bakufu*. The *Kurama Tengu* fought against the *Shinsen-gumi* on behalf of the Emperor. In this series, the star persona of Arashi became established as that of a loyal vassal of the Emperor. *The Kurama Tengu* series had been particularly popular during the war period as it was considered a good illustration of the ideals of loyalty and martial spirit. In keeping with his star persona and in the same year as *Daitōyō Sensō to Kokusai Saiban* was released, Arashi went on to star as Emperor Meiji in the film *Meiji Taitei to Nogi Shōgun* (*The Great Meiji Emperor and General Nogi*).

The construction of Tōjō's character in these films as 'tragic hero' is dependent on the allegoric meanings the films associate with his death. *Seppuku*, within the 'tragic hero' tradition, is encoded as a sincere demonstration of the acceptance of responsibility for one's actions. Satō (1976) has argued that this conception became institutionalised at the time of the *Chūshingura* incident and in subsequent fictionalised accounts. Tōjō's case is therefore problematic because unlike General Anami, heroically portrayed by Mifune Toshirō in Okamoto Kihachi's *Nippon no ichiban nagai hi* (*Japan's Longest Day*) 1967, he did not die by his own hand. In *Dai Nippon Teikoku*, this impediment to the film's ascription of General Tōjō's status as heroic 'tragic hero' is overcome in a crucial scene between the Minister of War, General Shimomura Sadamu, and Tōjō Hideki. In this scene occurring immediately following documentary footage of General MacArthur's arrival in Japan on 30 August 1945, General Shimomura asks Tōjō what his intentions are:

Tōjō: I feel a great responsibility to the Emperor and the people. Death is the only means by which I can apologise. (*Owabi wa shi o motte suru shika nai.*)

Shimomura: I fully understand your feelings. However, would you not consider changing your mind? The Occupation Forces are likely to hold an International Tribunal in order to establish responsibility for the war. If they proceed, you are the only person who could answer the charges. If you are not here, the trial will have an extremely adverse affect on the country. As a soldier, I fully appreciate the pain of living with dishonour, but please won't you stop thinking of taking your life and stand up in court. General Tōjō, it is clear that the Allied Powers intend to put the responsibility for the war on to the Emperor and to thereby destroy the foundation of our country's *kokutai*. Will you take the witness stand and tell the court of the Emperor's truly pacifist sentiments? There is no other way to save His Majesty. For the sake of His Majesty, for the sake of Japan's future, please bear this shame ...

Within the context of this dialogue, Tōjō's impending death takes on two interconnected meanings: (a) by his death the Emperor will be saved and (b) his death is linked to Japan's future. Within this discourse, his failed attempt to take his life just prior to his arrest, becomes a public statement of his sincerity and his true desire to make restitution through *seppuku* which for political reasons he cannot perform. The above quoted scene and the attempted *seppuku* thus coalesce to give Tōjō the prerequisite criteria for entry into the heroic tradition. General Yano in *Watashi wa kai ni naritai* expresses a similar willingness, as the officer in command at the time of the execution of the American airmen, to take responsibility through his own death. This is evident during the trial scene and later when he makes an appeal on behalf of Shimizu.

Cinematically, in war-retro films of this genre the deaths of General Tōjō, General Anami and various 'war criminals' are stylistically linked to Japan's post-war reconstruction through lighting motifs and the juxta-positioning of shots to signify historical closure and rebirth. In *Daitōyō Sensō to Kokusai Saiban* after Tōjō's death scene, characterised by the dark lighting symbolic of trial and execution scenes generally, the camera cuts to a shot of the sky and a flock of birds in full flight. This is followed by a series of shots of modern Tokyo including one of the Imperial Palace as the voice-over narration enjoins the Japanese people never to allow the nation to go to war again. The film ends with a shot of Mt Fuji over which the title 'the end' is superimposed. In *Nippon no ichiban nagai hi*, prior to his death, General Anami tells Takeshita and another officer present that, from this point on, Japan's history will change and that if all Japanese, whatever their position, work hard, Japan can be rebuilt. 'Not only that, but the people who survive must ensure that Japan never faces such a wretched day again.' After his protracted death, the camera cuts to a shot of the morning sun, resembling the Japanese flag (*Hi no maru*). *Dai Nippon Teikoku* concludes with a similar shot of the sun filtered through the palm trees. This shot follows immediately after the executions of Tōjō and Egami, a minor war criminal.

The visual codes of lighting and the juxtaposition of images in these scenes form coherent syntagmatic units of meaning complementing the dialogue. They reinscribe former wartime iconography, such as the rising sun, Mt Fuji and the Imperial Palace, into post-war popular culture inflecting these icons with new meanings that encourage the view that the war and the trials were a caesura and that Tōjō, Anami and other 'war criminals' sacrificed themselves and thereby made restitution for the excesses of the war. Onuma (1993) feels that the trials had a negative effect on the population in general. The trials separated in people's minds the 'bad' Japanese who were held responsible for the war from the general populace. This, Onuma argues, led to a sense of complacency in that 'I was not indicted, therefore I have been exonerated and need not question the extent to which I participated in the war effort.' This, combined with the general view that the trials were hypocritical in that the Allied Powers were unwilling to face up to their own 'crimes', such as the atomic bomb attacks and the Soviet Union's violation of its neutrality pact with Japan, led to an attitude amongst post-war Japanese which was not conducive to self-reflexive thought. This attitude was further compounded by the general sense of victimisation (*higaisha ishiki*) encouraged by the trials and reflected in films and the media in general.

By casting his own wartime experiences within a conflicting duality of law and morality, Katō (1994) contains his account within a 'tragic hero' mythic structure in which Ōishi Kuranosuke and the forty-six were also confronted with the same choice. This is a point the Confucian scholar, Ogyū Sorai, who was brought in to advise the *bakufu*, recognised in the following remarks:

> By righteousness we mean the path of keeping oneself free from any taint, and by law we mean the measuring rod for the entire country. A man controls his heart with decorum and his actions with righteousness. For the forty-six samurai to have avenged their master on this occasion shows that they are aware of shame, as becomes men who are samurai; and since they have followed the path of keeping themselves free from taint, their deed is righteous. However, this deed is appropriate only to their particular group; it amounts therefore to a special exception to the rules. The persons connected with the vendetta considered Kira to be their enemy because Asano Naganori was punished for his disorderly behavior in the palace, and they deliberately planned an act of violence without official permission. *This is not to be tolerated under the law.* If the forty-six samurai are pronounced guilty and condemned to commit *seppuku,* in keeping with the traditions of the samurai, the claim of the Uesugi family [the family of Kira's wife] will be satisfied, and their loyalty will not have been disparaged. This must therefore be considered as a general principle. If general principles are impaired by special exceptions, there will no longer be any respect for the law in this country. (quoted in Keene 1971:2-3) (my emphasis)

However, although Katō rationalised his own position and the positions of other 'war criminals' from within this figurative structure, his decision to violate morality condemned him and, through him, Shimizu, to the role of unheroic 'tragic hero'. Ōishi and the forty-six chose to violate the law and thus remained true to a nativist Confucian ethic which, as has been argued in preceding chapters, is highly valued. Shimizu's status as unheroic 'tragic hero' is reflected in the choice of actor to play the part. In the 1958 TBS version and the 1959 Tōhō remake, Sakai Furanki-Frankie, played the part of Shimizu and in the 1994 version, Tokoro Jōji took on the role. Both of these actors are comedians and could therefore, according to the dictates of their star persona, take on this non-heroic role.

The construction of Shimizu's character as non-heroic victim within this drama places *Watashi wa kai ni naritai* in a category of films which includes the Hiroshima and Nagasaki bomb films. In particular, films such as *Ashita (Tomorrow)* 1988,[15] while not actually depicting the horror of the attacks through a survival story such as *Genbaku no ko (Children of the Atomic Bomb)* 1952 or *Kuroi ame (Black Rain)* 1989, instead dwell on the everyday lives of ordinary people prior to the attacks. These films emphasise the innocence of the victims and the simplicity of their lives. In them, the spectator is constantly put in the place of the character and encouraged to feel as that character does. Therefore, they do not encourage the spectator to review the past critically nor to analyse the choices for the future; instead they instil a sense of horror of war.

These two chapters have analysed how the 'tragic hero' mythic narrative became the dominant figurative structure through which the events of the war and defeat were interpreted in war-retro films. As Hayden White explains:

How a given historical situation is to be configured depends on the historian's subtlety in matching up a specific plot structure with the set of historical events that he wishes to endow with a meaning of a particular kind. This is essentially a literary, that is to say a fiction-making, operation. And to call it that in no way detracts from the status of historical narratives as providing a kind of knowledge. For not only are the pregeneric plot structures by which sets of events can be constituted as stories of a particular kind limited in number . . . but the encodation of events in terms of such plot structures is one of the ways that a culture has of making sense of both personal and public pasts. (White 1985:85)

The reader, or in this instance the film spectator, gradually comes to a realisation that the events being portrayed on the screen fit into a particular narrative structure. Once this realisation occurs, we experience the effect of having the events explained to us.'They are rendered comprehensible by being subsumed under the categories of the plot structure in which they are encoded as a story of a particular kind' (White 1985:86).

The 'tragic hero' narrative, as an established *jidai geki* structure, provided a ready-made sequence of positive metaphorical identifications through which the war and defeat could be explained. These include 'purity of spirit' (*makoto*) expressed through a willingness to die for a cause – as in the case of the *kamikaze*, or, as in the case of *seppuku*, the willingness to accept responsibility for one's actions as, for example, Generals Anami and Tōjō or in fictional terms, Kaji. The allegoric meaning of death within this pregeneric structure is similarly flexible in its potential for interpretation as either sacrifice or, as in the case of Shimizu and the victims of the bombs, as victimisation (*higaisha ishiki*).

As a symbolic structure the 'tragic hero' pregeneric narrative form provided in fictionalised accounts of the war an avenue of exculpation from a foreign-imposed sense of guilt that accompanied the war trials. This was aided by popular discourse on the hypocrisy of the courts of the Allied Powers which failed to examine their own roles in the war. As Kaji says to the Soviet camp commander who is accusing him of war crimes, 'I acknowledge what I have done. I want to show you what you are doing', referring to the scenes of brutality he had witnessed on his long journey through Manchuria. Justice Pal's dissent provided a legitimating vehicle through which films could construct a counter argument, turning Japan's entry into the war into a defensive action, thus further exonerating Japan's wartime leaders. As has been stated above, popular discourses on the war and defeat are complex and often conflicting as the trajectory of the development of the image of General Tōjō in popular films illustrates. In the immediate post-war period, he was blamed for the hardships the populace had suffered during the war (Onuma 1993). However, as a backlash developed against the criminalisation of Japan through her wartime leaders, by 1982 Tōjō's image had emerged as a fully fledged 'tragic hero' in *Dai Nippon Teikoku*, a film which was screened twice in 1995 on the television as part of the fiftieth anniversary of defeat. This would suggest that this has become the dominant image associated with him.

CHAPTER 4

Facts, Fictions and Fantasy

Myth flourishes at the point where the social and the psychoanalytic overlap, redolent of fascination and anxiety and generating both creative energy (stories, images) and the 'taming and binding' process through which collective contact with the unconscious is masked. (Mulvey 1987:10)

Iji ga jiga o umu no de aru. (The ego is born from pride.) (Satō 1976:50)

Bushidō to iu wa, shinu koto to mitsuketari. (The meaning of *bushidō* is found in death.) (Yamamoto *Hagakure* 1993:58)

The preceding two chapters concentrated on a political analysis of the 'tragic hero' pregeneric narrative form. I argued that this narrative form was the principal figurative structure through which World War II was depicted in Japanese popular film. In this chapter, I shift the analysis to a socio-psycho-analytic perspective in order to shed light on the libidinal politics of violence in the post-war yakuza genre. This leads to a discussion in the following concluding chapter on the relationship between historicity and the sensual imperative of images of masculinity in post-war Japanese genres targeted at male audiences.

Broadly speaking, the analysis in this chapter will follow an historical trajectory by focusing on two highly popular series of films. The first, the 1960s *Abashiri bangaichi* series, stars Takakura Ken and centres on the lives and adventures of the inmates of a cell in the prison at Abashiri. Fourteen films were made. The principal director and originator was Ishii Teruo (1924–), who directed ten of the films made between October 1964 and December 1967. The second series is the 1970s *Jingi naki tatakai* (*War Without Morality*) which stars Sugawara Bunta (1933-) among others and which is based on the internecine wars of Hiroshima-based yakuza in the post-war period. The principal director was Fukasaku Kinji (1930-), who was responsible for eight of the nine films made between 1973 and 1979. Finally, this chapter will conclude with a brief discussion of the films of Kitano (Beat) Takeshi (1948-), bringing the survey up to the 1980s. However, prior to an analysis of the films, it is first necessary to discuss the relationship between fantasy and the ego (*moi* in Lacanian terms) in relation to the panoptic nature of social relations set out in chapter two and alluded to by Satō in the epigram that opens this chapter.

The *Nagare-mono*: Takakura Ken, Metaphorical Representation of *Iji*

Satō stresses the importance of *iji* (pride) as a central concept for an understanding of both the motivating force and the popularity of the 'tragic hero' in Japanese popular culture. He defines *iji* as does Ikegami, in terms of honour (*meiyo*), an individual's need for public acknowledgement of the righteousness of one's life and actions. He makes the point that *iji* as a concept in Japanese has two, often contradictory, meanings. The first, he links to the desire people have to receive public acknowledgement of their 'righteousness'. Although he explains this 'impulse' from within a discourse of 'nature' when he says, 'Human beings are living creatures who have an impulse to prove their righteousness' (*Ningen wa, jibun no tadashisa o shōmei shitai to iu shōdō o motsu ikimono de aru to iu koto*), he also acknowledges the social, i.e. constructed nature of this concept, when he links it to morality and the individual's desire to live a 'righteous life' (Satō 1976:45). The second meaning is with 'stubborn pride', *ijippari*. In explaining the meaning of this negative aspect of the concept, he refers to a proverb, *dorobō nimo sanbun no ri aru*, which loosely translates as 'even a robber has his reasons'. However, *sanbun no ri* translated literally means 'three-tenths of the truth', and as Satō goes on to argue, someone expressing stubborn pride, *ijippari*, 'tramples on his opponents seven-tenths' (Satō 1976:49). Satō proposes that this 'stubborn pride' is a central ethic in Japanese popular culture.[1] In answering

– 159 –

the question why, despite a logical understanding of the negative meanings attached to this concept, Japanese people have such a deep affection for 'tragic heroes' who display 'stubborn pride', he argues that it is an empathetic response to an almost universal experience of childhood.

> A young child at the time he first distinguishes between 'good' and 'bad' becomes confused, when by mistake or caprice, he is unfairly corrected by an adult or an older child. At such a time, the child learns obstinacy and stubborn pride. Why stubborn pride? As the child cannot explain the situation logically, he has two possible reactions, the expression of stubborn pride or doing exactly what he is told and thereby losing his sense of himself. Put another way, it is at this juncture that the ego is awakened. (Satō 1976:50)

Translated into the adult world, Satō's explanation can be interpreted as an expression of the contradiction between the mechanisms of social restraint that often appear arbitrary, and the social expectations of masculinity which evolve around domination and power. This study demonstrates that historically in Japanese cinema one of the dominant forms of idealised masculinity has been encoded within a discourse of untamed nature and a naïve innocence, as for example Muhō Matsu in the *gendai geki*, *Muhō Matsu no isshō*. There are many more examples from the *jidai geki*, such as *Miyamoto Musashi*, the blind samurai Zato-ichi, and Kurosawa's Sanshirō, to name a few. This image of masculinity is at odds with a society founded on a utilitarian system of restraint – the subordination of individual desires and needs for the greater good of the group and/or the avoidance of shame (*haji*) in Ikegami's conception. In an article on the *Abashiri* series written in 1966, Tayama makes the point that most of the films' spectators in the mid sixties were men who had secure jobs and were enmeshed in the social system (*kikō no naka ni kumikomare*). However, he goes on to say in the most negative terms that 'most are sinking in the reality of a stagnant tepid pool. Enduring the pressures of work, they live dull and wretched lives.' (Tayama 1966:135).

The inmates of the Abashiri prison represent a powerful masculinity that, in the examples of Tachibana (Takakura Ken) and the archetypal patriarch Onitora (Arashi Kanjurō), is predicated on physical strength and stoicism. The prison, the shackles, and the guards provide potent images of social restraint against which Tachibana and his friends struggle, while the vast expanses of the inhospitable Hokkaido winter landscape connotes the freedom denied to the heroes when in prison, and by extension, to society at large. The use of open landscape as a metaphor for male freedom was used to great advantage in the war period in the films of Rikoran (see chapter one). As Tayama's article stresses, the conditions of work in an advanced industrial society reduce most men to a state of dependency and powerlessness. This is in some sense compensated for in the family through the role of household head as provider. However, this is a double-edged sword as the family also represents a constraint to male freedom. Furthermore, in a society in which women are increasingly entering the work-force, this source of masculine esteem is further undermined. From within a scenario in which the yakuza's code of morality (*jingi*) is brought into confrontation with what is perceived to be an unjust restraint to his freedom, Tachibana displays a 'stubborn pride' that refuses compromise. Within this archetypal *nagare-mono* narrative, Tachibana closes the gap between the ideological image of masculinity and social experience, thus offering a vicarious solution to the eternal contradiction lived by most men. For example, in the opening sequences of the fourth film of the series *Abashiri bangaichi Hokkai-hen* (*Abashiri Bangaichi: The North Sea Episode* 1965), Tachibana is incarcerated in the prison at Abashiri. One of his fellow inmates is suffering from consumption and, while out at work on a chain-gang, he collapses. Tachibana intervenes as a guard maliciously begins to beat him. He tells the guard that the consumptive is ill and should be sent to hospital, at which point the guard turns on Tachibana who easily fends him off. At this moment, another member of Tachibana's inner circle, Nakada (Tanaka Kunie), intervenes offering the requisite apologies to the guard and generally placating the situation. If, as had seemed likely, Tachibana had attacked the guard, he would not have been released the following day. In this scene, Nakada compromises his own masculine status to save Tachibana. This is acceptable because of the comic status of the star persona of Tanaka Kunie who in this series relies on the sexual ambiguity of the Nakada character as a source of humour. Within this relatively minor scene, all the elements of the greater discourse of *iji* and its relation to *jingi* are present. The guard, representing law and 'culture', is clearly shown to be acting out of malice, while Tachibana, following the code of *jingi*, intervenes spontaneously with no thought for self. He is only saved further punishment when Nakada intervenes, adopting a subordinate position. Thus Tachibana's status as the representative of the ideal dominant male is not compromised, nor in this example is he punished.

The appeal to male spectators of *jingi*, upon which Tachibana and the other inmates of the prison base their conduct and by which they judge their own and the conduct of others, is nostalgia based. It is a Confucian derived term used predominantly in the Tokugawa period and, according to popular conception, it was first adopted by manual labourers before being taken over by yakuza in the post-war period as part of their attempts to legitimise their social position through historical continuity (Kasahara 1973:138). *Jingi* is a conservative value system in the films; it governs male-male relations and is in fact synonymous with the more commonly accepted moral code of *giri ninjō* (*Kōjien*), both of which can be rendered in English as 'justice and humanity'. The term 'justice' here refers to a nativist Confucian ethic as discussed in the preceding chapter and should not be confused with western juridical derived definitions of the concept. The male spectator is, through the homosocial sub-text, encouraged to sympathise with this value system. However, the fact that Tachibana, with whom the spectator is encouraged to empathise, is a 'tragic hero' and thus doomed to failure, also alerts the spectator to the need to adjust his own values to the new 'reality'. The principal difference between practitioners of the code of *jingi* and those of *giri ninjō*, is that they exist in a community which operates on the margins of 'legitimate' social institutions, as the word *bangaichi* in the title of the *Abashiri* films indicates. *Bangaichi* literally means 'land that has no address' (*banchi no nai tochi*) which clearly applies to the country around Abashiri, one of the remotest parts of the northern island Hokkaido. However, *banga*i by itself is defined in the *Kōjien* as, 'outside the ordinary', and carries metaphorical meanings of the social outsider in phrases such as *'kare wa bangai da'*. The use of this word in the promotional trailers for the films gives some indication of this metaphorical use in the context of the films, eg., *'bangaichi otoko wa doko e iku'* (Where will the outsider go?) and *'bangaichi otoko kokyō Nagasaki ni tatsu'* (The outsider will make a stand in his home town of Nagasaki). Tachibana, as the *bangaichi* man, exists on the fringes of mainstream society and lives by the yakuza code of *jingi*. However, the social reference group of this out-group which is both constituting of and constituted by the individual is just as exacting in the demands it makes on the individual as 'legitimate' *seken* of the world of the company and the family. Through its emphasis on physical strength and stoicism, continually tested by competitive violence as in the above example, the fantasy world of the *nagare-mono* offers a nostalgia-based solution to the incongruities between male role prescriptions of a powerful spontaneous masculinity and the experiential reality of men's lives.

Ikegami, also refers to the defining role played by concepts of 'honour' in relation to the individual's sense of self and his role in Japanese society.

> When a samurai regulates his own behavior based upon considerations of what is deemed 'honorable', he has an imagined community, or a symbolic reference group, in his mind that carries his reputation and social dignity. The power of this aspect of the honor community is informal and symbolic insofar as it ultimately resides in each subject. (Ikegami 1995:38)

Satō makes a similar point: the ego (*jiga*) is born from pride (*iji*), linking the socially defined classifications of what an individual's subjectivity should be and the formation of his ego. Furthermore, shades of the panoptic are evident, as pride (*iji*) is predicated on the self as object of another's gaze: one is exposed to either praise or censure. This social aspect – the role of the *seken* – as Lebra (1994) reminds us, can be either real or imagined, thereby complying with established Lacanian theories of the development of the ego or *moi*. In his essay on "The Mirror Stage", Lacan states that:

> the total form of the body by which the subject anticipates in a mirage the maturation of his power is given to him only as *Gestalt,* that is to say, in an exteriority in which this form is certainly more constituent than constituted. (Lacan 1993:2)

The western belief in the individual as an autonomous being is linked to Christian philosophies which, at the ideological level, are defined in metaphysical rather than social terms. In contrast, as Lebra has indicated, the Japanese sense of 'self' is predicated firmly in the social. Ikegami provides the historical context when she states:

Unlike the medieval Church, which asserted the existence of universal standards of truth and justice that were greater than the secular sovereignty of any one European country, the medieval Japanese Buddhist temples did not establish normative and transcendental values to which the secular authority should, in theory, be subject. (Ikegami 1995:186-187)[2]

Nor did it establish 'normative or transcendental values' that superseded the social. As such, the Japanese lexicon is comprised of many more words and phrases which compare the individual to the social norm or *seken-nami*. Lebra cites such examples as 'unable to face the *seken*' (*seken ni kao muke ga dekinai*) and 'have no face to meet the *seken*' (*seken ni awaseru kao ga nai*). On the obverse side of this equation are words and phrases which are used to describe a person or action in relation to the *seken*: *seken-nami* (conformative to *seken* standard, or ordinary), *seken-banare* (incongruent with the *seken*, or eccentric), and *seken-shirazu* (unaware of *seken* rules, or naïve) (Lebra 1994:107). In western society the interpolation of the individual into the social is often masked through metaphysical references, both legal and political, to the 'inalienable rights' and the 'nobility' of the individual. Alternatively, this process has been mythologised in Japan through references to 'nature' as the defining principle of human subjectivity, an example of which is the construction of the character, Muhō Matsu, as analysed in chapter one, or a more recent example, the deaf and dumb hero in Kitano Takeshi's *Ano natsu no ichiban shizukana umi* (released in the UK as *A Scene at Sea* 1992). This naturalisation of individual subjectivities along socially prescribed patterns or standards is evident also in western philosophical thought since the Enlightenment. However, I maintain that the Christian definition and influence have remained dominant, as the continued use of the Bible in legal proceedings and the prayers which open parliamentary sessions attest. The ultimate effect, in both traditions, whether Christian-based individualism or Japanese-based nature, is similar: the mythologising through fantasy of the accommodation of the individual to the socially symbolic order or, in Marxist terms, the mode of production. In both traditions the interpolation of the individual into socially and sexually specific codes of self-perception and behaviour occurs through the Oedipus complex. However, in the Japanese context, due to the Confucian precept of primogeniture, the male/female distinction upon which western social roles and subjectivities are defined is further complicated by the distinction between first and secondary sons. This, when linked to the paternal structure of Japanese pseudo-filial group relations, raises many problems for the hierarchical ordering of dominant and subordinate roles. This is reflected in the structure of the honorific language (*keigo*) itself, often explained wrongly in grammars purely as a distinction between feminine and masculine forms, when in fact, as Jordan explains, it can and does often represent the relative positions of dominance and subordination.

> Given the socialization process which trains Japanese women to be polite and subservient to men, it follows that women use the honorific and formal varieties of the Japanese language more frequently. This does not mean that the forms themselves are feminine, but rather that their frequent use and occurrence in certain social situations are typical of female usage. Thus, a polite form that would be used by a man only when talking to a person of extremely high position might be used by a woman in talking to a casual acquaintance. (Jordan 1983:251)

The *Nagare-mono* and the Symbolic Meaning of Violence

The *nagare-mono's* struggle to maintain and reaffirm his sense of self as defined by *iji* is played out in the *Abashiri bangaichi* series from within the structuring opposition of *jingi* (humanity and justice) and culture. Within this scenario of the heroic 'tragic hero', the nativist Confucian ethic of *jingi* is upheld at the expense of culture and the rule of law. Katō puts it another way, 'Due to justice and humanity (*giri ninjō*), a law (*okite*) is often violated and, in order to uphold the law, *giri* and *ninjō* are at times abandoned. This is the cause of many of society's tragedies and one of society's great contradictions' (1994:51-52). When Tachibana (Takakura Ken) is forced to choose between his morality (*jingi*) and the law, unlike Shimizu (*Watashi wa kai ni naritai*), he chooses morality and receives the punishment prescribed by the law, returning invariably to the prison at Abashiri in the final sequences of each film. Within this series, Takakura Ken, the heroic yakuza, fights to preserve the social order of the gambling community and, as 'a member of the gang which honours traditional values, he kills his rivals who trample on the morals (*moraru*) that the yakuza are supposed to uphold. He is faithful to the point of sacrificing his life for the *oyabun* whom he trusts, for his gang and for his brother yakuza. He is the embodiment of a heroism that saves the weak and fights the strong' (Satō 1996 vol 3:52).

Violence, within this scenario, is the visual enactment of an essentially abstract conflict located in the mind. In the final scenes, carrying his sword under his trench coat, Tachibana enters the rival gang's headquarters and is asked what he has come for. He replies in the politest of terms, 'To receive your life'. This is the symbolic representation of the abstract conflict between two antithetical positions: a nativist Confucian ethic, *jingi*, which requires the death of the rival *oyabun*, and the law which if upheld requires the individual to renounce his moral code. The final scene in each *Abashiri* film builds on iconic symbols scattered throughout each scenario. These symbols clearly identify Tachibana in harmony with traditional Japanese values; for example, he is often depicted with his friends participating in *matsuri* (festivals) into which the rival gang, dressed in loud Hawaiian shirts, intrudes. Tachibana prefers swords and knives as his chosen weapons while his opponents often brandish guns. Even food carries symbolic meaning, as in the 1965 *Abashiri bangaichi: Hokkai-hen*, when Tachibana eats huge *onigiri* (rice balls) while his opponents eat sandwiches. These films uphold nostalgia-based values in contemporary society through a ritualised social conflict resolved through violence.

At the level of personal inter-male relations, violence is the symbolic vehicle through which power relations are maintained and renegotiated both within the group and in wider society. In contemporary western popular culture, Russell argues that a denial of death has lead to its encodation as failure. 'The contemporary denial of death is coextensive with the depletion of mythical assurances of its meaningfulness. In so many stories about victims and criminals, this meaninglessness has been codified as failure in a culture devoted to progress' (Russell 1995:8). In the 1960s *nagare-mono* films that star Takakura Ken, however violence is a narrativised form of power-play between the dominant and the subordinate which ultimately restores the mythical meaningfulness of death as sacrifice. In traditional Hollywood genres of the detective, gangster, and cowboy films, conflict evolves around those who represent the law and the status quo, and those who seek to upset the social balance. Within these scenarios, as Fiske points out, 'Violence enacts social, rather than personal relations; it takes place between personalized moralities ... rather than between individual people *per se*' (Fiske 1989:179). At the level of the structuring opposition between a nativist Confucian ethic and western-based culture, a similar codification of character types is discernable in Japanese genres targeted at male audiences. At the level of inter-personal relations, violence in the yakuza and *nagaremono* films forms part of an internecine war between rival factions or gangs and is therefore symbolic of competitive power relations within a given field. Nakane (1972) argues that, due to the vertical structure of Japanese group relations (rather than horizontal class or interest-based alliances), competition is always between parallel groups. These 1960s yakuza films thus can be analysed as sites where academic *nihonjinron* discourses are fictionalised in popular form. Contestation is reflected in the films as struggles, not as in western Hollywood dramas between the 'good' and 'bad' *per se*, but between competing organisations or factions which are cast in either 'good' or 'bad' roles depending on their commitments to tradition. This has long been evident in war-retro films where violence is a symbolic representation of inter-personal or interdivisional rivalries and not between the enemy and the Japanese.

The personnel structure of yakuza organisations, as depicted within these films, can be compared metaphorically with Japanese corporate structures. As Nakane makes clear, in a situational (*ba*) based framework of inter-personal relations the vertical, i.e. hierarchical ordering of the group, dominates over and above horizontal ties between people who share the same attributes. This, she argues, is a characteristic ideal of Japanese group-relations and is evident in the structure of social relations in the family, village and more recently in the company. 'The new employee is in just about the same position and is, in fact, received by the company in much the same spirit as if he were a newly born family member, a newly adopted son-in-law or a bride come into the husband's household' (Nakane 1972:14). The opening sequences of the first *Abashiri bangaichi* film (1965) where Tachibana and a group of new prisoners are brought to the Abashiri jail, are parodies of the initiation of the new company recruit. These sequences reflect the often-painful initiation of new recruits (and new brides) into the group. Order is established only towards the end of the film, through the establishment of the authority of a strong patriarchal figure, Onitora (Arashi Kanjurō 1903-). After initial processing by the authorities, the new prisoners are placed in a cell with three other prisoners who, in order to establish the hierarchical ranking of each new cell member, proceeds to interrogate them on the nature of their various crimes. Yoda reminds them, 'You are all newcomers to this cell. Don't forget that the cell leadership has been established' (*senpai o taterutte koto wasurene*). The seriousness of the crime committed and the length of the sentence received establish rank. This introductory scene also functions to introduce the main characters and their idiosyncrasies to the spectators. The character types established in this opening sequence of this first film remain constant throughout the series. Yoda played by Abe Tōru (1917-), the archetypal villain of Japanese cinema who also took the part of a *kenpeitai* officer in *The Human Condition*, continues in his villainous role. Tanaka Kunie is established in these sequences as a comic character whose constant oscillation between extreme displays of machismo and sexual ambiguity provides much of the humour. It is interesting to note that within the series the names of secondary characters change but their star personas as character types remain constant. In the case of Tanaka Kunie, his character type transferred easily to the 1970s *Jingi naki tatakai* series, albeit with a minor shift in emphasis from the comic to the pathetic.

The first film of the *Abashiri* series thus establishes character types and the ranking of individuals within this group. This is reflected in linguistic terms of address which, as the list below demonstrates, is in direct correlation to terms used in companies and other 'legitimate' organisations.

Yakuza
Kumichō-oyabun
(both terms used to address a yakuza gang leader).

Aniki
(familiar term for a senior, literal meaning 'elder brother').

Omae-kimi
(terms of address to a subordinate).

Company
Buchō-shachō
(section head and company president).

Senpai
(a form of address to one's senior colleague).

Kun
(a prefix attached to the name of a subordinate).

(It should be noted that these lists are not mutually exclusive and that some overlap does occur; for example, in films based on 'salarymen', it is not uncommon to hear a *senpai* address his junior as *kimi*.)

The hierarchical structure portrayed in the films parallels Nakane's explanation that,

> relative rankings are ... centred on the ego and everyone is placed in a relative locus within the firmly established vertical system. Such a system works against the formation of distinct strata within a group, which, even if it consists of homogenous members in terms of qualifications, tends to be organized according to hierarchical order. (Nakane 1972:28)

The functioning of this hierarchical system is played out in two early scenes and revolves around a cigarette butt. In the first, just after Tachibana and the new prisoners arrive and while out on a work party, Otsuki (Tanaka Kunie) manages to retrieve a cigarette butt discarded by some passer-by. During their break, Yoda, claiming the rights of the *senpai* and reminding the others that, 'It is an established convention that any delicacy (*gochisō*) be given first to the senior and then handed down', proceeds to smoke the butt by himself. The scene immediately cuts to a long shot of the prison with the words 'Two years later' superimposed on the screen after which the previous cigarette scenario is repeated, only this time Tachibana and his friends have moved up the scale and, according to rank, share the cigarette butt. Cigarette butts represent continuity, and more importantly as markers of time, reflect the integration of the new recruits into the group.

Within the series as a whole the antagonistic division drawn between Tachibana and the new inmates who arrived with him, and Yoda who was already there, are maintained. The actor Abe Tōru who plays the part of Yoda in this first film, despite various guises in other films in the series, continues to play the part of the scheming entrepreneur who works against Tachibana and his allies in subsequent episodes. These films underline the importance attached to relationships and alliances established when one first enters a group. It is only in these relationships that true intimacy is possible, a point brought out in my earlier analysis of *kamikaze* films. Therefore, within the *Abashiri* series as a whole, the Abashiri prison cell acts as a reference point in much the same way as the *gakubatsu* (school clique) theoretically does in mainstream Japanese society. As Nakane explains, the *gakubatsu* 'denotes the group consciousness deriving mainly from a common university or college background. Graduates of the same university or college share an in-group feeling, a ready familiarity in face of others' (Nakane 1972:128). Unlike the *gakubatsu* which Nakane argues is only second to 'institution or place of work in degree of function and is more effective than either family or local background', the cell affiliation in the *Abashiri* series transcends yakuza gang affiliations. Therefore, in the 1966 film *Abashiri bangaichi: Nankoku no taiketsu* (*Abashiri Bangaichi: Showdown in the South Country*), when Tachibana finds himself and some of the former cell inmates temporarily working for opposing sides, they can in the final stages of the film join forces to defeat the exploitative 'bad' leader. This is a crucial point of divergence between the films and society at large. The moral code of *jingi* demands as a point of honour (*iji*) that once a relationship has been formed at this level, it transcends all other considerations. Ozu took up this same theme in his 1932 silent film *Seishun no yume ima izuko* (*Where are the Dreams of Our Youth?*), that is, the strains placed on male friendships due to the burdens of contemporary (1930s recession-hit Japanese) society. In the *Abashiri* series, conflict between obligations of *jingi* and demands of society are always resolved in favour of *jingi*. This is possible because, as the term *nagare-mono* (drifter) implies, the heroes are free from conventional social ties and responsibilities and can therefore remain true to the codes of brotherhood. In mainstream society the criteria of entry into a *gakubatsu* are intellectual; in the marginal *nagare-mono* world, they are physical and moral. Within both systems, male relationships are similarly stratified along a dominant–subordinate division as the list of comparative forms of address indicates. In the corporate world of 'legitimate' society, power relations are maintained and re-negotiated through political manoeuvreings, whereas in the marginal world of the *nagare-mono*, these same power relations are maintained and contested through physical violence. Thus, at the level of inter-personal male/male relations, the violence in these films can be read as a symbolic representation of the maintenance and readjustment of dominant/subordinate relations.

'Reflexive Masochism' and the Aesthetics of Violence

At the level of spectator pleasure, sadism forms the erotic component in the enactment of these symbolic relations of dominance/subordination. Cinematically, this is evident in the fetishisation of these scenes through the use of close-ups, freeze-frames and slow motion shots. Symbolically, it is evident in violent scenes where, as part of the attack, objects are rammed into opponents' mouths. For example, a slipper is stuffed into Kaji's mouth by a senior soldier in *The Human Condition*, and in the first film of the Abashiri series, Tachibana stuffs rice into his stepfather's mouth, a scene he repeats in the 1966 *Abashiri bangaichi: Ōyuki hara no taiketsu* (*Abashiri Bangaichi: Showdown on the Snowcovered Plains*), only in this latter example, the recipient is a prison guard. In more recent examples, such as the films of Kitano (Beat) Takeshi, guns are forced into people's mouths. There is also a trend to depict actual male rape scenes, as for example in the Fuji Television telemovie *Shinjuku nemuranai machi* (*Shinjuku the Town that Never Sleeps*) and the 1990 Kitano Takeshi film *3-4 × 10 gatsu* (released in the UK as *Boiling Point*). In violent scenes through cinematic and thematic devices such as these, the spectator is offered an eroticised, vicarious pleasure in the hero's physical assertion of his power.

Stephen Neale, in his seminal essay 'Masculinity as Spectacle' (1993), emphasises the 'process of narcissistic identification' as an important site of spectator pleasure. He argues that it is especially significant in 'current ideologies of masculinity' that involve 'aggression, power and control', all of which are important themes in the *nagare-mono* film. As Mulvey has indicated, narcissistic identification in male genres involves fantasies of power and omnipotence.

> As the spectator identifies with the main male protagonist, he projects his look on to that of his like, his screen surrogate, so that the power of the male protagonist as he controls events coincides with the active power of the erotic look, both giving a satisfying sense of omnipotence. A male movie star's glamorous characteristics are thus not those of the erotic object of the gaze, but those of the more perfect, more complete, more powerful ideal ego conceived in the original moment of recognition in front of the mirror. (Neale 1993:12).

Neale, however, makes the suggestion that, while the ideal 'model' (the film hero) may be a subject with whom the spectator identifies and to which he aspires, he may also be the cause of spectator-anxiety in as much as that ideal is something to which the male spectator is never adequate. Neale infers that this form of identification can entail a concomitant masochism in the relationship between the spectator and the image, and further, that the male image can involve an eroticism, 'since there is always a constant oscillation between that image as a source of identification, and as other, a source of contemplation' (Neale 1993:13). This then, Neale suggests, is one of the reasons why western male genres often involve 'sado-masochistic themes, scenes and phantasies', through which the male hero can legitimately become an 'object of an erotic gaze' (Neale 13).

In Japanese male genres, I shall argue that there is indeed a masochistic element in the relationship between the spectator and the ideal image of the hero; however, the following analysis will show that this masochism does not revolve around a form of passive masochism, but is 'reflexive' and is therefore active and in keeping with dominant images of a powerful masculinity. Furthermore, the display of 'reflexive masculinity' in these films is a narrative device which shores up the contradiction between an ideological view of masculinity predicated on power and authority, against a social economic structure which required employees to work long and gruelling hours in the name of self-sacrifice and post-war economic recovery. I shall demonstrate that these films codify competitive male relations of domination and subordination along a passive/ active division which, through the inclusion of homosexual characters in the narratives, is further codified as a feminine/ masculine distinction. This narrative trend, although obvious in Japanese male genres since the late 1950s, is only now becoming evident in western male genres in the films of directors such as Quentin Tarantino. Secondly, in these films, as Neale suggests, the male body is offered as an object of display but its eroticism is linked to a subversion of the dominant power relations of the panoptic gaze of the *seken*. In a society that advocates adherence to the norm, displays of difference can be liberating. Hence the bodily display of tattoos.

Silverman (1992), following on from Freud's analysis in the 'Three Essays on the Theory of Sexuality', makes the point that although masochism often provides a 'centrally structuring element of both male and female subjectivity, it is only in the latter that it can be safely acknowledged'. She concludes, in patriarchal societies which are based on a clear delineation between the sexes 'the male subject ... cannot avow feminine masochism without calling into question his identification with the masculine position ... [T]his is another way of suggesting that what is acceptable for the female subject is pathological for the male' (Silverman 1992:189-190). Therefore, it is reasonable to suggest that, although identification with the passive masochistic position within the image is possible, this is in fact a socially aberrant reading and is not the principal position that the narrative structure of the films encourages the male spectators to adopt. This point is further in evidence in the hugely popular films, novels and *manga* of the S/M pornographic genre. In this genre, unlike its counterpart in the west, men are always depicted in the dominant/sadistic position and the female in the passive/masochistic. Furthermore, within the *Abashiri* series, the inclusion of passive homosexual characters, constructed in negative terms, deters the spectator from identifying with the subordinate position. In the 1966 film *Abashiri bangaichi: Ōyuki hara no taiketsu*, two passive homosexual characters compete for the affections of another inmate of their prison cell at the Abashiri jail. These homosexual characters, although depicted as parodying women through the exaggerated use of 'feminine' gestures and honorific speech forms, are in fact metonymic constructions that represent the antithesis of the ideal of masculinity represented by Takakura Ken. Thus their inclusion in the group is to provide a negative counterpoise to Tachibana's positive characteristics. This binary opposition can be illustrated as below:

Tachibana	**Homosexual Characters**
physically strong	physically weak
handsome	ugly
honest	devious
silent	over-talkative
uses plain forms of address	uses honorific forms of address

Within the series as a whole, the passive homosexual characters take on subordinate roles normally assigned to women and junior males. For example, when a prisoner is ill, they take on the role of carer and nurse the patient. They also take on a subordinate mediative role in a scene which is a reworking of the scene discussed above from the 1965 film *Abashiri bangaichi*: *Hokkaihen* in which Tachibana intervenes on behalf of a consumptive who is being beaten by a guard. In the 1966 film *Abashiri bangaichi*: *Ōyuki hara no taiketsu*, this scene is repeated and again it is a sexually ambiguous character who adopts the mediative position and apologises on Tachibana's behalf. In the domestic world of the family, it is usual for the wife to take on this mediative role when her husband is involved in any form of altercation or conflict. In the company, a secretary or a junior male adopts this same mediative role. A scene from Kitano Takeshi's 1989 film *Sono otoko kyōbō ni tsuki* (released in the UK as *Violent Cop*), provides a good example. Kitano, the 'violent cop', is in pursuit of a criminal when his car swerves narrowly missing a woman on her bicycle, however, the driver of the car, a senior policeman, does not apologise, his junior does. By limiting this mediative function to sexually ambiguous characters, the *Abashiri* series clearly defines this role as non-masculine by linking it to its opposite, the feminine. However, the films do not define femininity using women as a reference point, but define it as a negative binary opposition to an esteemed masculinity. Therefore, the negative imaging of these subordinate characters in the Abashiri group deters spectator-identification with these characters. To paraphrase Silverman (1992): to empathise with them would call into question the spectator's identification with the masculine position.

While the thematic structure of the masculine discourse of the films deters spectator-identification with the passive subordinate position, it does encourage identification with a 'reflexive masochistic' position which, as the following analysis of the character, Tachibana Shinichi, will demonstrate, is in fact active and therefore compatible with dominant social conceptions of masculinity. It is this 'reflexive masochistic' position, or in Japanese terms the display of *shinbō* (endurance or stoicism), that these films privilege and cast as a defining characteristic of an ideal masculinity. As Satō (1996 vol 3) argues, the Takakura Ken star persona is the 1960s' equivalent of the *kabuki shinbō tateyaki* in that he displays a stoic perseverance in order to preserve 'traditional virtues' (*bitoku*).

In the essay "Instinct and Their Vicissitudes", Freud (1991f) sets out the 'principle of instinctual reversability', in which sadism is transformed into masochism.

In the case of the pair of opposites sadism-masochism, the process may be represented as follows: (a) Sadism consists in the exercise of violence or power upon some other person as object. (b) This object is given up and replaced by the subject's self. With the turning round upon the self the change from an active to a passive instinctual aim is also effected. (c) An extraneous person is once more sought as object; this person, in consequence of the alteration which has taken place in the instinctual aim, has to take over the role of the subject. Case (c) is what is commonly termed masochism ... [In case (b)] There is a turning round upon the subject's self *without* an attitude of passivity towards another person ... The desire to torture has turned into self-torture and self-punishment, not into masochism. The active voice is changed, not into the passive, but into the reflexive, middle voice. (Freud 1991f:124-125)

According to Freud's three stages, the first, the sadistic stage, mutates into the following stage when the object is given up and replaced by the subject's self; and finally, in the third stage, a new object that becomes the subject (i.e. the one who will inflict pain) is sought. Within this process at the first stage, the sadistic, the infliction of pain is not an aim in itself, as Freud concludes

Psychoanalysis would appear to show that the infliction of pain plays no part among the original purposive actions of the instinct. (Freud 1991f:125)

It is only after the transformation into masochism takes place, 'the pains are very well fitted to provide a passive masochistic aim'. The pain in itself is not pleasurable but 'entrenches' upon sexual excitation and produces a pleasurable condition.

When once feeling pains has become a masochistic aim, the sadistic aim of *causing* pains can arise also, retrogressively; for while these pains are being inflicted on other people, they are enjoyed masochistically by the subject through his identification of himself with the suffering object. (Freud 1991f:126)

The Tachibana character in the *Abashiri* series displays the characteristics described by Freud in case (b), that is, the 'reflexive middle voice'. Within the series this form of active masochism manifests in two narrative patterns. The first and most common is a display of Tachibana's ability to dominate his opponents by being able to withstand greater amounts of pain. The second is in the form of remonstrance which, if taken to the point of death, is traditionally referred to in Japanese as *shi no kōgi* (a protest death). The two patterns however, are not by any means mutually exclusive and are often combined.

The following example from the second film of the series *Zoku Abashiri bangaichi* (*Abashiri Bangaichi Continued*) 1965 provides a good example of stoic masochism as a vehicle of domination. Tachibana the wandering yakuza, following the code of *jing*i, goes to the regional gang headquarters of the yakuza who control the area to introduce himself. He bows formally and begins his oration to the effect that he is Tachibana Shinichi a wandering yakuza come to pay his respects to the local *oyabun*. The underlings guarding the entrance, unschooled in the code of *jingi*, ignore Tachibana before throwing him a handout and telling him to be off. He returns the money saying, 'I have come according to the code of *jingi*, and not as a beggar.' He turns to leave only to be called back by a low ranking yakuza (*chinpira*) who proceeds to slap Tachibana's face from left to right. The sequence of shots is as follows:

> Medium long shot from behind the *chinpira*, the camera focusing attention on Tachibana's face. Cut to medium close-up from behind Tachibana, highlighting the exertion in the *chinpira*'s face as he slaps Tachibana with all his might. Again a close-up reaction shot of Tachibana's impassive face. The *chinpira* at this stage stops exhausted. Cut to close-up of Tachibana, blood oozing from the corner of his mouth as he says, 'Is that the best you can do?'

This sequence is followed by a series of reaction shots of the now fearful onlookers. Tachibana then picks up an iron bar which he offers to the *chinpira* telling him to have a go with this. The *chinpira* and the others back off clearly frightened by this display of stoic masculinity. Tachibana then proceeds to introduce himself again; this time the *chinpira* respectfully responds according to the code of *jing*i. In this montage sequence, Tachibana makes his point through his greater capacity to withstand pain; at no stage does he threaten his opponents with actual physical violence. The camera supports Tachibana's dominating position with low-angle shots and reverse-cut reaction shots.

Similarly in the first film of the series, the true patriarchal *oyabun* of the series establishes his position within the hierarchical structure of the prison cell and the series as a whole through his total lack of fear of death and his potential to endure pain beyond the limits of the other prisoners. In an earlier scene described above, Yoda (Abe Tōru) the villain of the series, had established himself falsely as the senior figure (*senpai*) of the cell. In a subsequent scene in which the pecking order of the cell hierarchy is again re-negotiated, Hachi-nin Koroshi Onitora (Arashi Kanjurō) reveals himself as 'The Demon Tiger who has killed eight people'. He disarms one of his attackers of his makeshift knife and then proceeds to tell the others that one old man could not withstand an all-out attack, but that he would take one of them with him. He approaches each opponent individually asking him if he would be willing to join him on the road to hell. The others all weaken in the face of death. Onitora, through his acceptance of death, conquers his enemies without resorting to physical violence. This scene provides an excellent illustration of Mishima's explication of the statement in the *Hagakure* that 'The meaning of *bushidō* is found in death' (Mishima 1977:50).

> I discovered that the Way of the Samurai is death. In a fifty-fifty life or death crisis, simply settle it by choosing immediate death. There is nothing complicated about it. Just brace yourself and proceed. Some say that to die without accomplishing one's mission is to die in vain, but this is the calculating, imitation samurai ethic of arrogant Osaka merchants. To make the correct choice in a fifty-fifty situation is nearly impossible. We would all prefer to live. And so it is quite natural in such a situation that one should find some excuse for living on. But one who chooses to go on living having failed in one's mission will be despised as a coward and a bungler. This is the precarious part. If one dies after having failed, it is a fanatic's death, death in vain. It is not, however dishonourable. Such a death is in fact the Way of the Samurai. (Mishima 1977:48-49)[3]

In Mishima's example, honour (*meiyo*) and pride (*iji*) are preserved through death: in the case of Onitora, victory is gained over enemies through a stoic rejection of the fear of death.

The final sequence in the 1966 film, the fifth in the series, *Abashiri bangaichi: Arano no taiketsu* (*Abashiri Bangaichi: Showdown in the Wilderness*), provides an excellent example of the second narrative sub-plot through which 'reflexive masochism' becomes the vehicle of remonstrance, *shi no kōgi*. In the dénouement, Tachibana and his group ride to the rival *oyabun*'s stud farm to seek redress in this quasi-cowboy style yakuza drama. During the scene, Shimamoto, the son of a man cheated out of his property and driven to his death by the entrepreneurial villain Gonda, threatens Gonda's daughter. At this point, Tachibana intervenes stepping in front of the daughter and arguing that it would be wrong to shoot an innocent girl who could not be held responsible for her father's actions. In this montage sequence, there is a series of reverse-cut medium close-up shots between Tachibana and Shimamoto (see figures 29 and 30). Tachibana remains undaunted as Shimamoto counts to three and then shoots,

Figures 29–30: *Abashiri bangaichi: Arano no taiketsu* 1966

wounding Tachibana, after which Tachibana regains his composure and again places himself between the girl and Shimamoto, only this time Onitora and the other members of the group move into the centre of the frame, supporting Tachibana's position and further isolating Shimamoto. This is followed by a series of medium close-up reaction shots depicting Shimamoto's weakening resolve, as his grimaces turn to smiles and harmony is restored (see figures 31, 32 and 33). In this scene as in others throughout the series, the endurance of pain becomes one of the mechanisms of male bonding.

I have argued that the Tachibana character, and in fact Takakura Ken's star persona as a whole, can be deconstructed according to Freud's case (b), as set out in *Instincts and Their Vicissitudes*, that is, by a display of stoic masculinity (*shinbō*) through which moral victory is gained in defeat, or in Mishima's terms, honour is found in death. Within the *Abashiri* series, Tachibana is never depicted playing out a sadistic-masochistic scenario. These narrative themes are vicariously played through the sadistic objects of the villains of the various films that make up the series; for example, young children – *Abashiri bangaichi: Bōkyō-hen* (*Abashiri Bangaichi: The Homesickness Episode*) 1965 and *Abashiri bangaichi: Nankoku no taiketsu* 1966; and animals – an example of which and perhaps one of the most disturbing sequences of the entire series is when an old horse is beaten to death on camera by a man with a shovel in the 1967 film *Abashiri bangaichi: Fubuki no sensō* (*Abashiri Bangaichi: War in a Blizzard*). Unlike the later heroes of the yakuza genre Sugawara Bunta of the 1970s and Kitano (Beat) Takeshi of the 1980s, Takakura Ken's star persona is constructed as a sympathetic character, therefore he cannot be depicted in violent scenes in the negative terms of sadism. Thus his violence either revolves around 'reflexive masochism' or is played out in scenes with opponents who are his equal and with whom he invariably becomes a close friend. The violence in such scenarios is simply the device through which each tests, and reaffirms his relative status and position vis-à-vis the other. He is also often depicted in scenes in which he takes on and defeats a vast number of opponents. This narrative convention was incorporated into the *nagare-mono* and yakuza films from the *jidai geki* and demonstrates the hero's superior physical and spiritual power.

In the pre-war period traditional conceptions of masculinity were brought into question, and women often became the focus of

Figures 31–33: *Abashiri bangaichi: Arano no taiketsu* 1966

male discontent, as for example, in the films discussed in chapter one, *Tōkyō no onna* and *Konjiki yasha*. In the early post-war period, as Tayama (1966) explains, men's powerlessness in an oversecure world was a cause of discontent. Salarymen felt isolation and alienation when transferred from region to region, often alone and without their families. In one sense all such salarymen became *nagare-mono*. At another level with the post-war continuing growth of urbanisation, people often found themselves isolated from family and friends.[4] Hence the enormous popularity of the sentimental theme-song sung by Takakura Ken from the *Abashiri* series, which according to Tayama echoed out from myriad karaoke bars throughout Japan in the 1960s. Tayama concludes that the reason for the success of the series and the genre as a whole in the 1960s was that the films symbolically addressed the all too real problems faced by men in their everyday lives. Satō (1996 vol 3) on the other hand, attributes their popularity to the fact that they upheld traditional values at a time of rapid economic growth when profit and self-interest were the dominant concerns. Satō argues that these films played on spectator nostalgia (*nozutarujia*) for a former time when, at least at the ideological level of 'popular memory', relationships between people were based on vertical *oyabun-kobun* structures.

Jingi naki tatakai and the Crisis of the Patriarchy

Within the *Abashiri* series, the relationship between Tachibana and Onitora (*oyabun/kobun*) established from the first film, is central to the narrative. Flashbacks insert Tachibana's difficult childhood into the contemporary narrative of the Abashiri group with Onitora as the omnipotent *oyabun*. Tachibana's father died when he was a small child. His mother remarried and her husband, the archetypal cruel stepfather, beats Tachibana and his mother. The film depicts the rejection of the stepfather and the adoption of the more perfect father as a simultaneous action. These scenes carry two distinct meanings; the first is the clichéd but poignant connection between a deprived childhood minus a father and Tachibana's entry into the criminal world of the yakuza. The second, is in a sense liberating as Tachibana is free to choose a man as his surrogate father who is worthy of his loyalty, therefore their relationship can extend beyond the bounds of Confucian-based concepts of obligation (*giri*). This relationship between Tachibana and Onitora is cemented in an exchange of glances held in medium close-up between the two as Tachibana leaves the prison on the back of a truck and looks back at Onitora who must remain behind. This poignant scene of 'non-verbal' communication is overlaid with Tachibana's voice-over expressing his inner thoughts at their parting. This scenario is repeated in a later film, the 1967 *Abashiri bangaichi: Aku e no chōsen* (*Abashiri Bangaichi: The Evil Challenge*), only in this film it is a youth, Takeshi, who rejects his stepfather, forcing a bottle of lemonade (in Tachibana's case, it was rice) into his stepfather's mouth before leaving home and adopting Tachibana as his mentor. A few scenes later, Onitora ties a piece of string around Tachibana's and Takeshi's thumbs as a symbol of their union. Towards the end of the film, Takeshi is killed living up to the ideals of the homosocial brotherhood (*jingi*) symbolised by the string. In each case the relationship between the two men is established without words (voice-over narration of inner thoughts is often instrumental to this process), through close-up and reverse-cut shots which carry connotations of *ishin denshin* (the immediate communication of truth from one mind to another) (see figures 34, 35, 36, 37 and 38). The giving of, and the denial of food also carry great connotations for male bonding. In both the above examples, the stepfather's denial of food sparks the revolt

Figures 34–35: *Abashiri bangaichi* 1965

FACTS, FICTIONS AND FANTASY

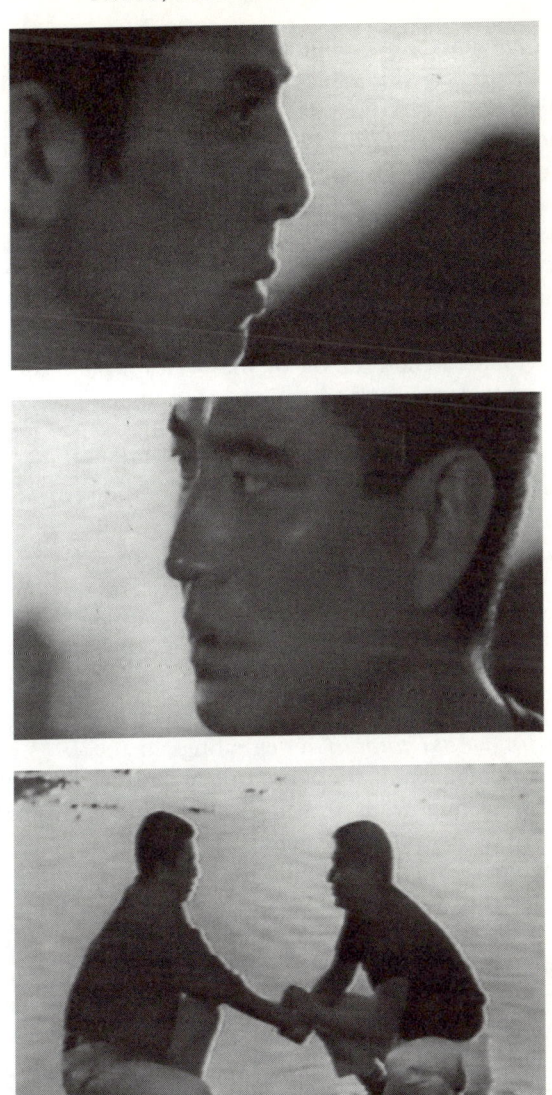

Figures 36–38: *Abashiri bangaichi: Aku e no chōsen* 1967

from the sons. Within the patriarchal structure of the films which rigidly delineates gender roles, the stepfathers clearly transgress in failing as providers. In the first film of the series, Tachibana, while attempting to eat his food with his hands tied across his back in solitary confinement, is reminded of a scene from his youth when his stepfather refused his sister a second helping of rice. Similarly, in the 1973 film based on the autobiography of Taoka Kazuo, *Yamaguchi-gumi sandaime* (*The Third Leader of the Yamaguchi Gang*), food becomes the metaphor which binds the young Taoka (Takakura Ken) to the gang and the *oyabun*. Following conventions established in the *Abashiri* series, this film also draws on flashbacks of Taoka's deprived childhood at the hands of a cruel stepmother who denies him food.

In the *Abashiri* series the omnipresent authority of the *oyabun* is central to the whole ethos of the series which continues to promote male homosocial bonding as a traditional virtue and principal site of male pleasure in much the same way as the wartime productions of Tasaka Tomotaka and the post-war films of the *kamikaze* genre discussed above. Within the vertical structure of social relations presented in the films and echoed in the *nihonjinron* academic discourse of Japanese scholars such as Nakane, the *oyabun/kobun* relationship is central. However, the 1970s *Jingi naki tatakai* series takes an antithetical position by presenting masculinity beset in a world devoid of the archetypal patriarch. With this crisis of the patriarchy that came in the 1970s and the Tōei Studio's break for 'realism' which earned two films from the *Jingi naki tatakai* series ratings in the 1973 and 1974 *Kinema Junpō* top ten, the structure of loyalty depicted in the yakuza film shifted from the vertical to the horizontal, as all successful *oyabun* came to be depicted as scheming entrepreneurs. The archetypal 'bad' *oyabun* of the *Jingi naki tatakai* series Yamamori (Kaneko Nobuo 1923-), who by the fourth film reaches the ultimate heights of yakuza authority in Hiroshima, is portrayed as a weak man who resorts to tears and tantrums as a means of imposing his will. As Sakai (Matsukata Hiroki 1935-) says as he resigns from the Yamamori gang, 'Yamamori was like a *mikoshi* (portable shrine) which he had been burdened with all these years'. Yamamori is therefore suitably depicted throughout the series counting money, powdering his nose with a gold compact and in later films surrounded by young mistresses.

The second film of the series, *Jingi naki tatakai: Hiroshima shitō-hen* (*War Without Morality: Mortal Combat in Hiroshima*), centres on the betrayal of a young man, Yamanaka, (Kitaoji Kinuya 1943-) by his *oyabun*. As a young man leaving prison in the early post-war period, Yamanaka is set upon by a group of yakuza only to be saved by the intervention of Muraoka (Nawa Hiroshi 1932-) an *oyabun* of a rival gang. After rescuing the young Yamanaka, Muraoka proceeds to manipulate him until Yamanaka, towards the end of the film, realises the truth and shoots himself in despair.

The *Jingi naki tatakai* series draws heavily on conventions established in the 1960s *Abashiri* series, particularly in the inclusion of the prison as the only possible setting left in a corrupt world where male bonding can occur. In both series the prison environment represents a utopia outside mainstream society where men can form friendships that transcend the material concerns of 'legitimate' society. In an early sequence in the first film of the series, Hirono Shōzō (Sugawara Bunta) finds himself caught up in a riot over the poor quality and meagre rations of food given to prisoners. He is placed in a cell with the instigator of the riot, a young yakuza, Wakasugi (Umemiya Tatsu 1938-). Wakasugi informs Hirono that he intends to attempt suicide by cutting his stomach (*hara o kiru*). This is not, as within the traditional 'tragic hero' discourse, an act of atonement or an act of self-sacrifice, but a cynical play to force his *oyabun* to pay the requisite bail-bribe to secure his release. Wakasugi asks Hirono to call the guards when he attempts suicide and to perform the *coup de grâce* for him, if for some reason his plan fails and he is left to die in pain. As a reward for his help, Wakasugi promises to raise the necessary bail-bribe money to secure Hirono's release. To seal the pact and in lieu of the fact that they do not have any *sake*, Wakasugi makes a cut in both their arms and they drink each other's blood (see figure 39). Wakasugi's plan succeeds and both men are released. However, as

Figure 39: *Jingi naki tatakai* 1970

fate would have it, both men, after intricate plot manoeuvres, find themselves in different gangs allied to scheming entrepreneurial *oyabun* who ultimately betray them. Therefore, in this example, as in subsequent sub-plots throughout the series, the hero, Hirono, is bonded to a man of similar age and status rather than to his *oyabun*. In the second film of the series mentioned above, Hirono similarly bonds with the young Yamanaka while in prison. Again, a riot is the cause of Yamanaka's punishment in solitary confinement and again, it is the food which Hirono brings him that bonds the two.

In both the *Abashiri* and *Jingi naki tatakai* series, the repression experienced by the yakuza at the hands of the guards, while serving to bind the group or individuals to each other, is also representative of the social forces which restrict spontaneous male freedom. However, in the *Abashiri* series where these scenes served to lighten the dramatic tension as Tachibana and his group get the better of the guards, in *Jingi naki tatakai,* these scenes form part of the sadistic power-play of the guards who represent legitimate authority at its most arbitrary. This is particularly evident in scenes which depict intimate body searches and therefore increases the sense of powerlessness of the yakuza victims involved.

The myriad micro-narratives of individuals interwoven throughout the series are contained within the meta-narratives of defeat, the Occupation, the Korean and Vietnam wars and the Ampo demonstrations. The films are set in Hiroshima and are punctuated by shots of the Hiroshima Dome, symbol not only of defeat but also of social discourses of victimisation (see figure 40). These shots

Figure 40: *Jingi naki tatakai* series – Hiroshima Dome 1970

often follow a funeral of one of the 'traditional' yakuza whose death, often in vain, was caused by the scheming machinations of a corrupt *oyabun*. Their deaths are thus visually linked to the war and victimisation. The hero, Hirono, and various other yakuza with whom he comes into contact are all either demobbed soldiers or, as in the case of Yamanaka, the 'tragic hero' of the second film who was too young to actually be sent to war, were reservists trained in *kamikaze* tactics of self-sacrifice to save the home islands. As Yamanaka says towards the end of the film, 'This is my *zero-sen*', referring to his pistol as his suicide plane thus predicting his own suicide.

The narrative structure of the series as docu-drama emphasises the sense of 'reality' the films project. Drawing on conventions established in war-retro films such as *Dai Nippon Teikoku* and *Nippon no ichiban nagai hi*, the series makes ample use of cinematic devices such as iconic news(*real*) footage and stills, newspaper headlines, voice-of-god narration and captions giving details regarding each character. The struggles of the various gangs and right-wing politicians are thus linked to the disorder and chaos of the immediate Occupation period. This is reinforced by the jerky use of hand-held cameras and the occasional splashes of blood that hit the camera lens as someone is stabbed. Picking up on post-war anti-American discourses, the films clearly associate Japan's post-war social problems with American foreign policy – the Korean and Vietnam wars and the Ampo demonstrations. This theme is further reinforced from within the micro-narrative of Hirono, who in the opening sequence of the first film, saves a Japanese girl from being raped by three American servicemen.

Publicity material and articles written by the screenplay writer, Kasahara, emphasise the fact that the films were based on the prison writings of Yoshino Kōzō, a former Hiroshima *oyabun*. In an article written for the film journal *Shinario* (*Scenario*) in 1974, he recounts his various meetings with Hiroshima yakuza as part of the research he carried out for the films. He states, 'we could not say that the films were a true record in the publicity material', however in another section of the same article he writes, 'the films are close to a true record (*jitsuroku ni chikai*)'. The sense that the films are factual is further in evidence, when in the same article he states that the Yamanaka narrative was based on an actual Hiroshima yakuza, Yamakami Koichi. Kasahara continues,

I intended to write an elegy to Yamanaka, a youth trained in the military tradition, but too young to have actually gone to war. He offers his *oyabun* the loyalty he once offered the state. He uses his twenty-four-caliber pistol, a substitute *zero-sen* freely, as he assassinates people while whistling a military tune. (Kasahara1974:111).

Having stated earlier that he himself had been a reservist too young actually to be sent to the war, but nonetheless trained to defend the home islands, he concludes that through the films, 'in reality I had wanted to expel the vestiges of that time which remained within me' (Kasahara 1974:111), further authenticating the narrative as a true reflection on a past 'reality'.

Satō (1974) argues that the appeal of the *Jingi naki tatakai* series lay in its depiction of the transformation of yakuza organisations from groups involved primarily in gambling enterprises to the modern-day organisations which form part of the quasi-legitimate world of Japanese political and economic life. He argues that in the early post-war period right-wing politicians employed yakuza to disrupt demonstrations and to act as strike-breakers. This alliance between right-wing politicians and the yakuza, based on a mutual dislike of any form of Communism or Socialism, became the vehicle through which yakuza organisations gained a place within legitimate society. It is this transformation that the *Jingi naki tatakai* series documents, therefore, 'it is possible to write the history of modern Japan by documenting the rise and fall of yakuza organisations ... The majority of young men who climbed up through yakuza organisations came from the lowest and most discriminated against social classes' (Kasahara 1974:112).

While the earlier Takakura Ken style of yakuza fought against the entrepreneurial, self-interested *oyabun*, the yakuza organisations depicted in the *Jingi naki tatakai* world have become the mainstay of that same corrupt society. The 'tragic heroes' of this series, like Takakura Ken, exist on the margins of mainstream society; however, they take on a pathetic pathos because, unlike Takakura Ken, they have no secure base such as the utopian Abashiri prison where the values of *jingi* are still adhered to and to which they can return. Their struggles are solitary against monolithic organisations which collude with 'legitimate' authority and which ultimately destroy them. Within the 1960s genre conventions through the hero's death or his confinement in prison (known colloquially as *jigoku chū*-time in hell), the values of *jingi* are upheld and a sense of harmony is restored, giving death or confinement a mythical meaning of sacrifice. From the 1970s and the institution of 'realist' yakuza films, such as the *Jingi naki tatakai* series, the hero often dies, but the system which causes his death remains unaltered and if anything continues stronger than ever.

Kitano (Beat) Takeshi, in his two films *Violent Cop* and *Sonatine*, has perhaps perfected this image of masculinity beset. Both films are, despite differing narrative content, based on the same dual story-line structure. In *Violent Cop*, Takeshi plays Azuma, a policeman who fights corruption in the police force and the drug barons in the society. On one level, the film portrays the disintegration of the work-group ethic through corruption, self-interest and profit, while on the other, it maintains the conventional detective story-line of a policeman fighting crime. In *Sonatine*, the narrative has a similar dual structure. First, Takeshi is brought into conflict with his *oyabun* who is conspiring with Takahashi, another yakuza from the same organisation, to kill him and take over Takeshi's 'patch'. Secondly, the plot evolves around the conventional theme of yakuza films, that is, inter-gang warfare. In both films, Takeshi, the hero, exists on the margins of society as he adheres to traditional values no longer relevant in today's individualistic and profit-orientated society. In the opening sequences of *Violent Cop*, we see Azuma arriving at work, he sits alone reading a newspaper while his fellow policemen are all attending a meeting where the new police chief is giving a speech. Takeshi's rejection of the work group is soon legitimated as potential corruption scandals are gradually revealed and as it becomes evident that what the new police chief says and does are two quite distinct and separate things. The chief's skill with words and subsequent insincerity contrasts with Takeshi's monosyllabic discourse and protracted silences both of which connote sincerity. Takeshi's inability to adapt to the new consumer society is evident in his lack of skill in driving, the car being perhaps the ultimate icon of masculine consumer culture. As Jameson explains, 'the new model car is essentially an image for other people to have of us, and we consume, less the thing itself, than its abstract idea, open to all the libidinal investments ingeniously arrayed for us by advertising' (Jameson 1992:12). In *Violent Cop* while out chasing a suspect in his car, Takeshi continually confuses the switches for the windscreen wipers and the indicators. In *Sonatine*, while driving his girlfriend home, he runs the car off the road and into a ditch, thereby seemingly rejecting contemporary definitions of 'masculinity' mediated through consumption and advertising. Within the Takakura Ken traditions of stoic 'masculinity', he dominates his opponents by showing no fear of death and in his ability to withstand greater amounts of pain. In both films, he has to die because he is an anomaly in the modern world where there is no place for him, no utopian Abashiri prison where the last vestiges of a once valued 'masculinity' can find respite. In the final sequences of *Violent Cop*, it is only too evident that, despite Azuma's death, the system will continue as Takeshi's young assistant, Kikuchi, accepts the bribe from the dead drug baron's assistant now promoted to the position of *oyabun*. In fact it is possible to read the entire sequence of events in the final scenes as being orchestrated by this yakuza. After Azuma kills Nitō the *oyabun*, he goes to Kiyohiro's hideout in a large warehouse where, in a protracted shoot-out, he succeeds in killing him. As he turns to leave, the new *oyabun* steps out of the shadows and shoots Takeshi. The new *oyabun*, surveying the dead bodies says, 'They were both mad,' before turning off the light switch and throwing the scene into darkness. These final scenes bring the film back full circle to the opening shots of a group of youths beating and killing an old tramp, followed by shots of a group of primary school boys throwing empty cans from a bridge at the helmsman of a passing barge.

Kitano (Beat) Takeshi's star persona is predicated on a spontaneous masculinity which draws on iconic meanings of stoicism and 'reflexive masochism' institutionalised in the 1960s through the star persona of such heroes as Takakura Ken and the 1950s idol Ishihara Yujirō. His extreme use of violence in his single-minded dealings with opponents is justified by the violent society in which the films are set and the perceived degeneration of modern youth depicted in the films. Extreme situations call for extreme remedies. On the other hand, violence in the *Jingi naki tatakai* series, is a physical manifestation of wider organisational political struggles. Therefore, the lists of dead, injured and imprisoned given at the end of the fifth film in the series, are in fact just tallies which confirm the extent of the conflict in much the same way as did the figures given at the end of the war-retro film *Nippon no ichiban nagai hi*. Just as the acquisition of money functions as a marker of success in the modern corporate world, the numbers of dead and injured, similarly, become scores by which failure and success are measured. Therefore, it can be argued that, apart from the micro-narratives of such figures as Wakasugi and Yamanaka, death in this series has been codified as failure without 'nobility', as Russell (1995) has argued it is in western fiction. To understand why this occurred, it is necessary to look at the *Jingi naki tatakai* series and its relationship to history and 'popular memory'.

Satō (1974) argues that the appeal of the *Jingi naki tatakai* series lay in its depiction of the transformation of the role of yakuza organisations from feudalistic gangs, involved primarily in gambling, to the multi-million dollar organisations that have penetrated all forms of Japanese political and economic life. Thus, it can be argued that the yakuza organisations depicted in this series are in fact metaphorical representations of 'legitimate' business organisations. As such, the films present an historical rewriting of Japanese post-war corporate and political culture from the perspective of the Tanaka Kakuei dominated 1970s. Tanaka Kakuei, a self-made man who prided himself on his rags-to-riches image, was Prime Minister from 1972 until his enforced resignation over bribery charges in relation to the Lockheed scandal on the 26 November 1974, after which he continued to dominate Japan's ruling LDP Party from behind the scenes until he suffered a stroke in the early 1990s. Tanaka who made his fortune through war contracts was known to have extensive connections with yakuza *oyabun* such as Kodama Yoshio. During the period in which he dominated Japanese politics, the term *kinken seiji* (money-power politics) was coined. The structure of the *Jingi naki tatakai* series as docu-drama encourages this reading of the films, as the development of the yakuza organisations is paralleled with historical landmarks of the post-war recovery. Thus, by the fourth film of the series which takes its historical reference point from the 1964 Olympics, which symbolised Japan's re-entry into the international community, the yakuza organisations are similarly transforming themselves through alliances into powerful international organisations. By the fifth film in the series and the twentieth anniversary of the dropping of the atomic bombs on Hiroshima, the organisation is portrayed as having sufficient legitimacy for its leaders to lay a wreath at the memorial shrine as part of the official ceremonies.

The *Jingi naki tatakai* series marks a distinct change in the narrative tradition of the yakuza genre sparking off other series such as 1977 *Nihon no don* (Japan's Leaders). In the title of this series, there is a pun on the word *don* which is usually pronounced as *shuryō* (leader). *Don* being the pronunciation that refers to yakuza *oyabun*, thus the title of the film overlaps and confuses the two uses of the word. This change in the yakuza genre, first instituted by the *Jingi naki tatakai* series, is evident in a shift to a perceived 'realism' both in the adoption of the docu-drama format and in its portrayal of death, not from within mythological discourses of sacrifice, but in its encodation as failure.

Conclusions

Historicity and the Sensual Imperative of Imaged Masculinity[1]

> The whole life of those societies in which modern conditions of production prevail presents itself as an immense accumulation of *spectacles*. All that was directly lived has become mere representation. (Debord 1995:12)

> What is inauthentic about nostalgia films and texts ... can best be dramatized in another way by which (*sic*) I will call the cult of the glossy image, as a whole new technology (wide-angle lens, light-sensitive film) has allowed its lavish indulgence in contemporary film. (Jameson 1992:85)

This study grew from the initial premise that *Chūshingura* established an important sub-text within Japanese popular culture. After viewing some 1,500 Japanese films, and drawing on the theories of Claude Lévi-Strauss (1962, 1968, 1990), Northrop Frye (1957) and Hayden White (1985), it became evident that the narrative structure of the 'tragic hero', implicit in *Chūshingura*, is in fact the principal structure through which aspects of modern Japanese history have been codified and interpreted in popular film. Therefore, chapters two and three examined the role of the 'tragic hero' pregeneric narrative form as a figurative structure through which the Japanese people could interpret the events of the Second World War and defeat. These films offered spectators both an avenue of exculpation from a foreign-imposed sense of guilt and, relatedly, formed part of a discourse which developed as a backlash against the criminalisation of Japan through her wartime leaders.

These chapters analysed the ideological construction of the filmic 'tragic heroes' and their relationship to the popular interpretation of historical events. War-retro films were examined from the contextual perspective of a structuring opposition between a nativist Confucian ethic, and culture as defined in terms of western 'civilisation' and encoded in the War Crimes Charter. Chapter 1 traced the roots of this opposition to the formation of a nationalist consciousness through the invention of the *kokutai* in the late nineteenth and early twentieth centuries as a psychological force to counter the threat of western imperialism. Post-war films, such as the tele-movie *Watashi wa kai ni naritai*, narrativised this opposition through the dilemma faced by Shimizu, the unheroic 'tragic hero' who was forced to make a choice between his morality, as defined by the nativist Confucian ethics of *giri ninjō*, and the law, symbol of culture/civilisation.

Films which take their themes from historical events, as well as academic histories (Carr 1990, White 1985), resonate with the values and concerns of the times in which they were produced. Therefore, it can be argued that they should be analysed on two levels; first, through their appeals to historicity, they can be analysed as texts which purport to comment on times past; and secondly, and perhaps more importantly, as cultural artefacts which contribute to the cultural discourses of the times in which they were produced. It is this second aspect which has been the dominant concern of this study and it is my conclusion that mainstream war-retro films, cast within the 'tragic hero' narrative form, recount the past and, in so doing, re-position the spectator for the future. My analysis has demonstrated that in the *kamikaze* films of the 1950s, the allegorical meaning of death as sacrifice is distanced from overt wartime propaganda, and is instead re-articulated as a site of purification in which the old was expunged so that the new, and by definition better, could come into being. Visually this theme is conveyed through motifs of light and darkness symbolising historical closure and rebirth and through images of falling *sakura* (cherry blossoms). In the 1960s, the images of Japan's wartime leaders, such as General Tōjō and General Anami, similarly emerged as 'tragic heroes' who sacrificed themselves for the *kokutai* and Japan's future. Only in films such as *The Human Condition* and the avant-garde *Nikudan* are attempts made to challenge this hegemonic discourse by questioning established cultural meanings of death. With the 1990s and the fiftieth

CONCLUSIONS

anniversary of the war, tele-movie remakes, such as *Watashi wa kai ni naritai*, invite the audience to make comparisons between Japan's role in the Second World War and defeat, and the Allies' foreign policy during various Cold War struggles, such as the Korean and Vietnam wars, thus contemporising the debate by asking the question, 'Was Japan any worse than the Allies in her pursuance of foreign policy through aggression?'

Chapter 4 analyses the 'tragic hero' through a focus on the fantasy world of the *nagare-mono* (drifter) or yakuza film. The analysis revealed the existence of a fundamental structuring opposition, manifested between the yakuza moral code of *jingi*, which translates literally as humanity and justice, and the restraints to spontaneous male freedom imposed by culture and the law; the law in this instance being both the coercive juridical institutions and the more subtle constraints imposed by social institutions, such as the family. Following Fiske's (1991) analysis of "Gendered Television: Masculinity" in *Television Culture*, I argued that one of the reasons for the great popularity of these films in the 1960s was their ability to offer meanings which men could employ to reach an understanding of the contradictions that existed between the reality of their everyday experiences and the 'ideological construction of masculinity which [was] offered as the way to make sense of those experiences' (Fiske 1991:198). One aspect of this was an analysis of the symbolic meaning of violence in these films. The examination revealed that violence is a narrativised physical expression of competition in relationships of domination and subordination. Thus, while the earlier chapters were concerned with an ideological deconstruction of the 'tragic hero' in war-retro films, chapter four was concerned with an analysis of masculine subjectivity as defined in the films of the yakuza genre, from a socio-psycho-analytic perspective.

In this final concluding chapter, I want to return to the two central questions raised in the introduction: what is the relationship between history, myth and memory? And, how are individual subjectivities defined in relation to the past? Despite the claims of most mainstream war-retro films to represent the past objectively (a claim made implicitly by their docu-drama structure, and explicitly in their publicity material), they have in fact codified their subject matter within traditional collective mythical structures. Most filmmakers chose to cast their heroes and, by extension, Japan itself (in the films of the atomic bombs and the Okinawa assault), as the 'tragic hero', thus rendering the inexplicable and traumatic, both familiar and understandable. I have argued that one of the reasons for the appeal of the 'tragic hero' form is to be found in the politics of defeat and the criminalisation of Japan through her wartime leaders.

But what about individual subjectivity? Lipsitz (1994) reminds us that we construct our identities at least in part 'in dialogue with the past'. Films therefore, help to 'locate our own private stories within the larger collective'. In Japanese cinema at the structural level, the individual spectator is encouraged to do just that, by the docu-drama format of most mainstream war-retro films and the 1970s 'realist' yakuza films, such as the *Jingi naki tatakai* series. This structure allows for the micro-narrative of individuals to be contained within the meta-narratives of war, defeat and post-war reconstruction. I would suggest that, in the case of contemporary audiences of the 1950s and 1960s war-retro films, that is, those who had actually experienced the war, this invitation to slot themselves into the narrative would have been quite powerful. Informal interviews I have carried out with people from this generation after screenings of these films confirm this view. The huge audience response to *The Human Condition* in the form of letters to the director Kobayashi Masaki, similarly shows the engagement of contemporary audiences with the character Kaji (Mellen 1976:185). Rose explains, 'new technologies change the nature of the memorial processes':

> A video or audiotape, a written record, do more than just reinforce memory; they freeze it, and in imposing a fixed, linear sequence upon it, they simultaneously preserve it and prevent it from evolving and transforming itself with time. (Rose 1992:61)

It can be argued that the Japanese proclivity for the almost identical remake of films based on experiential accounts of the war confirms this fixation of memory through technology. *Himeyuri no tō (Memorial to the Lilies)* provides a good example. Written shortly after the war, the book recounts the trials and deaths of a group of Okinawan female students aged between sixteen and twenty who were seconded to work as nurses in Japanese field army hospitals. The book recounts their experiences from March 1945 until Japan's acceptance of the Potsdam Declaration in August of that same year.

The majority were killed or committed suicide. A few survived, including Nakasone Seizen one of their teachers who wrote the book. Imai Tadashi made two films based on this book; the first in 1953 was in fact a political act to counter American demands for Japan's re-armament (Satō 1996 vol 3). In 1982 he remade the film in colour as part of Tōhō Studio's fiftieth anniversary celebration of the founding of the studio. In 1995 an almost identical remake was released by the Tōhō Studios to commemorate the fiftieth anniversary of the end of the war. At the time of this latter release and as part of the film's promotion, NHK interviewed one of the few survivors. She had worked as an advisor on the film, her principal function being to authenticate the film. Despite being made by a different director, the fact that the 1995 remake was so close to Imai's versions, similarly helps to demonstrate its authenticity as fact. Any changes even in character type at the level of casting would have brought into question the 'reality' of the world the films portray. Therefore, the 'reality' of the experiences of this group of girls as 'tragic heroes' of their age has become fixed within this narrative structure and the collective memories of the war generation who saw the films.

The first version, directed by Imai, was the largest grossing film of the year breaking box office records and earning a place in the *Kinema Junpō* top ten ratings for 1953. Despite the comments made by the survivor during the NHK interview to the effect that the 1995 remake was produced largely in the hope that the younger generations who had not actually experienced the war would come to see the film and thereby realise the full horror of war, there is little evidence to suggest any real interest in the film from this targeted audience; nor in fact in any of the other remakes (*Kike wadatsumi no koe-Listen to the Roar of the Ocean*) released at this time. It can be argued that these films have stayed fixed within the generational memories of people who did actually experience the war. Jameson's assertion with regard to the reception of pop music, appears just as applicable to the reception of cinema in the context of repetition and generational consciousness:

> The passionate attachment one can form to this or that pop single, the rich personal investment of all kinds of private associations and existential symbolism which is a feature of such attachment, are fully as much a function of our own familiarity as of the work itself: the pop single, *by means of*

repetition, insensibly becomes part of the existential fabric of our own lives, so that what we listen to is ourselves, our own previous auditions. (Jameson 1992:20). (my emphasis)

The example of *Himeyuri no tō* demonstrates how cinematic genres, just like pop music, are generationally linked.[2] However, as this study has shown, the 'tragic hero' narrative operates on another level, that of the pregeneric or mythic; thus it has remained popular by crossing genre boundaries. Therefore, it can be argued that repetition in popular Japanese cinema functions at two levels: first, it is generationally linked, that is, in terms of genre and mise-en-scène; and secondly, at the level of myth, as an interpretive framework it provides a link which binds generations by providing (imaginary) resolutions to real contradictions, thus, in the words of Lévi-Strauss, insuring 'the permanency of the group'. With regard to *Chūshingura* and films based on what is commonly referred to as the contemporary *Chūshingura*, that is, films based on the 26 February 1936 attempted uprising of a group of young army officers (fourteen films were made based on this incident), there is room within the mise-en-scène for contemporaneous interpretations which appear to make these films relevant to young audiences. The film critic Nomura Shusuke (1988), writing on the release of the 1988 Gosha Hideo version of the 26 February incident film, *226*, was surprised when his young son appeared to so enjoy the film. He was surprised because, as he explains in 'this age of plenty' (*hōshoku no jidai*) he did not think the story relevant. However, in this article which he wrote for the film journal *Eigageijitsu*, he went on to elaborate on an incident that occurred at his son's school. The relevance of the film was thus linked to questions of failure and the necessity for a man to accept responsibility for his actions regardless of the consequences. In short what Nomura is implying is that the perceived qualities of masculinity associated with the 'tragic hero' are still relevant for contemporary youth.

At the psychological level of spectator pleasure, I have argued that, in films based on the 'tragic hero' narrative pattern, a libidinal investment is made in the homosocial sub-text and the related displays of violence. In more recent films, such as those of Kitano (Beat) Takeshi, the ideological divisions between the homosocial sub-text and displays of violence no longer exist within the filmic discourse, as dominant homosexual characters exist openly within the films' narratives (*Violent Cop* and *Boiling Point*). This libidinal engagement is encouraged not only in the thematic concerns of the films, but perhaps more powerfully, in the 'sensual imperative' of the aesthetic construction of images. It is at this point that 'nostalgia' becomes the dominant emotion through which a 'libidinal politics' (*jouissance*) of desire is channelled into the post-war group ethos. Tayama (1966) and Satō (1996 vol 3) have both argued that the popularity of yakuza films of the 1960s was based on a 'nostalgia' for a past which is portrayed as promising male camaraderie. In these yakuza films, what was formerly constructed as wartime feelings of collectivity and solidarity are translated into civilian economic life. In both yakuza and war-retro films of the *kamikaze* sub-genre, this 'nostalgia'-based collective sentiment is structured as a critique of what is defined within the films as western style individualism and the materialism of modern society. In the *Jingi naki tatakai* series and in the films of Kitano (Beat) Takeshi, this critique is overtly connected to anti-American sentiments. In the *Jingi naki tatakai* series Japan's social problems are, through the docu-drama structure, linked to the Occupation and American foreign policy. In Kitano (Beat) Takeshi's films, Okinawa is the place where American servicemen sell illegal arms to yakuza and corrupt Japanese women. Through appeals to 'nostalgia', these films contribute to *nihonjinron* discourses of the group nature of Japanese society. Through 'nostalgia', the work-group ethos of the post-war economic recovery period is endowed with a reconstructed positive image of 'traditional' Japanese values based on a libidinal investment of the sensuality of the image. In chapter two, I gave a detailed outline of the penultimate sequence of *Kumo nagaruru hateni* as an example of how cinematically the relationship between Otaki and Fukami was eroticised. In terms of violence, scenes of death and sexuality are similarly constructed to link the two, as a comparison of figures 41 and 42 demonstrates.

Finally, the two latest film versions of *Chūshingura*, both released in 1994 to celebrate one hundred years since the birth of cinema, and the 1988 film *226*, continue the trend established in the 1960s to emphasise loyalty to the group and horizontal ties between men. In the two latest *Chūshingura*, *Shijūshichi-nin no shikaku* (*The Forty-seven Assassins*) and *Chūshinguragaiden Yotsuyakaidan*, Asano, while symbolic, is not the true focus of loyalty for the forty-seven *rōnin*. Their primary loyalty is to each other. It is a loyalty that is built up and maintained in the face of adversity, in that they have reached a state of relative equality by all

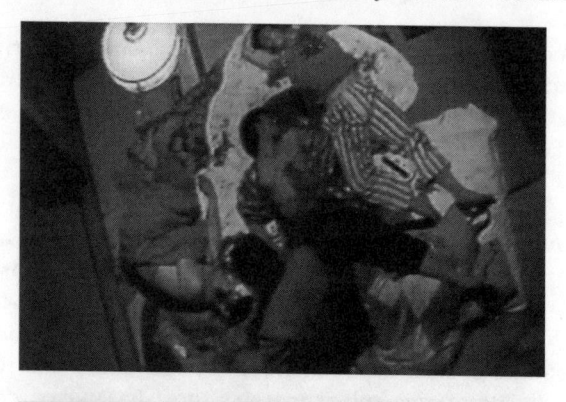

Figure 41-42: *Jingi naki tatakai* 1970

being subjected to the same repression. This aspect of loyalty echoes the relationship between the soldiers in the Tasaka Tomotaka war films of the 1940s. Only now, the development of cinematic technology (wide-angle lens and light-sensitive film) has made it possible to capture scenes of iconic significance as pure spectacle, the interpretation of which requires a libidinal engagement on the part of the spectator. Thus, a film like Gosha Hideo's *226* can be made without a significant plot. Images resonating of the 'tragic hero' are strung together, and we, the spectators, recognise them as such in all their glossiness and piece the narrative together from our iconic memory.

In short, in this study I have argued that within Japanese popular cinema the 'tragic hero' pregeneric narrative has, through repetition, reached mythic significance. It is both an interpretive structure through which explanations of the war and defeat have

CONCLUSIONS

become fixed within the collective memory, and the principal strategy through which a particular concept of 'masculinity' is constituted as 'reality'. The theme of this study, although political, delved into the psychic to explain the individual's relation to the image of the 'tragic hero' and the dominant (ideo)logic of a Japanese conception of masculinity.

Notes

Introduction

1 In 1932 the first Shanghai Incident sparked off hostilities between Chinese and Japanese forces. During the ensuing battle, three soldiers became immortalised as 'human bullets' (*nikudan*). They carried bombs to the perimeter fence of the Chinese army camp and, in the process of blasting a hole through the fence, blew themselves up. Shimizu (1994) states that although they were made into heroic figures, becoming the heroes of six films made about the incident, their deaths were in fact an accident.

2 *Yoidore tenshi*: Dr Sanada says, 'Things have changed a lot since you were thrown in jail. Your feudal ideas are out of date. Calling her your wife doesn't make her that, unless she wants to be. Women have the same rights as men.'

3 Barthes made a similar point in *Mythologies* (1981):

> ... pictures, to be sure, are more imperative than writing, they impose meaning at one stroke, without analysing or diluting it. (110)

4 It should be noted however that Althusser makes the point that neither the institution of the Repressive State Apparatus nor the Ideological State Apparatus function purely as independent agents of repression and ideology respectively. Rather institutions of the Repressive State Apparatus function 'predominantly by repression (including physical repression), while functioning secondarily by ideology. Althusser makes the point that 'there is no such thing as a purely repressive apparatus'. He cites the Army and Police as examples – they 'function by ideology both to ensure their own cohesion and reproduction, and in the "values" they propound externally' (Althusser 1971:145).

Similarly, but inversely,

NOTES

the Ideological State Apparatuses function massively and predominantly by *ideology* but they also function secondarily by repression, even if ultimately, but only ultimately, this is very attenuated and concealed, even symbolic. (There is no such thing as a purely ideological apparatus.) Thus Schools and Churches use suitable methods of punishment, expulsion, selection, etc., to "discipline" not only their shepherds, but also their flocks. The same is true of the Family ... The same is true of the cultural I[deological] S[tate] Apparatus (censorship, among other things), etc. (Althusser 1971:145)

5 This photograph has reached iconic significance through its constant reproduction in both western and Japanese film history texts.
6 The dates here are taken from the lunar calendar.
7 This is now known as Hyōgo prefecture in the Kinki district.
8 In the Edo period, one hundred and four cases of revenge were recorded. (Satō 1976:11)
9 There was only one recorded instance where a maid took revenge for her dead master. (Satō 1976:ll)
10 The Soga Brothers. Soga Sukenari (1172-1193) and Soga Tokimune (1174-1193). Their father, Sukeyasu, was murdered in 1177 by a relative, Kudō Suketsune. Their mother re-married Soga Sukenobu who adopted the two boys. When they were still children, they vowed to avenge their father. However, Kudō Suketsune enjoyed the patronage of Yoritomo who had fallen out with the Soga brothers' grandfather. Yoritomo ordered the boys to be brought to Kamakura where they were to be put to death. After the intervention of various noblemen, the two were spared and returned to their mother. When Yoritomo was on a hunting trip, they penetrated into his camp and killed Kudō Suketsune. Sukenari (Jūrō), the elder brother, was killed instantly, but Tokimune (Gorō) was arrested. According to popular discourse, Yoritomo, admiring the boldness of the act, was inclined to spare Tokimune. However, Kudō Suketsune's son intervened and Tokimune was executed.
11 Sugawara Michizane (845-903) was a minister in the Imperial Court of the Emperor Uda. He sought to re-establish the authority of the Emperors who had increasingly come under the influence of the Fujiwara clan through marriage politics. As a result of their activities, the Fujiwara orchestrated his downfall and in 901 he was exiled. He died two years later.
12 Kusunoki Masashige (1294-1336) supported the Emperor Go-Daigo against the Hōjō whom he fought in many battles before being defeated at Hyōgo. It is reported that during this battle, he sustained eleven wounds and finally committed *seppuku* with his brother Masasue.

After his death, the Emperor conferred on him the title of *Sakon-e-chūjō* and the rank of *shō-sa ni*. After the restoration, he was raised to the rank of *jū-ichi-i* and in 1871, a temple (Nankō-san) was erected in his honour on the spot where he died for the cause of the legitimate sovereign. (Papinot 1984:334)

13 Sakura Sōgorō was the village headman (*nanushi*) of the village Kōzu. The local *daimyō*, Hotta Masanobu, had raised the taxes causing great suffering throughout the prefecture. All the village heads met and decided to take a petition to the Shōgun Ietsuna in Edo. Sakura Sōgorō was chosen as their representative. At this time, it was against the law for a common person to appeal directly to the shōgun. As a result, Sakura Sōgorō and his entire family were arrested and executed in 1655.
14 Some early *bunraku* and *kabuki* versions cast Kira in the role of lecher.

Chapter 1

1 *Kokutai* as a concept is very important in the study of Japanese nationalism. *The Kodansha Nihongo Daijiten* (*Japanese Dictionary*) comments:

> From the *bakumatsu* period to the Second World War [*kokutai*] was employed as a concept to signify both the unique family state over which the Emperor reigned from a line unbroken, and racial supremacy.

This dictionary also gives an English translation for *kokutai* as 'national polity' which is the way it is generally translated into English. However, there are problems with this translation, as 'polity' refers both to 'civil order' and a 'particular form of political organization', whereas the Japanese definition above implies a stronger sense of 'nationalism' which does not always come through in the translation 'national polity'.

Maruyama in *Nihon no shisō* (*Japanese Thought*) gives a better account of how the concept of *kokutai* actually functioned in Japanese society in the pre-war years as an illusory community which carried with it powers of social regulation. In this extract, he is discussing the village *kyōdōtai* (community) which was at one time regarded as the smallest cell of the *kokutai*.

> [The village *kyōdōtai*] is a group whose emotional immediacy and cohesiveness checks any overt conflict of interests, obscures the locus of decision-making, and disallows the autonomy of the individuals within it. It is also there that the tradition of 'indigenous belief' originates. Through the control of irrigation and common lands and the web of personal *oyakata-kokata* relationships, the village produces an absolute unity of authority and feelings of mutual obligation. It is thus the very 'model' of traditional human relationships and the smallest 'cell' of the *kokutai*. In *kyōdōtai* at the base, as in *kokutai* at the apex, of society all ideologies - whether 'totalitarianism', parliamentary 'democracy', or harmonious 'pacifism' - are necessarily subsumed. (quoted in *The Culture of the Meiji Period*, Irokawa Daikichi, 1985:273)

NOTES

2   This is not to imply, as subsequent chapters will demonstrate, that there was a total rejection of things and concepts western, but rather only of those aspects associated with bourgeoisie individualism which were construed as potentially divisive.
3   Ikegami supports this view when she states that 'By the late seventeenth century, a full-blown national market economy flourished' (1995:173)
4   [A] law enacted by the Tokugawa Shōgun which obliged all the *daimyō* to reside alternately in their domains and in Edo, and to leave their wife and children as hostages in that city. The time of residence was not strictly determined but most of the daimyō remained one year at Edo and one year in their domains. Those of the Kwantō [Kantō] province changed their residence every 6 months. This law [was] enacted in 1634 by the Shōgun Iemitsu, [and] was abrogated in 1862. (Papinot 1984:541)
5   It was Max Weber who first defined the state as the agency which possesses the monopoly on legitimate violence.
6   For a detailed discussion of the unifying effects of education particularly mass literacy, see B. Anderson, *Imagined Communities*, London: Verso 1993.
7   Gluck makes the point that

> despite the social myth of the middle-class, disparities of net wealth, employment security, and social equality affect the lives of those 95 out of 100 Japanese who identify themselves in that category. (Gluck 1992:xli)

8   It should be noted that prior to and during the election campaign of 1890, party politics and politicians, who associated themselves with the new constitutional government, were given a negative image linked to a western-style individualism and self-interest (*rigai kankei*) in the press. At first this view was perpetuated by the oligarchs who became increasingly alarmed by the characteristic social problems (*shakai mondai*) of industrialisation – the new proletariat, a massive increase in urbanisation and the establishment of the Popular Rights movement. In the 1870s, there was a phenomenal growth in the People's Rights Movement. Sims locates the origins of this movement in the *shizoku* (a descendant from a samurai) opposition to the Meiji government. In January 1874, a petition was presented to the government

> advocating the immediate establishment of a representative assembly (or assemblies) to limit the arbitrary nature of the regime, they argued that by uniting government and people this would produce greater stability and national strength. (Sims 1991:50)

Although this petition was rejected, it did, as Sims points out, provoke the first public debates on constitutionalism. At about this time, the same group of discontented samurai formed Japan's first political society, the *Aikokukōtō* (The Public Patriotic Party). This was followed by the establishment of several other regional parties which, while able to influence government at the local level, failed to gain support at the national level. However, the failure of the Satsuma rebellion did encourage the *Risshisha* (Self-Help Society) to take up the call for a national assembly. According to Sims, by 1880 the People's Rights Movement had reached a peak with the lodgement of an estimated 130 petitions calling for a national assembly.

The reasons for the awakening of political consciousness at this time are attributed by Sims to 'the rapid development in communications and social mobility...' In particular, the increase in newspapers critical of the government which 'allowed, for the first time in Japan, informed public debate of national affairs'. The newspapers in the late 1870s were more like 'the organs of political clubs' than the mass-circulation dailies of the post-World War One era. By 1878, 225 titles were being printed with an annual circulation of 37 million.

> Through them, and through the speech-making tours by the leaders of political societies and by liberal lawyers and journalists, the third strand of the People's Rights movement – the urban intellectuals – made its impact on the country at large. (Sims 1991:53)

Furthermore, the oligarchs were also concerned to secure their own power base before the promulgation of the Constitution of 1889 which would (even if only on a very limited scale) effectively open up politics. The oligarchs sought to raise themselves above politics so that they would not be subject to the 'mandate of heaven', a Confucianist precept allowing for the removal of a ruler if he were found to be unjust. By linking themselves to the Emperor and not politics, their positions became like that of the Emperor, similarly 'inviolable'.

The introduction in 1889 of the 'Regulations for Public Meetings' effectively banned teachers, military personnel, police officers, students, agricultural and technical apprentices from joining political associations. This prohibition was extended to women and minors in July 1890. Legal restrictions were reinforced by direct ideological injunction. The 'Rescript to Soldiers and Sailors' of 1882 enjoined the military to 'neither be led astray by current opinions nor meddle in politics but with a single heart fulfill your essential duties of loyalty (*chūsetsu*).' (quoted in Gluck 1985:53) The purpose of this passage was to keep the military, like the Emperor, above politics. Therefore, the Rescript was given from the Emperor 'to his – not the state's soldiers' (Gluck 1985:54). This reinforced the personal nature of the relationship between the Emperor and his soldiers and provided the very justification to which the young officers of the 26 February Incident were to appeal in the late 1930s. They argued they had acted not in the name of politics, i.e. self-interest, but in the higher cause of the Emperor, i.e. a non-partisan neutrality (*fuhen futō*). Gluck comments:

NOTES

> Through universal conscription and the growth of the reservist associations the exclusion and denigration of politics by the military were messages that over the years reached large numbers of Japanese. (Gluck 1985:54-55)

The Imperial Rescript on Education of 1890 became the ultimate ideological mechanism establishing a personal relationship between each individual and the Emperor. Like the Rescript to Soldiers and Sailors, it bypassed politics as it was issued as a 'personal moral utterance' of the Emperor and not as a law of the state (Gluck 1985:122). It was a mixture of Mito School historical mythology (for a detailed discussion of the Mito School, see H.D.Harootunian, *Toward Restoration: The Growth of Political Consciousness in Tokugawa Japan*, 1984:47-128), combined with Confucian ethics linking the *kokutai* to loyalty and filial piety, and modern injunctions to civil obedience and national sacrifice.

The oligarch's view that politicians were corrupt was strengthened in the popular press during the election campaign of 1890, as journalists sought to expose cases of opportunism and corruption. They placed politics in the context of the traditional *kan* (government official)/*min* (the people) dichotomy and accused candidates of attempting to play one off against the other to advance their own self-interest. Gluck (1985) makes the point that this view was in fact distorted as scholars considered the election of 1890 to have been relatively fair. However, it must be borne in mind that the electorate comprised only 1.1 percent of the population who were eligible to vote due to the fifteen *yen* per annum tax requirement. Therefore, the electorate was mostly comprised of rural landowners. Consequently, urban dwellers were vastly under-represented. These rural landowners were mostly village officials and so the *kan*-politician combination further strengthened the popular image of corruption. Moreover, the newly elected dietmen were lampooned in the popular press because of their western ways.

> the connection with western fashions ... brought the politicians into range of the reaction against superficial westernization that was both part of the cultural nationalism of the time and, more viscerally, of the glaring differences in lifestyle between the social elite and the rest of the population. (Gluck 1985:70)

9 The suppression of popular participation in politics by the Meiji oligarchy runs counter to the western political tradition by which Hobsbawm argued:

> The very act of democratising politics, i.e. of turning subjects into citizens, tends to produce a populist consciousness which, seen in some lights, is hard to distinguish from a national, even a chauvinist, patriotism - for if 'the country' is in some way 'mine', then it is more readily seen as preferable to those of foreigners,

especially if these lack the rights and freedom of the true citizen. (1992c:88)

In the 1870s, the Japanese opposition parties argued along these same lines – participation meant commitment, western nations were strong for this reason. The Meiji government countered saying that the 'Japanese people were politically immature' (Lehmann 1982:249) and therefore not ready for popular participation in government. Even after the Second World War, the elite led by Yoshida, sought to limit the effects of universal suffrage on the Japanese polity.

10 An anti-American sub-text is evident in the 1964 *Nikutai no mon (The Gates of Flesh)*, directed by Suzuki Seijun. In this version which was based on a best-selling novel by Tamura Taijirō and earlier made into a film by Makino Masahirō in 1948, the rape of a Japanese woman becomes a metaphor for the rape of Japan by the American Occupation Forces. Recently, Gosha Hideo has made yet another version. Interestingly, this sub-text is prevalent in South Korean films made after the Korean War of 1950–1953, particularly in the 1955 version of *Ch'un Hyang-chŏn (The Story of Ch'un Hyang)*. Within the first two months of its release, ten percent of the population of Seoul had been to see it.

11 Censorship Law.

June 1939 – directors, assistant directors, script writers, cameramen and artistic directors formed a single Union of Cinema Personnel (*Nippon Eiga Renmei*). (Hamada 1995:102)

October 1939 – The Japanese Film Law was put into effect. In total this law comprised twenty-six articles. Hamada summarises the main points as follows:

> All scripts were to be subject to pre-production censorship; a film industry licensing system was introduced; minors fourteen or under were prohibited entry to cinemas; only films which increased public education would be authorised; a distinction was to be made between general and non-general films; the screening of news and culture films was made compulsory; and actors and technicians had to be registered. (Hamada 1995:103–104)

The first article of the law stated that

> The aim of this law is to encourage the development of a healthy film industry that will produce a qualitatively high standard of films which promote the national culture. (quoted in Hamada 1995:104)

Hamada criticises the declared aims of this law, arguing that its true purpose was related to the prosecution of the war and the maximisation of the 'effective use of the country's strength'. He goes on to say that it was a blatant attempt to regulate culture (*bunka tōsei*) and ideology (*shisō tōsei*). However, I would suggest that it is important when condemning the Japanese wartime Film Laws to bear in mind that in the immediate post-war period, under American auspices, a similarly draconian law was introduced to effectively regulate 'culture' and 'ideology'. For a further discussion of the film laws, see Sakuramoto 1993: 66-92; Satō vol. 2, 1995:21-37. In English, see Hirano 1992:13-24.

12 The film version was based on the prize-winning novel by Iwashita Sunsaku.

13 As Mishima explains in his book on the *Hagakure:*

> The ideal presented in *Hagakure* may be summed up in one expression, 'secret love', and *Hagakure* maintains flatly that once love has been confessed, it shrinks in stature; true love attains its highest and noblest form when one carries its secret to the grave. (1977:28)

14 Ozu again used the giving of *kozukai* in *Tōkyō monogatari* to symbolise Noriko's filial attitude to her parents-in-law. This is contrasted with the failure of their children to conform even to this symbolic tradition.

15 The film version of *Kaigun* was based on the novel *Tennō no kaigun* (*The Emperor's Navy*) by Iwata Toyō and was first serialised in the *Asahi Shinbun*. 'Special' was a euphemism for 'suicide'.

16 In this section, I have focused the discussion on *Kaigun* and *Rikugun* as they are representative examples of mainstream war films released in the early 1940s. They are also both excellent examples of the *kinen* film (films produced to commemorate an historic event such as Pearl Harbour - *Kaigun*, and the third anniversary of the Pacific War - *Rikugun*). Other examples include *Katō Hayashi sentō-tai* 1944, *Sensuikan ichi gō* 1941, *Hawai Marē okikaisen* 1942, *Aiki minami e tobu* 1943, and *Kimi koso tsugi no arawashi da* 1944.

17 In traditional Japanese theatre, the *Noh* and *Kabuki*, women have been contained through the institution of the *onnagata* (female impersonator). It was only with the advent of *shinpa* theatre and its closely related medium, the modern film, that actresses began to appear, driving *onnagata* from the screen completely in 1922. (Hamada 1995:55)

18 While *Hōrō zanmai* effectively contains the female character within an idealised feminine image, the hero's estranged mother in Inagaki's 1931 film *Banba no Chūtarō mabuta no haha* is in the reality of the film's narrative found to be very different from the image the hero held of her in his mind's eye (*mabuta*). Although set in the late Tokugawa period, the film reflects the unpredictability of changing social roles brought about by rapidly changing economic relations. The title, freely translated in Burch (1979) as *The Mother He Never Knew*, in fact carries greater significance for the narrative when *mabuta*, which literally means eyelid, is read in its metaphorical sense as in phrases such as *mabuta ni nokoru* (live in one's memory) or *mabuta ni*

ukabu (float back into one's memory). It is this sense of memory that both the visual narrative and the *benshi* (narrator) dwell on in the final climactic scenes when Chūtarō, after many months of searching, finally finds his mother only to be rejected by her before a reconciliation is reached. (This film was re-released on video as part of a series of six classic films recorded with *benshi* voice-over narration.)

19 The *shinpa* movement that appeared in the latter half of the Meiji period refers to a 'realistic' theatrical trend that broke with the stylised traditions of *Noh* and *Kabuki* and was inspired by such western playwrights as Ibsen.

20 Said in *Orientalism* describes the west's response to the Oriental world in terms of an often negative sexuality, as he observes when discussing Flaubert.

> Woven through all of Flaubert's Oriental experiences, exciting or disappointing, is an almost uniform association between the Orient and sex. In making this association Flaubert was neither the first nor the most exaggerated instance of a remarkably persistent motif in Western attitudes to the Orient. (Said 1991b:188)

He continues at various other points in his analysis to refer to the threatening nature of this sexuality particularly in relation to the Islamic world. A similar discourse is evident in Bornoff's account of sexuality in Japan, *Pink Samurai* (1991). However, the Japanese discursive pattern evident in the Riko-ran films is most definitely not of a threatening nature, but rather the opposite, alluring. At the time these films were produced, it was government policy to encourage migration to Manchuria. As Hamada states, 'These films were made in order to strengthen Sino-Japanese relations and to deepen friendship and goodwill' (Hamada 1994:146). Even in spy films, such as the 1942 *Kanchō kida shisezu*, directed by Yoshimura Kōzaburō (1911-), the hero, a young Chinese spy, is not portrayed as a threatening enemy but as a misguided younger brother who ultimately sees through the evil machinations of his American masters.

21 Satō in *Nihon Eiga to Nihon Bunka* (1989) devotes the first few pages of chapter one to a discussion of why Japanese couples do not exchange verbal expressions of love, particularly in public. He offers several explanations; first, that in the family, relations between husband and wife are secondary to those between parent and child. Also, in the case of an extended family, the open display of affection between the married son and his wife would be seen as the young couple putting their happiness above their duty to their parents.

22 In this discussion of the wartime films of Yamaguchi Yoshiko, I have referred to her throughout as Riko-ran rather than addressing her by the names of the characters she portrays in the films. Her manufactured star persona and her political significance as Riko-ran over-road the individual characters she portrayed on the screen.

23 War films, such as *Shingun,* by portraying the rise of a young farm boy from rags to officer status, linked social mobility to a military education.

NOTES

Chapter 2

1 Yoshino Kosaku in his study *Cultural Nationalism in Contemporary Japan: a Sociological Enquiry* quotes from a survey carried out by the Nomura Research Institute which found that 'approximately seven hundred books were published between 1946 and 1978 on the theme of Japanese peculiarities' (1995:227)
2 *Against the State: Politics and Social Protest in Japan* by David E. Apter and Nagayo Sawa (Harvard University Press) 1984 is an excellent study of this movement.
3 The women's movements of the 1970s is sensitively documented in Kurihara Noriko's film *Ripples of Change* 1993.
4 'Akira: Postmodernism and Resistance' *The Worlds of Japanese Popular Culture: Gender, Shifting Boundaries and Global Cultures* ed. D.P. Martinez, Cambridge University Press, Australia (October 1998).
5 The utilitarian political philosopher, Jeremy Bentham (1748-1832), designed a penal system which he called the panopticon, the main purpose of which was to induce in its inmates, through an architectural configuration of surveillance, 'a state of conscious and permanent visibility that [would ensure] the automatic functioning of power' (Foucault 1991:201). He who is subjected to a field of visibility, and who knows it, assumes:

> responsibility for the constraints of power; he makes them play spontaneously upon himself; he inscribes in himself the power relation in which he simultaneously plays both roles; he becomes the principle of his own subjection. (Foucault 1991:202-203)

The architectural design of the panopticon was to have created a sense of unverifiable visibility of the inmates. Hence, the administration of power would become automatic as continual visibility became the mechanism for control.

> The essence of [the panopticon] consists ... in the *centrality* of the inspector's situation, combined with the well-known and most effectual contrivances for *seeing without being seen*. As to the *general form* of the building, the most commodious for most purposes seems to be the circular ... Of all figures ... this you will observe, is the only one that affords a perfect view, and the same view, of an indefinite number of apartments of the same dimensions: that affords a spot from which, without any change of situation, a man may survey, in the same perfection, the whole number, and without so much as a change of posture, the half of the whole number, at the same time ... (Bentham 1995:43)

Bentham envisaged an open penitentiary where members of the public and interested parties could freely come and observe the inmates in a similar manner to the French asylums of the eighteenth century. He felt that this would ensure that the observers were themselves subject to observation and would therefore have to maintain a degree of vigilance. Hence, the panopticon's ability to 'autonomize and disindividualize power'.

> Power [therefore] has its principle not so much in a person as in a certain concerted distribution of bodies, surfaces, lights, gazes; in an arrangement whose internal mechanisms produce the relation in which individuals are caught up. (Foucault 1991:202)

As a configuration of power, it therefore becomes a self-perpetuating mechanism for control which anyone can operate for any purpose. (Bentham envisaged its use beyond the penitentiary to include workhouses for the poor, hospitals, schools and factories among other applications.) Its implications for social control as power reduced to an ideal form extend far beyond a penal application. It is in fact a 'political technology' that can be detached from any specific use.

The utilitarian philosophical position from which Bentham designed his panopticon, when viewed from a moral or ethical position, is very close to a traditional Japanese Confucian-based ethic of the maintenance of social harmony through a rigid set of social relations. Bentham defined the principle of utility:

> By the principle of utility is meant that principle which approves or disapproves of every action whatsoever, according to the tendency which it appears to have to augment or diminish the happiness of the party whose interest is in question: or, what is the same thing in other words, to promote or to oppose that happiness. I say of every action whatsoever; and therefore, not only of every action of a private individual, but of every measure of government. (Bentham 1988:2)

Semple (1993) makes the point that in western terms this was a revolutionary concept of morality as it was not based on a metaphysical notion of divine concepts of good and evil nor was it based on natural law. Bentham clearly acknowledges in the above statement the role of society in the construction of a social morality – a point the Confucianists have always recognised.

6 Ikegami identifies three aspects of change in the nature of the 'honour culture' of the samurai during the Tokugawa period:

> The first transition, *a shift in the expression of honor*, parallels the demilitarization of the concept of samurai honor. During this process, honor was reconceived as *less associated with violence and more with virtuous self-discipline* ... The second shift ... involved a change in *the locus of honor, which moved from personal to organizational* ... the *o-ie* or organization of the master's house, moved to the center of the vassals' sense of loyalty. In the mind of the Tokugawa samurai the *o-ie* was not simply the house of the master's family; rather, it embraced all the

NOTES

samurai united to it in a sense of shared destiny and commitment
.... The third ... concerns *the changing source of honor from performance to status* ... [T]he Tokugawa samurai's position became largely hereditary, and there was only a small range of open career possibilities that could be affected by effort and achievement, in order to change one's position in the samurai hierarchy. (Ikegami 1995:343-345)

7 Nakane gives an example of the sense of competitiveness that this form of social partitioning encourages, the Japanese obsession with collateral ratings. In traditional village society, an annual list of households was made (the *kotohyo*),

... in which all households of the village were listed in order from top to bottom, with an internal grading into several classes, according to actual wealth and income, and efficiency in handling money. (Nakane 1972:88)

She goes on to provide anecdotal evidence as to how families would try to make their households more productive than their neighbours' in an attempt to increase their rating.

The degree reached by such competition even prompted inhumane excesses. I was told by one old woman in a comparatively poor village that it was the greatest pleasure of her life when her neighbour's store building caught fire. (1972:89)

This competitive ethos extends to companies, schools, and universities, in fact to all collateral groups within Japan. Nakane acknowledges the fact that:

Such competition among enterprises certainly contributes to economic development by concentrating the energies of individual enterprises, and competition is both an important element in toughening the intra-group unity towards which Japanese managers are always aiming and a powerful factor in encouraging independence and isolation. (Nakane 1972:89-90)

In the 1960s, the Daiei Film Company produced a series of ten films that are known as the *Kuro* (black) films. They are all based on the theme of industrial espionage and the personal costs to the individual who literally sells his soul for the company. Kurosawa Akira made a film on a similar theme in 1960, *Warui yatsu hodo yoku nemuru* (released in the west as *The Bad Sleep Well*).

8 It is interesting to note that the Japanese police allow youths who participate in *bōsōzoku* activities (car and motorcycle gangs) a degree of latitude until they reach the age of twenty, when 'penal law rather than juvenile law' is applied (I. Satō, *The Kamikaze Biker* 1991:159,

University of Chicago Press). Built into the Japanese penal code is an acknowledgement that youths sometimes engage in anti-social behaviour as part of the process of maturing and in such cases, reclamation rather than punishment is the rule. It would seem that this approach is effective for, according to Satō's informants, few youths continue in *bōsōzoku* gangs after the age of twenty, when they are increasingly subject to the process of group control.

9 Kondo, as a Japanese American engaged in field-work in Japan provides ample anecdotal evidence in her chapter "The Eye-I" of the pressures placed upon her to conform to the social ideals of what a Japanese woman should be. Her use of the 'eye' in the title of her chapter confirms that she was the object of a panoptic disciplining gaze. As she states:

> I was 'always already' caught in webs of relationships, in which loving concern was not separable from power, where relationships define one and enable one to define others. (Kondo 1990:26)

Lebra makes a similar observation when she describes the disciplining role of the *seken* as

> the generalized audience or jury surrounding the self in an inescapable way. Two features of the *seken* make the self especially vulnerable to its sanction. In parallel with the 'face'/focused self, the *seken*/other is equipped with its own 'eyes', 'ears' and 'mouth', watching, hearing and gossiping about the self. This body metaphor contributes to the sense of immediacy and inescapability of the *seken*'s presence. On the other hand, the *seken* itself is immediately invisible and ill-defined and thus can make the self defenceless. (Lebra 1994:107)

Takami Kuwayama, in his article on the mechanisation of agriculture in a small Japanese village, argues that a 'mechanism of mutual observation' functions as a disciplining agent. He goes on to explain that:

> This kind of situation is particularly conducive to two patterns of thought. First, people constantly evaluate one another and determine each person's worth by relative standards of excellence. Certainly, one's performance is judged only in relation to that of others because there is no such thing as an absolute standard of excellence. (Kuwayama 1992:134)

10 One of the standard techniques adopted in Japanese soft-porn films is a third person poking a hole with a moist finger through a paper screen to observe unseen the couple in the next room. A good example of this can be found in the 1983 version of *Narayama bushi-kō* (*The Ballad of Narayama*).

NOTES

11 The flow of Ozu's camera movements as he cuts from a low camera position from one room to another or focuses into a second room through open sliding doors, has become the hallmark of his style and has endeared his films to western audiences. The openness of his household sets is further reinforced as neighbours frequently appear outside looking in through window frames to converse with the inhabitants. In the opening scenes of *Tōkyō monogatari* (1953), as the old husband and wife are preparing for their trip to Tokyo, in the centre background is an open window frame into which a neighbour enters and proceeds to ask about their trip. A similar scene occurs at the end of the film, but this time the old man is alone as his wife has just died. Equally in *Sōshun (Early Spring)* 1956 and *Ohayō (Good Morning)* 1959, the rows of hastily constructed post-war suburban houses are designed so that one can see straight through from the kitchen of each house into the house opposite. Although Ozu's films depict an idealised view of Japanese family life, upholding ideologies of group harmony in an ever-changing world, it is possible to discern the mechanisms for control through the architectural configuration of space evident in his mise-en-scène. Even though harmony, despite changing social values and lifestyles, is the dominant theme of his films, there always exists under the surface a hint of conflict, as in the scene in *Tōkyō monogatari* when Shige, the hard-headed eldest daughter, tells her husband about her father's drinking and his resulting abuse of her mother when she was young. The characters in his films on the whole happily conform to the roles required of them by the family and society, but viewed from the perspective of the panoptic society, mechanisms for control can be seen at work in the form of camera movements and mise-en-scène.

12 *Kumo nagaruru hateni* is largely based on information taken from the letters, poems and extracts from diaries of actual members of the naval pilots of the Special Attack Forces. It also draws heavily on information provided by Iguchi Rikihei and Nakajima Tadashi in the final chapters of their book, *Kamikaze Tokubetsu Kōgeki-tai no Kiroku* 1947. This book was translated into English by Roger Pineau as *The Divine Wind: Japan's Kamikaze Force in World War II*.

13 I would suggest that in this scene the young pilot was parodying Vice-Admiral Ōnishi Takijirō's appeal to the naval pilots when the Special Attack Forces were first officially formed in October 1944.

> Japan is in a state of crisis. Neither ministers, generals nor senior officers can save the situation. Of course, an admiral such as myself cannot either. It is only young men full of vitality in its purest form who can save Japan. Therefore, in the name of one hundred million people of Japan, I make this request ... You are already gods. Because you are gods, you have no earthly desires (*yokubō*). But you will want to know that your sacrifice will not have been in vain. Because you will have settled into a long sleep, there is no way you will know nor is there any way to inform you. However, I assure you that the Emperor will hear of your sacrifice, so go in confidence. (quoted in Morimoto 1992:15)

14 The generally hostile attitude of Japanese to *yōshi* (adopted sons) who enter their wife's parents' home after marriage is reflective of the ambivalent position of secondary sons in the family and social hierarchy. Recently, as a compromise, there appears to be a trend whereby secondary sons enter the home of the wife's parents, but retain their own name, listing the names of their wife and children on their own *koseki* (family register).

15 *Ningen gyorai shutsugeki su* pre-empted the box office hits of a series of four films *Kaigun Heigaku monogatari aa Etajima (The Story from the Naval Academy, Ah Etajima)* 1959; *Aa Zero-sen (Ah, the Zero Fighter Plane)* 1965; *Aa Kaigun (Ah, the Navy)* 1969; *Aa Rikugun (Ah, All the Combat Units of the Army)* 1969, directed by Murayama Mitsuo (1920-1978) which all reassert a hyper-masculinity using the war context as a site of male bonding.

16 The AMPO riots of 1960 began 'when a coalition of various student and citizen protest groups opposed the revision of the US-Japan Security Treaty' (Apter and Sawa 1984:8)

> The great '*ampo* struggle' of 1960, in which many leftist groups united in their opposition to Prime Minister Kishi's handling of the extension of the US-Japan security treaty, represented the high-water mark for the Japanese anti-establishment movement and provided the authorities with a moral pretext to expand the powers of the police. The most eye-catching aspect of this has been the display of power by the *kidōtai,* or riot police. In their sense of a mission to safeguard the security of the nation, these heavily trained troups are the closest successors to the elite forces of the Imperial Army. (Karel van Wolferen 1990:198-199)

17 *Nikudan* was listed second in the *Kinema Junpō* top ten films for 1968, the year of its release.

18 Being made to train naked for a day was an established form of punishment for cadets of the Army Academy.

19 Watanabe and Iwata in *The Love of the Samurai: A Thousand Years of Japanese Homosexuality* make the point that Yamamoto Jōchō (1649-1719) in the original *Hagakure* was referring in this passage to male homosexual love and not love for a woman as Mishima has stated. Watanabe and Iwata quote from another passage in the *Hagakure* not commented on by Mishima.

> There is a proverb: a virtuous woman does not marry twice. It is the same for you *wakashu* [adolescent males]. You must have only one lover in your life; otherwise there would be no difference between you and prostitutes or worse. It is truly a shame for a samurai ... If you have had relations with your *nenja* [a man who loves adolescent males] for five years or so and you have found him to be really loyal, you must then put your trust in him completely. Because he is the person for whom you sacrifice your life, you must really see into his heart. (Watanabe and Iwata 1989:115)

However, as Mishima's interpretation is in keeping with popular discourses on sexuality in the 1960s, this error is not important.

20 *Kyomenka* is not a compound found in a dictionary, but the *kyo* is the first character in *kyomu* (nothingness) and carries the meaning of emptiness and unpreparedness. It is in this sense that Ozaki refers to in his article.
21 *Naraku* as defined in the *Japanese/English Kenkyūsha* dictionary is given only its Buddhist meaning as 'hell'. The *Sanseido Japanese/Japanese* dictionary gives a further meaning of 'hopeless situation' – *dōshōmonai, warui jōtai*.

Chapter 3

1 Joy Hendry illustrates this point in relation to changing attitudes to marriage with regard to the lower classes:

> ... as the samurai ethic spread, personal choice in marriage came to be viewed as 'barbaric or backward', 'a disruptive act, rebellious against both family and nation ... 'Gradually the marriage arranged by parents through the offices of a go-between became the normal and proper way to proceed. If parents were particularly 'understanding' they might ask a go-between to help stage an arranged marriage to make a 'love match' look respectable, but on the whole mate selection through love came to be thought 'immodest, or even immoral'. In 1930, one writer wrote that 'According to the traditional moral ideas, it is deemed a sign of mental and moral weakness to "fall in love" 'and Kawashima maintains that in the army and navy, until the end of the war, love was thought 'effeminate and unmanly' (*memeshii*). (Hendry 1989:24)

2 Joy Hendry makes the point that, despite the post-war changes to the laws of inheritance to allow for the equal distribution of property amongst siblings of whatever status or sex,

> A clause of the laws of succession admits of the necessity for an heir to be chosen to inherit the genealogical records and utensils of religious rites (Article 897), and several writers have described a practice whereby one son does in fact inherit particularly farm property because his siblings sign away their rights for the good of the *ie* [house]. (Hendry 1989:28)

As the existence of lengthy inheritance disputes indicates, the 'signing away' of siblings' rights is not always an entirely voluntary matter.
3 The choice of Rodin's *The Kiss* is poignant when viewed from the perspective of the controversial inclusion of kissing scenes in early

post-war films at the instigation of David Conde of the CIE censorship office. These scenes were clearly viewed by some Japanese as a transgression and therefore subjected to harsh criticism, or by others as liberating and therefore to be encouraged. In either case, they marked a clear break with the depiction of male-female relations in wartime productions. For a full account of the introduction of kissing scenes into the Japanese cinema, see Hirano (1992:154-164).

4 A 'structuring absence' refers to:

> an issue, or even a set of facts or an argument, that a text cannot ignore, but which it deliberately skirts round or otherwise avoids, thus creating the biggest 'holes' in the text, fatally, revealingly misshaping the organic whole assembled with such craft. (Dyer 1993:105)

5 As Joy Hendry has emphasised, in marriage even in post-war Japan, the emphasis is placed on the continuance of the *ie* rather than the happiness of the individuals concerned. She concludes that:

> marriage in a village like Kurotsuchi involves much more than a contract between individuals. Even for a couple living alone, ... or a newly formed branch house, marriage immediately establishes the house head as a member of the village assembly, and various obligations follow for the household. (Hendry 1989:228)

6 This was not exclusive to Japanese cinema; a similar process is evident in some post-war British films, such as David Lean's 1945 *Brief Encounter*.

7 It is interesting to note that Nitobe Inazō and Yanaihara Tadao were both Christians.

8 Ooms makes the point in a footnote that

> Modern scholarship on Ansai and his schools reached its peak in the 1930s and 1940s within a general political and intellectual climate that interpreted Ansai as the first in a long line of imperial panegyrics and ideologues of the *Yamato damashii* or Japanese spirit. (Ooms 1989:195)

9 Michel Foucault in *The Order of Things: An Archaeology of the Human Sciences* analyses a similar change in European thought in the seventeenth century:

> ... faced with existing and already written language, criticism sets out to define its *relation* with what it represents; hence the importance assumed, since the seventeenth century, by critical methods in the exegesis of religious texts; it was no longer a question, in fact, of repeating what had already been said in them, but of defining through what figures and images, by following what order, to what expressive ends, and in order to

declare what truth, God or the Prophets had given a discourse the particular form in which it was communicated to us. (Foucault 1992c:80-81)

10 In *The History of Sexuality*, volume 1, Foucault states:

> I have repeatedly stressed that the history of the last centuries in western societies did not manifest the movement of power that was essentially repressive. (Foucault 1990a:81)

I think that this point should also be taken into consideration when analysing Japanese history.

11 It is interesting to note that Kitano (Beat) Takeshi's two films *Violent Cop* (1989) and *Sonatine* (1993) are based on the same underlying narrative structure as *The Human Condition*. Both films (*Violent Cop* and *Sonatine*) set up two parallel sites of conflict - in *Violent Cop*, Azuma at one level takes on the drug barons, a conventional plot for a detective film; and on another level, he is confronted by corruption in the police force. Similarly, in *Sonatine* as a yakuza, the hero becomes embroiled in inter-gang warfare, again a conventional plot for a yakuza film, but on another level, he has to fight against corrupt factions within his own gang. The heroes in both films are besieged from all fronts. They are marginalised and/or excluded by the very groups that should offer them support. Just as Kaji in *The Human Condition* is beaten and betrayed by his fellow soldiers and officers, the heroes in *Violent Cop* and *Sonatine* are betrayed by the very work groups which should support them. The deaths of the heroes in both films reassert the powerlessness of the individual against the monolithic institutions that control society. The final scenes of *Violent Cop* where the new drug baron is in place and Kikuchi, Azuma's junior detective, accepts the bribe offered him, projects a bleak image of contemporary Japanese society in which the individual's only hope of survival is to conform. Those, like the heroes who take a high moral position are doomed to failure, and in the fictionalised world of the films, death.

12 The charter for the International Tribunal for the Far East included the following:

> Neither the official position, at any time, of an accused, nor the fact that an accused acted pursuant to order of his government or of a superior shall, of itself, be sufficient to free such accused from responsibility for any crime with which he is charged. (quoted in Minear 1971:42-43)

13 Onuma states that the Japanese cynicism in relation to the trials was strengthened when it became public knowledge that the atomic bombs were dropped as part of the implementation of the cold war policy to impress the Soviet Union. For an English language account of this policy, see Gar Alperovitz *Atomic Diplomacy: Hiroshima and Potsdam* 1994.

14 Rawls explains the traditional western view of the rights of man:

> It has seemed to many philosophers, and it appears to be supported by the convictions of common sense, that we distinguish as a matter of principle between the claims of liberty and right on the one hand and the desirability of increasing aggregate social welfare on the other; and that we give a certain priority, if not absolute weight, to the former. Each member of society is thought to have an inviolability founded on justice or, as some say, on natural right, which even the welfare of every one else cannot override. Justice denies that the loss of freedom for some is made right by a greater good shared by others. The reasoning which balances the gains and losses of different persons as if they were one person is excluded. Therefore in a just society the basic liberties are taken for granted and the rights secured by justice are not subject to political bargaining or to the calculus of social interests. (Rawls 1973:27-28)

The philosophical dilemma fictionalised in these Japanese war-retro films is also evident in some Hollywood films, such as Stanley Kramer's *Judgement at Nuremberg* 1961 and most recently in *A Few Good Men* 1992.

In *Judgement at Nuremberg*, utilitarian principles of the general good are couched in terms of patriotism, 'my country, right or wrong', and set against the 'inviolability' of the individual – the position taken by the American judge played by Spencer Tracy. As he says in his summing up, 'The men in the dock are responsible for their actions ... The court stands for justice, truth and *the value of a single human being*.' The film, in upholding this ethos is critical of the pragmatism that turned both the Nuremberg and Tokyo trials into an exercise in international politics as a result of the emergence of the cold war. This film, therefore, parallels many of the points raised in the Japanese trial films.

Like *Watashi wa kai ni naritai*, *A Few Good Men* puts into narrative form the conflict between a soldier's morality and his duty to obey orders.

15 *Ashita* was rated second in the *Kinejun* top ten films for 1988. Fuji Television also produced a version of *Ashita* to commemorate their thirty-fifth anniversary in August 1988.

Chapter 4

1 Kasahara, the author of the screenplays for the first four films of the *Jingi naki tatakai* series, states that to define a yakuza 'in good terms would be to describe him as a lone wolf, and in bad terms as an egoist (*egoisuto*) (Kasahara 1973:138).
2 Nakane makes a similar observation:

NOTES

> Japanese culture has no conception of a God existing abstractedly, completely separate from the human world. In the ultimate analysis, the Japanese consciousness of the object of religious direction grows out of direct-contact relations between individuals; it is conceived as an extension of this mediating tie. (Nakane 1972:139-140)

3 Mishima Yukio was apparently a fan of the yakuza genre. He greatly admired Takakura Ken and Tsuruta Koji, and in 1969, wrote an article for *Eigageijitsu* on the film *Jinsei no gekijō* (*The Theatre of Life*).
4 Horsley and Buckley comment on the rush to the cities of the 1960s:

> Everywhere in the regions young people were now rushing to seek a better life in the cities. Families broke up as their sons and daughters were recruited by the big industrial firms to work on the assembly lines of the new factories. The companies sent group recruitment trains around the country to transport school-leavers, most of them fifteen years old, into the cities. (Horsley and Buckley 1990:78)

Conclusions

1 The phrase 'sensual imperative of the image' was first used by Jean Baudrillard in *Symbolic Exchange and Death* (1993).
2 In western Hollywood cinema, the same phenomenon is evident in cult movies.

Bibliography

Allen, Robert C. and Douglas Gomery. (1985) *Film History: Theory and Practice,* London: McGraw-Hill.

Alperovitz, Gar (1994) *Atomic Diplomacy: Hiroshima and Potsdam,* London: Pluto Press.

Althusser, Louis. (1971) *Lenin and Philosophy and Other Essays,* (trans.) Ben Brewster. New York: Monthly Review Press.

—— (1990) *For Marx,* (trans.) Ben Brewster. London: Verso.

Anderson, Benedict. (1993) *Imagined Communities: Reflections on the Origin and Spread of Nationalism,* London: Verso.

Anderson, J.T. and D. Richie. (1959) *The Japanese Film: Art and Industry,* Tokyo: Tuttle.

Apter, David E. and Nagayo Sawa. (eds.) (1984) *Against the State: Politics and Social Protest in Japan,* Cambridge, Mass: Harvard University Press.

Ashihara, Yoshinobu. (1992) *The Hidden Order: Tokyo Through the Twentieth Century,* (trans.) Lynne E. Riggs, Tokyo: Kodansha.

Bachnick, Jane M. and Charles J. Quinn, (eds.) (1994) *Situated Meaning: Inside and Outside in Japanese Self, Society and Language,* Chichester: Princeton University Press.

Balázs, B. 'The Theory of Film: The Close-up'. *Film Theory and Criticism,* (1979) (eds.) G. Mast and M. Cohen. New York: Oxford University Press. p. 288-298.

Barrett, Gregory. (1989) *Archetypes in Japanese Film: The Sociopolitical and Religious Significance of the Principal Heroes and Heroines,* Selinsgrove: Susquehanna University Press.

Barthes, Roland. (1975) *The Pleasure of the Text,* (trans.) R. Miller, New York: Hill and Wang.

—— (1981) *Mythologies,* (trans.) Annette Lavers. 5th ed. London: Granada Publishing.

—— (1982) *Empire of the Signs,* (trans.) Richard Howard. New York: Hill and Wang.

Baudrillard, Jean (1993) *Symbolic Exchange and Death,* (trans.) Iain Hamilton Grant. London: Sage Publications.

Beasley, W.G. (1973) *The Meiji Restoration,* London: Oxford University Press.

—— (1989) *Japanese Imperialism 1894-1945*, Oxford: Clarendon Press.
—— (1990) *The Rise of Modern Japan*, London: Weidenfeld and Nicolson.
Behr, Edward. (1989) *Hirohito: Behind the Myth*, London: Hamish Hamilton.
Bentham, Jeremy. (1988) *The Principles of Morals and Legislation*, New York: Prometheus.
—— (1995) *The Panopticon Writings*, (ed.) Miran Bozovic. London: Verso.
Bordwell, David. (1988) *Ozu and the Poetics of Cinema*, London: BFI Publishing.
—— (1989) *Making Meaning: Inference and Rhetoric in the Interpretation of Cinema*, London: Harvard University Press.
Bordwell, David and Kristin Thompson. (1980) *Film Art: An Introduction*, 2nd ed. Reading, Massachusetts: Addison Wesley Publishing.
Bornoff, Nicholas. (1991) *The Pink Samurai: The Pursuit and Politics of Sex in Japan*, London: Grafton Books.
Braw, Monica. (1991) *The Atomic Bomb Suppressed: American Censorship in Occupied Japan*, London: M.E. Sharpe.
Buehrer, Beverley Bare. (1990) *Japanese Films: A Filmography and Commentary, 1921-1989*, London: St. James Press.
Bungei Shunjū (eds.) (1992) *Nihon Eiga Besuto 150: Daianketo ni yoru*, Tōkyō: Bungei Shunjū.
Burch, Noël. (1979) *To the Distant Observer: Form and Meaning in the Japanese Cinema*, London: Scolar Press.
—— (1983) *Theory of Film Practice*, (trans.) Helen R. Lane. 3rd ed. London: Martin Secker and Warburg.
Burgoyne, Robert. (1994) 'National Identity, Gender Identity and the "Rescue Fantasy" in Born on the Fourth of July.' *Screen*, vol.35, no.3, Autumn, p. 211-234.
Burnett, Ron. (ed.) (1991) *Explorations in Film Theory: Selected Essays from Ciné-Tracts*, Bloomington and Indianapolis: Indiana University Press.
Buruma, Ian. (1988) *A Japanese Mirror: Heroes and Villains of Japanese Culture*, 2nd ed. London: Penguin Books.
—— (1994) *Wages of Guilt: Memories of War in Germany and Japan*, London: Jonathan Cape.
Calman, Donald. (1992) *The Nature and Origins of Japanese Imperialism: A Reinterpretation of the Great Crisis of 1873*, London: Routledge.
Carr, E.H. (1990) *What is History?*, (ed.) R.W. Davies. 2nd ed. London: Penguin Books.
Chomsky, Noam. (1993a) *Deterring Democracy*, London: Vintage.
—— (1993b) *Necessary Illusions: Thought Control in Democratic Societies*, London: Pluto Press.
—— (1993c) *Year 501: The Conquest Continues*, London: Verso.
Cohan, S. and I.R. Hark. (eds.) (1993) *Screening the Male: Exploring Masculinities in Hollywood Cinema*, London: Routledge.
Corrigan, Timothy. (1991) *A Cinema Without Walls: Movies and Culture after Vietnam*, New Brunswick, New Jersey: Rutgers University Press.
Craig, S. (ed.) (1992) *Men, Masculinity and the Media*, California: Sage Publications.

Crowley, J.B. (1996) *Japan's Quest for Autonomy: National Security and Foreign Policy 1930-1938*, New Jersey: Princeton University Press.
Custen, G.F. (1992) *Bio-pics: How Hollywood Constructed Public History*, New Jersey: Rutgers University Press.
Dale, Peter N. (1990) *The Myth of Japanese Uniqueness*, London: Routledge.
Debord, Guy. (1995) *The Society of the Spectacle*, (trans.) D. Nicholson-Smith. New York: Zone Books.
Denzin, Norman. K. (1991) *Images of Postmodern Society: Social Theory and Contemporary Cinema*, London: Sage Publications.
Desser, David. (1988) *Eros Plus Massacre: An Introduction to the Japanese New Wave Cinema*, Bloomington and Indianapolis: Indiana University Press.
De Voss, George A. (1973) *Socialization for Achievement: Essays on the Cultural Psychology of the Japanese*, London: University of California Press.
Dissanayake, Wimal. (1992) 'Cinema, Nation, and Culture in Southeast Asia: Enframing a Relationship.' *East-West Film Journal*, vol.6, no.2, July, p. 1-22.
Dittmar, Linda and Gene Michaud. (eds.) (1990) *From Hanoi to Hollywood: The Vietnam War in American Film*, London: Rutgers University Press.
Doi, Takeo. (1981) *The Anatomy of Dependence: The Key Analysis of Japanese Behaviour*, London: Kodansha.
Dower, John. W. (1986) *War Without Mercy: Race and Power in the Pacific War*, New York: Pantheon Books.
—— (1988) *Empire and Afermath: Yoshida Shigeru and the Japanese Experience, 1878-1954*, London: Harvard University Press.
Dyer, R. *Stars*, (1992) 5th ed. London: British Film Institute.
—— (1993) *The Matter of Images: Essays on Representation*, London: Routledge.
Eagleton, Terry. (1991) *Ideology: An Introduction*, London: Verso.
Ellis, J. (1993) *Visible Fictions: Cinema, Television, Video*, London: Routledge.
Etō, Jun. (1995) *Senkyūhyakuyonjūrokunen Kenpō: Sono Kōsoku Sono Ta*, Tōkyō: Bungei Shunjū.
—— (1996) *Wasureta Koto to Wasuresasereta Koto*, Tōkyō: Bungei Shunjū.
Evans, D.T. (1993) *Sexual Citizenship: The Material Construction of Sexualities*, London: Routledge.
Firumuātosha (eds.) (1986) *Hon no Eigakan Bukku Shinematēku: Ozu Yasujirō o Yomu*, Tōkyō: Firumuātosha.
Fiske, John. (1991) *Television Culture*, 4th ed. London: Routledge.
—— (1994) *Media Matters: Everyday Culture and Political Change*, Minneapolis: University of Minnesota Press.
Fiske, John and John Hartley. (1989) *Reading Television*, London: Routledge.
Forgacs, David. (ed.) (1988) *A Gramsci Reader*, London: Lawrence and Wishart.
Foucault, M. (1980) *Power and Knowledge: Selected Interviews and Other*

BIBLIOGRAPHY

Writings 1972-1977, C. Gordon (ed.) Hertfordshire: Harvester Wheatsheaf.

—— (1988) *Politics, Philosophy, Culture: Interviews and Other Writings 1977-1984*. L.D. Kritzman (ed.) London: Routledge.

—— (1990) *The History of Sexuality, Volume 1, An Introduction*, London: Penguin Books.

—— (1992) *The History of Sexuality, Volume 2, The Use of Pleasure*, London: Penguin Books.

—— (1990) *The History of Sexuality, Volume 3, The Care of the Self*, London Penguin Books.

—— (1991) *Discipline and Punish: The Birth of the Prison*, (trans.) Alan Sheridan. Harmondsworth: Penguin Books.

—— (1992a) *Madness and Civilization: A History of Insanity in the Age of Reason*, (trans.) Richard Howard. 3rd ed. London: Routledge.

—— (1992b) *The Archaeology of Knowledge*, London: Routledge.

—— (1992c) *The Order of Things: An Archaeology of the Human Sciences*, London: Routledge.

—— (1993) *Language and Counter-Memory, Practice: Selected Essays and Interviews by Michel Foucault*, (ed.) Donald F Bouchard .(trans.) Donald F. Bouchard and Sherry Simon. 7th ed. Ithaca, New York: Cornell University Press.

Freud, Sigmund. (1991) 'Three Essays on the Theory of Sexuality (1905).' *On Sexuality*. vol.7: p. 33-170. (trans.) James Strachey, (ed.) Angela Richards. London: Penguin Books.

—— (1991) 'A Special Type of Choice of Object Made by Men (Contributions to the Psychology of Love 1, 1910.' *On Sexuality*, vol.7: p. 227-242. (trans.) James Strachey, (ed.) Angela Richards. London: Penguin Books.

—— (1991) 'Some Physical Consequences of the Anatomical Distinction Between the Sexes (1925).' *On Sexuality*, vol.7: p. 323-344. (trans.) James Strachey, (ed.) Angela Richards. London: Penguin Books.

—— (1993) 'A Child is Beaten. (A Contribution to the Study of the Origin of Sexual Perversions, 1919.)' *On Psychopathology*, vol.10: p. 159-194. (trans.) James Strachey, (ed.) Angela Richards. London: Penguin Books.

—— (1991) 'On Narcissism: An Introduction (1914).' *On Metapsychology*, vol.11, p. 59-98. (trans.) James Strachey, (ed.) Angela Richards. London: Penguin Books.

—— (1991f) 'Instincts and Their Vicissitudes (1915).' *On Metapsychology*, vol.11, p. 105-138. (trans.) James Strachey, (ed.) Angela Richards. London: Penguin Books.

—— (1991) 'Mourning and Melancholia (1917[1915]).' *On Metapsychology*, vol.11, p. 245-268. (trans.) James Strachey, (ed.) Angela Richards. London: Penguin Books.

—— (1991) 'Beyond the Pleasure Principle (1920).' *On Metapsychology*, vol.11, p. 269-338. (trans.) James Strachey, (ed.) Angela Richards. London: Penguin Books.

—— (1991) 'The Ego and the Id (1923).' *On Metapsychology*, vol.11, p. 339-408. (trans.) James Strachey, (ed.) Angela Richards. London: Penguin Books.

—— (1991) 'The Economic Problem of Masochism (1924).' *On Metapsychology*, vol.11, p. 409-426. (trans.) James Strachey, (ed.) Angela Richards. London: Penguin Books.
—— (1991) 'Group Psychology and the Analysis of the Ego (1921).' *Civilization, Society and Religion*, vol.12, p. 91-178. (trans.) James Strachey, (ed.) Albert Dickson. London: Penguin Books.
—— (1991) 'Civilization and its Discontents (1930 [1929]).' *Civilization, Society and Religion*, vol.12, p. 251-340. (trans.) James Strachey, (ed.) Albert Dickson. London: Penguin Books.
—— (1991) 'Why War? (1933 [1932]) (Einstein and Freud).' *Civilization, Society and Religion*, vol.12, p. 341-362. (trans.) James Strachey, (ed.) Albert Dickson. London: Penguin Books.
—— (1991) 'Totem and Taboo (1913 [1912-13]).' *The Origins of Religion*. vol.13, p. 43-224. (trans.) James Strachey, (ed.) Albert Dickson. London: Penguin Books.
Frye, Northrop. (1957) *Anatomy of Criticism: Four Essays*, Princeton: Princeton University Press.
Fukutake, Tadashi. (1981) *The Japanese Social Structure: Its Evolution in the Modern Century*, (trans.) Ronald P. Dore. Tokyo: University of Tokyo Press.
Fukuyama, Francis. (1992) *The End of History and the Last Man*, London: Penguin Books.
Gellner, Ernest. (1990) *Nations and Nationalism*, Oxford: Basil Blackwell.
Gilmore, David D. (1990) *Manhood in the Making: Cultural Concepts of Masculinity*, London: Yale University Press.
Gluck, Carol. (1985) *Japan's Modern Myths: Ideology in the Late Meiji Period*, Princeton: Princeton University Press.
Gluck, Carol and Stephen R. Graubard (eds.) (1992) *Shōwa: The Japan of Hirohito*. New York: Norton.
Gomikawa Junpei, (1990) *Ningen no Jōken Vol 1*, Tōkyō: Bungei Shunjū.
—— (1990) *Ningen no Jōken Vol 2*, Tōkyō: Bungei Shunjū.
—— (1989) *Ningen no Jōken Vol 3*, Tōkyō: Bungei Shunjū.
—— (1990) *Ningen no Jōken Vol 4*, Tōkyō: Bungei Shunjū.
—— (1990) *Ningen no Jōken Vol 5*, Tōkyō: Bungei Shunjū.
—— (1990) *Ningen no Jōken Vol 6*, Tōkyō: Bungei Shunjū.
Grant, Barry Keith. (ed.) (1990) *Film Genre Reader*, 3rd ed. Austin: University of Texas Press.
Hakuō Izokukai (eds.) (1992) *Sensō to Heiwa Shimin no Kiroku I: Kumo Nagaruru Hate ni: Senbotsu Hikōyobigakusei no Shuki*, Tōkyō: Nihon Tosho Sentā.
Halford, Aubrey S. and Giovanna M. Halford. (1983) *The Kabuki Handbook*, Tokyo: Tuttle.
Halpern, Ben. (1961) 'Myth and Ideology in Modern Usage.' *History and Theory* No. 1, p. 129-149.
Hamada, Yoshihisa. (1995) *Eiga Hyakunen, Sengo Gojūnen: Nihon Eiga to Sensō to Heiwa*, Tōkyō: Ichihosha.
Harootunian, H.D. (1984) *Toward Restoration: The Growth of Political Consciousness in Tokugawa Japan*, Berkeley: University of California Press.

BIBLIOGRAPHY

Harries, Meiron and Susie. Harries. (1991) *Soldiers of the Sun: The Rise and Fall of the Imperial Japanese Army 1868-1945*, London: Heinemann.
Harvey, Robert. (1994) *The Undefeated: The Rise, Fall and Rise of Greater Japan*, London: Macmillan.
Hauser, William. B. (1991) 'Women and War: The Japanese Film Image.' *Recreating Japanese Women*. (ed.) G. L. Bernstein. Oxford: University of California Press.
Hendry, Joy. (1989) *Marriage in Changing Japan*. Tokyo: Tuttle.
Hirano, Kyoko. (1992) *Mr. Smith Goes to Tokyo: Japanese Cinema Under the American Occupation, 1945-1952*. Washington and London: Smithsonian Institution Press.
Hobsbawm, E. J. (1992a) *The Age of Revolution 1789-1848*, London: Abacus.
—— (1992b) *The Age of Capital 1848-1875*, London: Abacus.
—— (1991) *The Age of Empire 1875-1914*. London: Abacus.
—— (1995) *Age of Extremes: The Short Twentieth Century 1914-1991*. London: Abacus.
—— (1992c) *Nations and Nationalism since 1780: Programme, Myth and Reality*. Cambridge: Cambridge University Press.
Hobsbawm, Eric and Terry Ranger (eds.) (1992) *The Invention of Tradition*. Cambridge: Cambridge University Press.
Horsley, William and Roger Buckley. (1990) *Nippon: New Superpower, Japan since 1945*, London: BBC Books.
Horsman, Mathew and Andrew Marshall. (1995) *After the Nation-State: Citizens,Tribalism and the New World Order*, London: Harper Collins.
Ichikawa, Kon & Yūki Mori. (1994) *Ichikawa Kon no Eigatachi*, Tōkyō: Waizu Shuppan.
Ienaga, Saburō. (1978) *The Pacific War 1931-1945*. (trans.) Frank Baldwin. New York: Pantheon Books.
—— (1994) *Taiheiyō Sensō*, Tōkyō: Iwanami Shoten.
Iguchi, Rikihei, Tadashi Nakajima and Roger Pineau. (1958) *The Divine Wind: Japan's Kamikaze Force in World War II* Annapolis, Maryland: United States Naval Institute.
Iguchi, Rikihei & Tadashi Nakajima. (1984) *Kamikaze Tokubetsu Kōgekitai no Kiroku*, Tōkyō: Sekksha.
Ikegami, Eiko. (1995) *The Taming of the Samurai: Honorific Individualism and the Making of Modern Japan*. London: Harvard University Press.
Ikemiya, Shōichirō & Kazuo Nawata. (1994) *Ikemiya Shōichirō ga Kataru Chūshingura no Subete*, Tōkyō: PHP Kenkyūjo.
Iritani, Toshio. (1991) *Group Psychology of the Japanese in Wartime*, London: Kegan Paul.
Irokawa, Daikichi. (1985) *The Culture of the Meiji Period*. (trans. and ed.) Marius B. Jansen. Princeton, New Jersey: Princeton University Press.
Ishii, Teruo & Kenji Fukuma. (1992) *Ishii Teruo Eiga Tamashi*, Tōkyō: Waizu Shuppan.
Itami, Mansaku. (1973) *Itami Mansaku Zenshū Vol. 1,2,3*, Tōkyō: Chikuma Shobō.
Itō, Kimio. (1994) *<Otokorashisa> no Yukue: Dansei Bunka no Bunka Shakaigaku*, Tōkyō: Shinyōsha.

Itō, Takashi. & Hiroaki Kita (1995) *Shintei 2-26 Jiken Hanketsu to Shōko*, Tōkyō: Asahi Shinbunsha.

Iwamoto, Kenji. & Tomonori Saiki. (eds.) (1988) *Kikigaki Kinema no Seishun*, Tōkyō: Libroport.

Iwamoto, Kenji. (ed.) (1991) *Nihon Eiga to Modanizum 1920-1930*, Tōkyō: Libroport.

Jameson, Fredric. (1981) *The Political Unconscious: Narrative as a Socially Symbolic Act*, Ithaca, New York: Cornell University Press.

—— (1992) *Signatures of the Visible*, London: Routledge.

Jeffords, Susan. (1989) *The Remasculinization of America: Gender and the Vietnam War*, Bloomington: Indiana University Press.

Johnson, Richard, G. McLennan, B. Schwarz and D. Sutton (eds.) (1982) *Making Histories: Studies in History Writing and Politics*, London: Hutchinson.

Jordan. E. (1983) 'Feminine Language' and 'Masculine Language', *Kodansha Encyclopaedia of Japan*, Vol. 2, p. 250-252 and Vol.5, p. 124-125 respectively.

Kasahara, K. (1973) *'Jingi naki Tatakai Hiroshima Shitōhen* e no Purorōgu: Yamakami Mitsuji Shōden', *Shinario*, June, p. 141-172.

—— (1973) 'Jingi Kangae', *Shinario*, October, p. 138.

—— (1974) 'Jitsuroku Shinario Taikendan *Jingi naki Tatakai* no Sanbyaku Hi', *Shinario*, February, p. 106-114.

Kasza, Gregory J. (1993) *The State and the Mass Media in Japan 1918-1945*. London: University of California Press.

Katō Hidetoshi. (ed.) (1960) *Japanese Popular Culture*. Tokyo: Tuttle.

Katō, Tetsutarō (1994) *Watashi wa Kai ni Naritai: Aru BCkyū Senpan no Sakebi*, Tōkyō: Shunjūsha.

Keene, Donald (ed.) (1956) *Anthology of Japanese Literature from the Earliest Era to the Mid-Nineteenth Century*. London: George Allen and Unwin.

—— (trans.) (1971) *Chūshingura: The Treasury of Loyal Retainers*. New York: Columbia University Press.

Kenkyūsha (1985) *New Japanese-English Dictionary*, 4th Edition, Tōkyō.

Kinema Junpō, (1988) *Nihon Eiga Terebi Kantoku Zenshū*, Tōkyō: Kinema Junpōsha.

—— (1991) *Nihon Eiga Haiyū Zenshū: Joyūhen*, Tōkyō: Kinema Junpōsha.

—— (1991) *Nihon Eiga Haiyū Zenshū: Danyūhen*, Tōkyō: Kinema Junpōsha.

—— (1993) *Sengo Kinema Junpō Besutoten Zenshi 1946-1992*, Tōkyō: Kinema Junpōsha.

—— (1994) *Besuto Obu Kinema Junpō / Jō 1950-1966*, Tōkyō: Kinema Junpōsha.

—— (1994) *Besuto Obu Kinema Junpō / Ka 1967-1993*, Tōkyō: Kinema Junpōsha.

—— (1994) *Chūshingura Eizō no Sekai*. 25 October, No 1145.

—— (1994) *Ishihara Yūjirō Eiga Korekushyon 1956-1987*, Tōkyō: Kinema Junpōsha.

Kirkham, P. and J. Thumin (eds.) (1993) *You Tarzan: Masculinity, Mores and Men*. London: Lawrence and Wishart.

BIBLIOGRAPHY

Kōjien (1991) 4th Edition, Tōkyō, Iwanami Shoten.
Kondo, Dorinne K. (1990) *Crafting Selves: Power, Gender and Discourses of Identity in a Japanese Workplace.* London: University of Chicago Press.
Kōno, Tsukasa. (ed.) (1993) *Ni-Niroku Jiken: Gokuchū Shuki Isho,* Tōkyō: Kawade Shobōshinsha.
Kosaka, Masataka. (1982) *A History of Postwar Japan.* 2nd ed. Tokyo: Kodansha.
Kritzman, Lawrence D. (ed.) (1988) *Michel Foucault: Politics, Philosophy, Culture, Interviews and Other Writings, 1977-1984.* (trans.) Alan Sheridan and others. New York: Routledge.
Kuwayama, Takami. (1992) 'The Reference Other Orientation.' *Japanese Sense of Self.* (ed.) Nancy R. Rosenberger. Cambridge: Cambridge University Press, p. 121-151.
Lacan, Jaques. (1993) *Écrits: A Selection,* (trans.) Alan Sheridan. London: Routledge.
La Capra, Dominick. (1992) *History and Criticism,* London: Cornell University Press.
Lebra, Takie Sugiyama. (1994) 'Self in Japanese Culture.' *Japanese Sense of Self,* (ed.) Nancy R. Rosenberger. Cambridge: Cambridge University Press, p. 105-120.
Lehmann, Jean-Pierre. (1982) *The Roots of Modern Japan.* London: Macmillan.
Lévi-Strauss, Claude. (1962) *The Savage Mind,* London: Weidenfeld and Nicolson.
—— (1968) *Structural Anthropology,* (trans.) Claire Jacobson and Brooke Grundfest Schoepf. Harmondsworth: Penguin.
—— (1969) *The Elementary Structures of Kinship,* (trans.) James Harle Bell and John Richard von Sturmer, (ed.) Rodney Needham. Boston: Beacon Press.
—— (1981) *The Naked Man: Introduction to a Science of Mythology,* vol.4. (trans.) John and Doreen Weightman. London: Jonathan Cape.
—— (1990) *The Raw and the Cooked: Mythologiques* vol.1. (trans.) John and Doreen Weightman. Chicago: University of Chicago Press.
Lipsitz, George. (1994) *Time Passages: Collective Memory and American Popular Culture,* Minneapolis: University of Minnesota Press.
McDonald, Keiko I. (1983) *Cinema East: A Critical Study of Major Japanese Films,* New Jersey: Associated University Press.
Martin, Luther H., Huck Gutman and Patrick H. Hutton, (eds.) (1988) *Technologies of the Self: A Seminar with Michel Foucault,* London: Tavistock Publications.
Maruyama, Masao. (1979) *Thought and Behaviour in Modern Japanese Politics,* (ed.) Ivan Morris. London: Oxford University Press.
Mast, Gerald and Marshall Cohen. (1979) *Film Theory and Criticism: Introductory Readings,* 2nd ed. Oxford: Oxford University Press.
Masters, Patricia Lee. (1993) 'Warring Bodies: Most Nationalistic Selves.' *East-West Film Journal,* vol.7, no.1, January, p. 137-148.
Mellen, J. (1976) *The Waves at Genji's Door: Japan Through Its Cinema,* New York: Pantheon Books.

Miles, R. (1992) *The Rites of Man: Love, Sex and Death in the Making of the Male,* London: Paladin.

Minear, Richard H. (1971) *Victors' Justice: The Tokyo War Crimes Trial,* Princeton, New Jersey: Princeton University Press.

Mishima, Y. (1977) *On Hagakure: The Samurai Ethic and Modern Japan,* London: Penguin Books.

Miyoshi, Masao and H.D. Harootunian (eds.) (1989) *Postmodernism and Japan,* Durham and London: Duke University Press.

Moeran, Brian. (1989) *Language and Popular Culture in Japan,* Manchester: Manchester University Press.

Monaco, James. (1977) *How to Read a Film: The Art Technology, Language, History and Theory of Film and Media,* New York: Oxford University Press.

Morimoto, Tadao. (1992) *Tokkō: Gedō no Tōsotsu to Ningen no Jōken,* Tōkyō: Bungei Shunjū.

Morris, Ivan. (1978) *The World of the Shining Prince: Court Life in Ancient Japan,* Tokyo: Tuttle.

—— (1980) *The Nobility of Failure: Tragic Heroes in the History of Japan,* Harmondsworth: Penguin Books.

Morton, W.F. (1980) *Tanaka Giichi and Japan's China Policy,* Folkstone, Kent: Dawson.

Mouer, Ross and Yoshio Sugimoto. (1990) *Images of Japanese Society: A Study in the Social Construction of Reality,* London: Kegan Paul.

Mulvey, Laura. (1975) 'Visual Pleasure and Narrative Cinema.' *Screen,* vol.16, no.3, p. 6-8.

—— (1981) 'Mulvey on Duel in the Sun.' *Framework,* 15-17, p. 12-15.

—— (1987) 'Changes: Thoughts on Myth, Narrative and Historical Experience.' *History Workshop Journal,* Issue 23, Spring, p. 3-19.

Myers, R.H. and M.R. Peattie. (eds.) (1984) *The Japanese Colonial Empire, 1895-1945,* Princeton, New Jersey: Princeton University Press.

Nakamura, Akira. (1994) *Daitōa Sensō e no Michi,* Tōkyō: Tentensha.

Nakane, Chie. (1972) *Japanese Society,* Berkeley: University of California.

Nakasone, Seizen. (1995) *Himeyuri no Tō o Meguru Hitobito no Shūki,* Tōkyō: Kadokawa Shoten.

Neale, Stephen. (1987) *Genre,* 3rd ed. London: British Film Institute.

—— (1993) 'Prologue: Masculinity as Spectacle, Reflections on Men and Mainstream Cinema.' *Screening the Male: Exploring Masculinities in Hollywood Cinema,* (eds.) Steven Cohan and Ina Rae Hark. London: Routledge p. 9-19.

Nolletti, Arthur Jr. and David Desser. (1992) *Reframing Japanese Cinema: Authorship, Genre and History,* Bloomington and Indianapolis: Indiana University Press.

Nosco, Peter (ed.) (1989) *Confucianism and Tokugawa Culture,* Princeton, New Jersey: Princeton University Press.

Okumura, Y. (ed.) (1993) *Gakuto-hei no Seishun: Gakuto Shutsujin Gojū-nen me no Tōan,* Tōkyō: Kadokawa Shoten.

Onuma, Yasuaki. (1986) 'The Tokyo Trial: Between Law and Politics.' *The Tokyo War Crimes Trial: An International Symposium,* (eds.) C. Hosoya, N Ando, Y Onuma and R. Minear. Tokyo: Kodansha.

BIBLIOGRAPHY

—— (1993) *Tōkyō Saiban kara Sengo Sekinin no Shisō e*, Tōkyō: Tōshindō.

Ooms, H. (1989) *Tokugawa Ideology: Early Construction, 1570-1680*, Princeton, New Jersey: Princeton University Press.

Ōshima, Nagisa. (1978) *Taikenteki Sengo Eizōron*, Tōkyō: Asahi Shinbunsha.

—— (1992) *Cinema, Censorship and the State*, (trans.) Dawn Lawson. London: The MIT Press.

—— (1993) *Ōshima Nagisa 1960*, Tōkyō: Seidosha.

Ozaki, H. (1968) 'Aitsu no Kiseki', *Art Theatre*, October, p. 12-13.

Ozu, Yasujirō. (1993) *Zen Nikki Ozu Yasujirō*, Tōkyō: Firumuātosha.

Papinot, E. (1984) *Historical and Geographical Dictionary of Japan*, Tokyo: Tuttle.

Penley, Constance. (1989) *The Future of an Illusion: Film, Feminism and Psychoanalysis*, London: Routledge.

Perkins, V.P. (1974) *Film as Film: Understanding and Judging Movies*, 2nd ed. Harmondsworth: Penguin Books.

Pinguet, Maurice. (1993) *Voluntary Death in Japan*, (trans.) Rosemary Morris. Oxford: Blackwell.

Radstone, Susannah. (1995) 'Cinema/Memory/History.' *Screen*, vol.36, no.1, Spring, p. 34-47

Rawls, John. (1973) *A Theory of Justice*, Oxford: Oxford University Press.

Reimer, R.C. and C.J. Reimer. (1992) *Nazi-Retro Films: How the German Narrative Cinema Remembers the Past*, New York: Twayne.

Richie, Donald. (1975) *Ozu*, Berkeley: University of California.

—— (1982) *The Japanese Movie*, Tokyo: Kodansha.

Rodowick, P.N. (1991) *The Difficulty of Difference: Psychoanalysis Sexual and Film Theory*, London: Routledge.

Rose, S. (1992) *The Making of Memory: From Molecules to Mind*, London: Bantam Books.

Rosenberger, N.R. (ed.) (1992) *Japanese Sense of Self* Cambridge: Cambridge University Press.

Rosenstone, Robert A (1995) *Visions of the Past: The Challenge of Film to Our Idea of History*, London: Harvard University Press.

—— (ed.) (1995) *Revisioning History: Film and the Construction of a New Past*, Chichester, West Sussex: Princeton University Press.

Rotundo, E. A. (1993) *American Manhood: Transformations in Masculinity from the Revolution to the Modern Era*, New York: Basic Books.

Russell, Catherine. (1995) *Narrative Mortality: Death, Closure and the New Wave Cinemas*, London: University of Minnesota Press.

Safouan, Moustafa. (1981) 'Is the Oedipus Complex Universal?' *M/F*, 5-6, p. 85-87.

Said, Edward W. (1991a) *The World, The Text and The Critic*. London: Vintage.

—— (1991b) *Orientalism: Western Conceptions of the Orient*, London: Penguin Books.

—— (1993) *Culture and Imperialism*, London: Chatto and Windus.

Sakuramoto, Totomio. (1993) *Daitōa Sensō to Nihon Eiga: Tachimi no Senchū Eigaron*, Tōkyō: Aoki Shoten.

Sansom, G.B. (1977) *The Western World and Japan: A Study in the Interaction of European and Asiatic Cultures*, Tokyo: Tuttle.
—— (1981) *A History of Japan: to 1334, 1334-1615, 1615-1867*, 3 volumes, 4th ed. Tokyo: Tuttle.
—— (1983) *Japan: A Short Cultural History*, 8th ed. Tokyo: Tuttle.
Satō, Ikuya. (1991) *Kamikaze Biker: Parody and Anomy in Affluent Japan* Chicago: University of Chicago Press.
Satō Tadao (1968) 'Nikudan', *Art Theatre*, October, p. 4-10.
—— (1974) *'Jingi naki Tatakai* Shirīzu no Omoshirosa', *Shinario*, August, p. 100-103.
—— (1976) *Chūshingura: Iji no Keifu*, Tōkyō: Asahi Shinbunsha.
—— (1986) *Nihon Eiga Shisōshi*, Tōkyō: Sanichi Shobō.
—— (1987) *Currents in Japanese Cinema*, (trans.) Gregory Barrett. Tokyo: Kodansha.
—— (1989) *Nihon Eiga to Nihon Bunka*, Tōkyō: Miraisha.
—— (1995) *Nihon Eigashi Vol 1: 1896-1940*, Tōkyō: Iwanami Shoten.
—— (1995) *Nihon Eigashi Vol 2: 1941-1959*, Tōkyō: Iwanami Shoten.
—— (1996) *Nihon Eigashi Vol 3: 1960-1995*, Tōkyō: Iwanami Shoten.
—— (1996) *Nihon no Eigashi Vol 4*, Tōkyō: Iwanami Shoten.
Segal, Lynne. (1990) *Slow Motion: Changing Masculinities, Changing Men*, London: Virago.
Selig, Michael. (1993) 'Genre, Gender and the Discourse of War: The A-Historical and Vietnam Films.' *Screen*, vol.34, no.1, Spring, p. 1-18.
Seidler, V.J. (1994) *Unreasonable Men: Masculinity and Social Theory*, London: Routledge.
Semple, Janet. (1993) *Bentham's Prison: A Study of the Panopticon Penitentiary*, Oxford: Clarendon Press.
Shimizu, Akira. (1991) ' Nihon ni Okeru Sensō Eiga' in *Nichibei Eigasen: Pāruhābā Gojūshūnen*, Tōkyō: Seikyūsha.
—— (1994) *Sensō to Eiga: Senjichū to Senryōka no Nihon Eigashi*, Tōkyō: Shakai Shisōsha.
Silver, Alain. (1983) *The Samurai Film*, Woodstock, New York: The Overlook Press.
Silverman, Kaja. (1992) *Male Subjectivity at the Margins*, London: Routledge.
Sims, R.L. (1991) *A Political History of Modern Japan 1868-1952*, New Delhi: Vikas.
Slotkin, Richard. (1973) *Regeneration Through Violence: The Mythology of the American Frontier, 1600-1860* Middleton: Wesleyan University Press.
Smith, Robert J. (1987) 'Gender Inequality in Contemporary Japan'. *The Journal of Japanese Studies*, vol.13, no. 1.
Spigel, Lynn. (1995) 'From the Dark Ages to the Golden Age: Women's Memories and Television Reruns.' *Screen*, vol.36, no.1, Spring, p. 16-33.
Stacey, Jackie. (1994) 'Hollywood Memories.' *Screen*, vol.35, no.4, Winter p. 317-335.
Standish, Isolde (1998) *'Akira:* Postmodernism and Resistance' in D.P. Martinez (ed) *The Worlds of Japanese Popular Culture: Gender, Shifting Boundaries and Global Cultures*, Cambridge: Cambridge University Press.

BIBLIOGRAPHY

Storry, Richard. (1957) *The Double Patriots: A Study of Japanese Nationalism*, London: Chatto and Windus.
—— (1982) *A History of Modern Japan*. 15th ed. Harmondsworth: Penguin Books.
The Sexual Subject: A Screen Reader in Sexuality, (1992) London: Routledge.
Suzuki, Seijun. (1991) *Kenkaerejii*, Tōkyō: Sanichi Shobō.
Takami, Kuwayama. (1994) 'The Reference Other Orientation' *Japanese Sense of Self*, (ed.) Nancy R. Rosenberger. Cambridge: Cambridge University Press, p. 121-151.
Tayama, R. (1966) *'Abashiri Bangaichi* Nagaremono no Erejī', *Shinario*, October, p. 134-137.
Thompson, John B. (1990) *Ideology and Modern Culture: Critical Social Theory in the Era of Mass Communication*, Cambridge: Polity Press.
Van Wolferen, Karel. (1990) *The Enigma of Japanese Power: People and Politics in a Stateless Nation*, London: Papermac.
Tōhō (eds.) (1992) *Kihachi Fōhīto no Aruchizan: Okamoto Kihachi Zensakuhinshū*, Tōkyō: Tōhō Shuppan Jigyōshitsu.
Ventura, Rey. (1992) *Underground in Japan*, London: Jonathan Cape.
Walsh, Jeffrey and James Aulich. (eds.) (1989) *Vietnam Images: War and Representation*, London: Macmillan Press.
Watanabe, Tsuneo. (1989) *Toransu Jiendā no Bunka: Isekai e Ekkyō suru Chi*, Tōkyō: Keisō Shobō.
—— (1991) *Datsudansei no Jidai: Andorojinasu o Mezasu Bunmeigaku*, Tōkyō: Keisō Shobō.
Watanabe, T. and J. Iwata. (1989) *The Love of the Samurai: A Thousand Years of Japanese Homosexuality*, (trans.) D. R. Roberts. London: GMP Publishers.
White, Hayden. (1985) *Tropics of Discourse: Essays in Cultural Criticism*, London: The John Hopkins University Press.
Willeman, Paul. (1981) 'Anthony Mann: Looking at the Male.' *Framework*, 15-17, p. 16-20.
Williams, Raymond. (1977) *Marxism and Literature*, Oxford: Oxford University Press.
—— (1981) *Culture*, London: Fontana Press.
—— (1988) *Keywords: A Vocabulary of Culture and Society*, 3rd ed. London: Fontana Press.
Yamamoto, Kikuo. (1990) *Nihon Eiga ni Okeru Gaikoku Eiga no Eikyō: Hikaku Eigashi Kenkyū*, Tōkyō: Waseda Daigaku Shuppanbu.
Yamamoto, Tsunetomo. (1993) Chūkō Bakkusu Nihon no Meicho 17: *Hagakure*, Tōkyō: Chūōkōronsha.
Yasukuni Jinja (eds.) (1994) *Izasaraba Ware wa Mikuni no Yamazakura: Gakuto Shutsujin Gojūnen Tokubetsuten no Kiroku*, Tōkyō: Tentensha.
Yoshida, Shigeru. (1961) *The Yoshida Memoirs: The Story of Japan in Crisis* (trans.) Yoshida Kenichi. London: Heinemann.
Yoshino, Kosaku. (1995) *Cultural Nationalism in Contemporary Japan: a Sociological Enquiry*, London: Routledge.
Zavarzadeh, Mas'ud. (1991) *Seeing Films Politically*, Albany: State University of New York Press.

Index

References to illustrations are in **bold** type.

Aa Kaigun 216
Aa Rikugun 216
Aa Zero-sen 216
Abashiri Bangaichi series 158, 160-3, 165-184, **178, 180, 182, 183,** 185, 186
Abe, Tōru 168, 169, 177
Aiki minami e tobu 209
Aikoku no hana 63-4, 123, 126
Ai no bōrei 6
Ai no kōrida 6
Althusser, Louis 'Ideology and the Ideological State Apparatus' 11, 202-3
Anderson, Benedict 28
Anderson, J.T. & D. Richie 7
Ano natsu no ichiban shizukana umi 164
anthropocosmic
 discourse 133-4
 world-view 128-132, 138-9, 140, 141, 143, 149
Aratama, Michiyo 121
Arashi, Kanjurō 152, 160, 168, 177
Ashihara, Yoshinobu 77
Ashita 156, 220
Asian Co-Prosperity Sphere 61
ATG (Art Theatre Guild) 6
Autumn Afternoon see *Samma no aji*

Bad Sleep Well, The see *Warui yatsu hodo yoku nemuru*

Balázs, B 68
Ballad of Narayama see *Narayama bushi-kō*
Banba no Chūtarō mabuta no haha 53, 209
Bandō Tsumasaburō 22, 35
Barthes, Roland 1
 Empire of the Signs 8
 Paris Match photograph 13
 Mythologies 202
Battleship Potemkin 51
Beasley, W.G. 25, 75, 151
Bentham, Jeremy 73, 74
 panopticon 70
 utilitarianism 211-2
Black Masked Reformer see *Kurama Tengu*
Black Rain see *Kuroi Ame*
Boiling Point 171, 198
Bordwell, David 7, 8, 38
 Ozu camera placement 42-3
Bornoff, Nicholas 210
bōzōzoku 73, 115, 213-4
Boy see *Shōnen*
Brief Encounter 218
Brothers and Sisters of the Toda Family see *Todake no kyōdai*
Burch, Noël 4, 7, 8
 To the Distant Observer 9

Carr, E.H. 1, 2, 15, 194
censorship
 kissing scenes 217-8

– 234 –

INDEX

Law 208-209
Chichi ariki 38-41, 45, 46, 48, 49, 51, 56, 59, 64, 81, 108, 119, 122, 123
Children of the Atomic Bomb see *Genbaku no ko*
Ch'un Hyang-chŏn 208
Chūshingura 3, 25, 37, 69, 115, 152, 193, 198, 199
  films 9
  myth or history? 15-23
Chūshingura/Ten no maki/Chi no maki 22
Chūshinguragaiden Yotsuyakaidan 21, 199
Civil Codes (1898 and 1912) 29, 30, 76-7
Civil Information and Education, Section (CIE) 6
comfort women 125-6, 136, 138
comradely love see *sen'yūai*
Constitution (1889) 30

Dai Nippon Teikoku 151, 152-4, 157, 187
Daitōyō Sensō to Kokusai Saiban 142, 146, 151-2, 153-4
Dale, Peter
  on *nihonjinron* 71
Death by Hanging see *Kōshikei*
Debord, Guy 193
Deer Hunter, The 32
Desser, David 7
Diary of a Shinjuku Thief see *Shinjuku dorobō nikki*
diegesis 35, 36, 64
diegetic process 4, 5
discourse 4, 23, 55, 79, 94, 95, 97, 116, 119, 133, 146, 147, 153, 157, 167, 185, 187, 199
  discursive traditions 7-11
  patriarchal (*Rikugun*) 49
docu-drama 196
  Kaigun 46, 48
  Jingi naki tatakai 187, 191, 192, 199
  Watashi wa kai ni naritai 145-6
Doi, Takeo
  Anatomy of Dependence 72

Dower, John W
  on racism 32
drifter see *nagare-mono*
Drunken Angel see *Yoidore tenshi*
Dyer, Richard
  definition of structuring absences 218
  structuring absences 124-5

Eagleton, Terry
  on ideology 13
Early Spring see *Sōshun*
Earth see *Tsuchi*
education system 27-8
Egawa, Ureo 55, 57
Eigageijitsu 198
Empire of Passion see *Ai no bōrei*
enemy within, the 119, 149

fantasy 158
February Incident (1936) 4, 206
  films 9, 198
Few Good Men, A 220
filiative/affiliative 33, 119-120
  Said on 19-20
Film Laws (1939) 5
film series 9
Fiske, John
  on masculinity 195
  on violence 167
Five Scouts, The see *Gonin no sekkōhei*
Forty-seven Loyal Retainers see *Chūshingura*
Forty-seven rōnin see *Genroku Chūshingura*
Foucault, Michel 4, 74, 76, 77, 78, 139, 144, 218-9
  Discipline and Punish 71
  on discipline 75
  on power 133
  on sexuality 122, 123
  panopticon 211-2
Freud, Sigmund 172, 174-6, 179
Frye, Northrop 2, 193
Fujiwara, Yoshie 32
Fukasaku, Kinji 159
Furukawa, Takumi 80, 96

Gates of Flesh see *Nikutai no mon*
Gellner, Ernest 29
  on education system 27, 28
  on nationalism 24, 26
Genbaku no ko 3, 156
Genroku Chūshingura 21, 22
Gluck, Carol 27, 29, 30, 31, 205, 206-7
  Japan's Modern Myths 12
Gokudō no onna/tsuma tachi series 93
Gomikawa, Junpei 10, 120
Gonin no sekkōhei 67, 69, 93, 94, 127
Good Morning see *Ohayō*
Gosha, Hideo 198, 200, 208

Hagakure 36, 45, 124, 158, 177, 209
  Watanabe and Iwata 216
Halpern, Ben
  'Myth and Ideology in Modern Usage' 12-3
Hamada, Yoshihisa
  on censorship 208-9
  on colonial film policy 210
  on directives to filmmakers (1938) 34
  on *onnagata* 209
Hasegawa, Kazuo 61
Hawai Marē okikaisen 66, 79, 101, 125, 209
Hendry, Joy
  on *ie* 218
  on marriage 217
Himeyuri no tō 3, 70, 127, 196, 197-8
history 1, 2, 10, 23, 25, 45, 46, 48, 76, 99, 146, 191, 194, 195
Hobsbawm, Eric 1, 31, 33, 207-8
  on nationalism 26
homosocial
  bonding 184
  brotherhood 52, 182
  chūgi (loyalty) 22
  kamikaze 79, 91, 108
  sub-text 95, 101, 198
  sub-text *nagare-mono* 162
Hōrō zanmai 52, 53-4, 209

Horsley, William and R. Buckley 221
Horsman, Mathew and Andrew, Marshall
  on nationalism 66
Hoshino, Yasumasa 48
Human Condition, The 3, 50, 83, 119-121, 123-141, **124**, **136**, **140**, 142, 144, 145, 148, 168, 171, 194, 196, 219
humanism 124, 141
  humanitarian impulses 131
  humanitarian perspective 120
  Kaji's humanism 134-5
  Kaji's humanitarian beliefs 127, 129, 130
  Kaji's intuitive humanitarian principles 133-4
  socialist ideals of 138

Ichiban utsukushii 93, 126
Ichikawa, Kon and Y. Mori 10
ideology 11-15
  filiative/affilative social relations 20
  in *Chichi ariki* 40
  tennōsei (absolute loyalty to the Emperor) 19
Ieki Miyoji 79
Iguchi, Rikihei and Tadashi Nakajima 10, 215
iji (pride) 159-160, 161, 170, 177
Ikegami, Eiko 16, 19, 20, 27, 159, 160, 163-4, 205
  honour culture 71, 73-4, 212-3
imagined cultural community see *seken*
Imago 11
Imai, Tadashi 3, 70, 83, 123, 127, 197
Imperial Rescript on Education (1890) 29, 123, 207
Imperial Rescript to Soldiers and Sailors (1882) 29, 123, 206-7
Inagaki, Hiroshi 34, 53-4
industrialism 121, 138
In the Realm of the Senses see *Ai no kōrida*
I Want to be Reborn a Shellfish see *Watashi wa kai ni naritai*

INDEX

Ishihara, Yujirō 96-7, 190
Ishii, Teruo 158
Ishii, Teruo and Kenji Fukuma 10
ishin denshin (non-verbal communication) 4, 22, 181, 182
Itami, Mansaku 10, 51-2, 63
Itō, Takashi and Hiroaki Kita 10
Itō, Tasaburō
  definition of *kokutai* (1945) 33
Iwamoto, Kenji and T. Saiki 10, 53
Iwashita, Shima 96

Jameson, Fredric 189, 193, 197-8
Japan's Longest Day see *Nippon no ichiban nagai hi*
Jeffords, Susan 66
  definition of masculine voice 53
Jingi naki tatakai series 159, 160, 181, 184-9, **185, 186,** 190-2, 196, 199, **200,** 220
jingi (yakuza code of morality) 161-2, 165-6, 170, 176, 188-9, 195
Jordan, E. 165
Judgement at Nuremberg 220
justice 138, 145
  giri/ninjō 162

Kaigun 3, 43-7, 48, 49, 64, 66, 79, 119, 122, 123, 209
Kaigun heigaku monogatari, aa Etajima 216
Kaisen no zenya 64-5, 123
kamikaze films 3, 43-7, 68-118, 119-120, 133, 144, 169, 184, 187, 194, 199
  documentary footage 150
Kanchō kida shisezu 210
Kaneko, Nabuo 184
Kasahara, K. 162, 187-8, 220
Kataoka, Chiezō 22, 54
Katō Hayashi sentō-tai 209
Katō, Tetsutarō 142, 144-5, 146, 148, 154, 155
  giri/ninjō 165
Kawabata, Yasunari 96
Kawasaki, Hiroko 59
Kawashima, Yūzō 37

Kenka erejii 123
Kike wadatsumi no koe 197
Kita, Ikki 129
Kimi koso tsugi no arawashi da 209
Kimi no na wa 50, 123
Kimura, Isao 81, 82, 96, 110
Kinejun see *Kinema Junpō*
Kinema Junpō 8, 116, 117, 120, 184, 197, 216, 220
Kinoshita, Keisuke 47, 49
  censors' criticism of 54
Kitano, (Beat) Takeshi 159, 164, 171, 174, 179, 189, 190, 198, 199, 219
Kataoji, Kinuya 184
Kobayashi, Masaki 120, 123, 146, 147, 196
Kodama, Yoshio 191
Kogure, Michiyo 63
kokutai 44, 45, 48, 64, 65, 72, 81, 84, 95, 115, 119, 121, 122, 123, 126, 129, 151, 153, 194
  Chichi ariki 40
  definition of 204
  invention of 24-34
Komori, Kyoshi 146
Kondo, Dorinne K. 115-6
  panoptic gaze 214
Konjiki yasha 59-60, 66, 180
Kōno, Tsukasa 10
Kōshikei 6
Kramer, Stanley 220
Kumo nagaruru hateni 68, 74, 79-80, 81-3, 87-96, **88, 91, 92, 93,** 99, 101, 106, 108, 109-110, 115, 116, 126-7, 150, 199, 215
Kuro series 213
Kurama Tengu series 52, 152
Kuroi ame 156
Kurasawa, Akira 6, 8, 93, 96, 160
Kuwayama, Takami 214

Lacan, Jaques
  on the ego 163
League of Nations 32
  Japan's withdrawal from (*Kaigun*) 46-7

- 237 -

Lean, David 218
Lebra, Takie Sugiyama
  on *seken* 78, 86, 87, 163, 164, 214
Lehmann, Jean-Pierre 28, 30, 31, 208
  on racism 32
  samurai-isation 29
Lévi-Strauss, Claude 1, 2, 119, 193
  on myths 13, 16, 21, 24-5, 198
Lipsitz, George 196
London Naval Disarmament Conference 1930 (*Kaigun*) 47

McDonald, Keiko 7
Makino, Masahiro 208
Manchurian Film Company 60, 66
Manshū Film Company see Manchurian Film Company
masculinity 43
  beset 184, 189
  break-down of relationships between men 57-9
  code of brotherhood 66-7
  consumer culture 189-190
  family as constraint 161
  feminisation of Chinese men 62
  Fiske on 195
  homophobic violence 131
  Kimura Isao 82
  male rape 132, 171
  male rite of passage 139
  masculine consciousness 59
  masculine discourse 174
  masculine fellowship 66
  masculine subjectivity 2
  masculine voice 53-5
  Neale Stephen on 171-2
  nurturing 51-3
  point of view 60, 126
  primogeniture 122
  pure self 34
  Okada Eiji 83
  secondary sons 96, 120
  sensual imperative of 158, 193, 199
  Tsuruta Kōji 83
  virgin fathers 109, 123,
  yōshi (adopted son-in-laws) 216

masochism 172
  feminine/passive 173
  Freud on 174-6
  reflexive 171, 172-3, 174-9, 190
Mata au hi made 50, 83, 123
Matatabimono 53
Matsubayashi, Shue 79
Matsukata, Hiroki 184
Max, Mon Amour 6
Meiji Taitei to Nogi Shōgun 152
Mellon, J. 7, 196
memory, iconic 22
Merry Christmas, Mr Lawrence 6, 123
Mifune, Toshirō 37, 152
Miles, R. 79, 82, 110
militarism 121, 138
Minear, Richard H. 151, 219
Ministry of Internal Affairs Censorship Office 1938 directives 34
Mishima, Yukio 216-7
  on *Hagakure* 109, 177, 209
  on yakuza 221
Mitsuda, Ken 48
Miyamoto Musashi 160
Mizoguchi, Kenji 8
Moeran, Brian 7
moga (modern girl) 59
Morimoto, Tadao 10, 68-9
  on Ōnishi Takijirō 215
Morris, Ivan 16
  on Heian legal code 122
  on *kamikaze* 94
Mother He Never Knew, The see *Banba no Chutarō mabuta no haha*
Mouer and Sugimoto group model 72-3
Mud and Soldiers see *Tsuchi to heitai*
Muhō Matsu 164
Muhō Matsu no isshō (1943) 34-7, 41, 42, 43, 45, 49, 51-2, 54, 63, 86, 108, 122, 123, 160
Muhō Matsu no isshō (1958) 37
multifarious relations of power 132-141
  Foucault's definition of 133

INDEX

Mulvey, Laura 158, 171
Murayama, Mitsuo 216
Myers, R.H. and M.R. Peattie 128
myth 11-5
  interpretive framework 198
  Lévi-Strauss on 16
  modern 32
  mythoi or generic plot 2

nagare-mono 159-171, 195
Nakadai, Tatsuya 121
Nakane, Chie 76
  collateral ratings 213
  Japanese society 72
  on *gakubatsu* 170
  on group relations 167, 169
  on religion 220-1
Nakasone, Seizen 10, 197
Narayama bushi-kō 214
nationalism 66
  Hobsbawm on 26
national polity *see kokutai*
Natsukawa, Daijirō 59
nature/culture 24-5, 34, 55, 65, 145, 167, 194
  law 161-2
  Muhō Matsu no isshō in 37
  nature untamed 160
Nawa, Hiroshi 185
Neale, Stephen
  on masculinity 171-2
Night and Fog in Japan see Nihon no yoru to kiri
nihonjinron 8, 23, 26, 70, 95, 149, 167, 184, 199
  Dale on 71
Nihon no don/shuryō series 192
Nihon no yoru to kiri 5
Nikudan 70, 99-108, **101, 106, 107,** 110-5, **112, 113, 114,** 117-8, 119, 150, 194, 216
Nikutai no mon 208
Ningen gyorai kaiten 79-87, **86,** 93-6, 99, 106, 109-110, 115, 116, 126-7
Ningen gyorai shutsugeki su 80, 96-9, 116, 216
Ningen no jōken see *The Human Condition*

Niniroku (226) 198, 199, 200
Nippon no ichiban nagai hi 151, 152, 187, 190
Nitobe, Inazō 128
Nomura, Hiromasa 61
Nomura, Shusuke 198

Ōba, Hideo 123,
Ogyū, Sorai 25, 155
Ohayō 41, 215
Okada, Eiji 83
Okada, Yoshiko 55
Okamoto, Kihachi 99, 111, 117, 118, 152
Ōnishi, Takijrō 94, 95, 215
Onuma, Yasuaki 3, 143-4, 147, 148, 149, 150-1, 157, 219
  on War Crimes Trials 154
Ooms, H. 129-130, 218
orientalism 61, 210
Ōshima, Nagisa 5, 8, 10
Otome no iru kichi 64, 126
Ozaki, Hideki 117-8
Ozu, Yasujirō 8, 10, 38-43, 55, 66, 77, 170, 209, 215
  silent films 53, 54

panopticon
  definition of 211-2
patriarchy 181
  archetypal patriarch 184
  patriarchal figure 168
  patriarchal structure 183-4
Perkins, V.P. 7
Platoon 139

racism
  European 32
  League of Nations 47
Rawls, John 145
  on rights of man 220
remakes 9, 197
Rescript on Education *see* Imperial Rescript on Education
Rescript to Soldiers and Sailors *see* Imperial Rescript to Soldiers and Sailors
reverse course policy 14
Richie, Donald 7

- 239 -

Riko-ran 60-3, 66, 161
  star persona 210
Rikugun 14, 47-51, 54, 122, 123, 209
Rodowick, P.N. 121
  romance 51-67
  in *kamikaze* films 109-113
  romanticism 117
  post-war rebirth of 121-8
Rose, S. 196
Russell, Catherine 166, 191
Russo-Japanese War (*Rikugun*) 48
Ryū, Chishū 38, 46, 48, 110

Said, Edward W. 210
  filiative/affilative 19-20
Sakai, Furanki/Frankie 155
Saito, Tatsuo 57
Sakuramoto, Totomio 10
Samma no aji 41
samurai-isation 29, 65, 75, 76
  of the lower classes 34-51
Sano, Shūji 38, 61, 63
Sanshirō (Sugata) 160
Sasaki, Keisuke 63
Sasaki, Kon 64
Satō, Ikuya 213-4
Satō, Tadao 10, 21, 34, 52-3, 66, 70, 152, 158, 159, 199, 203
  on anti-war films 95
  on *Abashiri* series 166, 181
  on *Chūshingura* 17-9, 22, 23
  on *Himeyuri no tō* 197
  on *iji* (pride) 159-160, 163
  on *Jingi naki tatakai* series 188, 191
  on Okamoto Kihachi 117-8
  on relations between sexes 210
  on Takakura Ken 174
Sawada, Kiyoshi 66
Sayon no kane 14, 63
Scene at Sea see *Ano natsu no ichiban shizukana umi*
Season of the Sun see *Taiyō no kisetsu*
Seishun no yume ima izuko 57-9, 60, 66, 170
seken 71, 75, 78, 86, 99, 133, 163, 164, 172, 214

Kumo nagaruru hateni 90
  shame 74
  spatial configuration of power 73
Senjō no merii kuriisumasu see *Merry Christmas Mr Lawrence*
Sensō to seishun 3
Sensuikan ichi gō 209
Sen'yūai 67, 70, 79-95. 115, 127
  Satō's definition of 69
Seven Samurai see *Shichinin no samurai*
Shanghai Incident 66, 202
Shichinin no samurai 96
Shijūshichi-nin no shikaku 199
Shimizu, Akira 5, 10, 60-1
Shimizu, Hiroshi 59, 63
Shinario 187
Shingun 65, 210
Shinjuku dorobō nikki 6
Shinjuku nemuranai machi 171
Shōnen 6
Silverman, Kaja 172-3, 174
Silverman, Serge 6
Sims, R.L. 205-6
Sino-Japanese War 32
Slotkin, Richard 1
Snow Country see *Yukiguni*
Sonatine 189-190, 219
Sono otoko kyōbō no tsuki see *Violent Cop*
Soshū no yoru 14, 61-3, 83
Sōshun 215
Special Attack Forces see *kamikaze*
Stacey, Jackie
  iconic memory 21
Stalinism 121, 138
Stone, Oliver 139
story of the forty-seven loyal retainers see *Chūshingura*
  sublimated love 63-5
Sugawara, Bunta 159, 179, 185
Suzuki, Seijun 10, 123, 208

Taiyō no kisetsu 96
taiyōzoku (subculture) 96-7, 99, 100, 109, 116, 118
Takakura, Ken 4, 109, 158, 173, 179, 181, 184, 188, 190, 221
  as Tachibana 159-162, 165-7

- 240 -

INDEX

Takihano Hisako 44
Tanaka, Kakuei 191
Tanaka, Kinuyo 14, 49, 54, 55, 57, 64
Tanaka, Kunie 108, 131, 161, 169, 181
Tange Sazen yowa hyakūman ryō no tsubo 52
Taoka, Kazuo 184
Tarantino, Quentin 172
Tasaka, Tomotaka 43, 66, 69, 93, 115, 184, 200
Tayama, R 160, 161, 180-1, 199
Terada, Minori 100
Teshigahara, Hiroshi 8
theories of Japaneseness *see nihonjinron*
Todake no kyōdai 41
Tōjō, Hideki 151-4, 157, 194
Tokoro, Jōji/Georgie 144, 155
Tōkyō monogatari 41, 209, 215
Tōkyō no onna 54, 55-7, 59, 60, 180
Tōkyō Saiban 146, 147
Tokyo Story *see Tōkyō Monogatari*
Tokyo Trials *see Tōkyō Saiban*
Tomijima Matsugorō den 51
Tōno, Eijirō 46
tragic hero 2, 3, 4, 16, 23, 25, 43, 44, 46, 95, 98, 99, 117, 120, 121, 144, 149, 151, 154, 156, 157, 158, 159, 160, 185, 187, 188, 193, 194, 195, 196, 197, 198, 200
heroic 165
nagare-mono 162
Tōjō 152-3
unheroic 145, 155
Triple Alliance (*Kaigun*) 47
Triple Intervention of (1895) 32
Rikugun 48
Tsuchi 5, 66
Tsuchi to heitai 67, 69, 127
Tsugawa, Masahiko 149
Tsuruta, Kōji 83, 221

Uchida, Tomu 5
Umemiya, Tatsu 185
uniformed politicians 116, 119, 150

utilitarianism 70, 75-8, 83, 87, 97, 119-120, 126, 129, 130, 144, 160
in *Ningen gyorai kaiten* 85
Jeremy Bentham 211-2
Utsui, Ken 81

violence 158, 195
aesthetics of 171-181
symbolic meaning of 165-170
Violent Cop 174, 189-190, 198, 219

Wa ga machi 37
war crimes 147
War Crimes Trials 3, 6, 116, 120, 121, 132, 141, 142-4, 146, 154
Charter 194, 219
criminalisation of Japan 151
Kaji's mock trail 137, 142
Tōjō's testimony 151
victor's justice 142
War from Hawaii to Malaya, The see *Hawai Marē okikaisen*
war-retro films 3, 12, 16, 23, 70, 119-120, 126, 127, 153, 156, 167, 187, 190, 194, 195, 196, 199
Warui yatsu hodo yoku nemuru 213
Washington Conference (1921) 47
Watanabe, Tsuneo and J. Iwata on *Hagakure* 216
Watashi wa kai ni naritai 3, 120, 141-2, 144-151, 153, 155-6, 165, 194, 195, 220
White, Hayden 1, 2, 15, 156, 193, 194

yakuza code of morality *see jingi*
yakuza films 3, 4, 12, 16, 23, 117, 158, 179
Yamaguchi-gumi sandaime 184
Yamuguchi, Yoshiko *see* Riko-ran
Yamamoto, Kikuo 10, 52-3
Yamanouchi, Akira 43
Yamakami, Koichi 187
Yamazaki, Ansai 129, 218

– 241 –

Yanagita, Kunio 24, 31
Yanaihara, Tadao 128
Yoidore tenshi 6, 202
Yoshida, Shigeru 14, 72, 150
Yoshimura, Kōzaburō 210
Yoshino, Kosaku 26, 71, 211

Yoshino, Kōzō 187
Yukiguni 96

Zato-ichi 160
Zavarzadeh, Mas'ud 5